Illinois Central College
Learning Resources Center

The Celluloid South

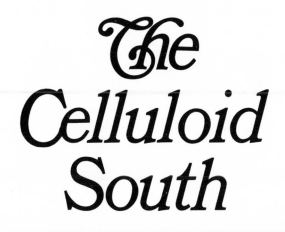

The Celluloid South

HOLLYWOOD AND THE SOUTHERN MYTH

by Edward D.C. Campbell, Jr.

THE UNIVERSITY OF TENNESSEE PRESS
KNOXVILLE

Clothbound editions of University of Tennessee Press books are printed on paper designed for an effective life of at least 300 years, and binding materials are chosen for strength and durability.

Frontispiece: Bill "Bojangles" Robinson and Shirley Temple in *The Little Colonel*. *The Museum of Modern Art/Film Stills Archives. Courtesy of 20th Century-Fox.*

Library of Congress Cataloging in Publication Data

Campbell, Edward D.C., 1946-
  The celluloid South.

  Bibliography: p.
  Includes index.
  1. Southern States in motion pictures.   I. Title.
PN1995.9.S66C3   *791.43'09'093275*   81–7457
ISBN 0–87049–327–2   AACR2

In Memory of

CHARLES BLACKFORD ROBERTSON, JR.

Contents

Illustrations

Preface

Hollywood in recent years has become the subject of ever-widening interest. There have been studies of the film images of women, masculinity, sex, horror, race, war, propaganda, romance, and the always popular cowboy, to name a few. Despite the varied views of the end-product, all have in common an abiding respect for the attraction of cinema. Whatever their drawbacks and inaccuracies, motion pictures possess the lure of a fascinating interlude. The same respect must be expressed when discussing films of the Old South, for though they were more often than not disappointing in their concept of history and race, they were nonetheless remarkable escapes. They well assessed the public's beliefs, desires, and needs in productions of unquestionable spirit and technique.

The impact of this cinematic antebellum culture was enormous, its mystique always evident. Once destroyed in the crucible of war, the Old South's ideals emerged some forty years later as a popular culture enjoyed both for its psychological and visual attractions. And as with popular culture in general, the preoccupation with the prewar lifestyle in flamboyant films revealed far more about contemporary society than it did about the subject itself.

For all the appeal of cinema, any conclusions about the significance of a particular film or theme can only be drawn with considerable caution and difficulty. Speculation is necessarily a part of any study into the intent or meaning of movies. What is even harder to fathom is the audiences' reaction to a certain production, viewed first as entertainment and only secondarily, if at all, as social commentary.

Perhaps most frustrating is the lack of standard research tools. To state the obvious, film audiences leave no letters, no collections of papers on which to depend for some revealing glimpse of motive and reaction. In this particular study, specific responses were culled from those few comments hidden in reviews and in theatre managers' reports in trade magazines.

The other alternative is to examine those sources which might offer some clue as to what the ticket holder expected from a given production. For example, for each film studios issued press releases aimed at trade and general publications, posters, lobby cards, press packages of suggested advertising gimmicks and visual aids, and even canned, unsigned reviews—naturally laudatory of the product.

Though predictable in its praise of any film, the studio's publicity is nonetheless invaluable. Whatever students of cinema may argue as to a specific director's and writer's intentions, the published advertising and teaser stories at least expose what a production company and distributor thought the public wanted and even how the industry intended the public to react.

Captions such as "Feel the bloody whip of truth" for *Slaves* in 1969 leave little doubt as to the distributor's concept of the product and, for business purposes anyway, of the institution of slavery itself. By the same token, advertisements decades earlier boasting of "a loveable, thrilling show of plantation life" for the 1939 film *Way Down South* left little doubt as to the movie's outlook and the desired audience reaction. In other words, the publicity departments attempted to mold what the audiences would perceive, enjoy, appreciate.

That is not to say that every moviegoer believed every public relations gambit, but at the least the industry's efforts provide information as to any film's supposedly most saleable aspects. Whether the ticket-buying public "bought" the theme is harder to determine. One way to gauge the popularity of a given movie is by referring to trade publications such as *Motion Picture Herald* or *Variety* which reveal how much a production grossed, how long it remained viable as a "first-run" offering, etc. But except for a few selected locales, the trade publications do not outline the response of a region. Here a wide sampling of local newspapers is essential; a total receipts figure or ranking of national popularity alone is not very significant.

A film may have grossed millions, been a box office leader, starred one of Hollywood's most adored contract players, but that does not necessarily mean the film was well received in every part of the country. This is particularly true of movies oriented to a particular topic or setting, such as those of the antebellum South.

An examination of local periodicals is crucial in deciding where a production was poorly or well regarded. The broad sampling reveals not only the success of a 1930s romance, but by following a paper's advertising for each film's run in addition to the reviews and particular reviewers themselves over several decades, patterns emerge for a community, regional, and finally national audience. Though the moviegoers may be silent, advertising tailored for one specific area, announcements of local premiere activities, evidence of extended runs, reviews, and sometimes even second reviews reveal much.

The study, therefore, is not of film as film per se, but of film as a reflection of popular perceptions of the South in plots, visual images, advertising, reviews—and how those perceptions may reveal the uses to which the region has been put and the needs the South has met in the popular culture of cinema. The mythology which surrounds and shrouds the South is revealed on the screen as not uniquely Southern but distinctly American in origin, use, and appeal.

E.D.C.C., Jr.

Richmond, Virginia
August 1980

⟨Acknowledgments

In the earliest stages of research, several individuals provided the encouragement and knowledgeable advice necessary for the project. In particular, Thomas L. Connelly as mentor and friend initiated an interest in popular culture and images of the South. His confidence, guidance, and suggestions were enormously helpful and much appreciated.

Anthony Slide, coordinator of the National Film Information Service of the Academy of Motion Picture Arts and Sciences, helped in locating many films. Benjamin Dunlap of the University of South Carolina and Calhoun Winton of the University of Maryland made numerous helpful suggestions for background readings, as did Thomas Cripps of Morgan State University, whose vast research into the black in film was of considerable aid.

Barbara Humphrys of the Library of Congress Motion Picture Section was an essential adviser, especially in procuring several overlooked copyright files. In the same department, Joseph Balian cheerfully searched for several films at a moment's notice. Elena Millie of the Library's Prints and Photographs Division literally searched from the institution's basement to attic for various movie posters important to the study. The Periodicals Section staff amiably met requests for the many newspapers needed.

At the Film Study Center of New York's Museum of Modern Art, Charles Silver and Emily Sieger generously welcomed many requests and questions while always showing an interest in the research. Lamia Doumado and Pearl Moeller of the Museum's library assisted in utilizing several collections of documents.

Mary Corliss and Carlos Clarens of the Film Stills Archives were gracious in their assistance.

MCA Corporation's Universal/16 Film Rentals was the source of otherwise unobtainable films, quickly procured by the extensive efforts of Gary Bordzuk. The staff of the International Museum of Photography/Eastman House in Rochester, especially Kathleen MacRae, was also helpful in arranging screenings. In addition, the staffs of the New York Public Library at Lincoln Center and the libraries of New York University, Columbia University, and the University of South Carolina pleasantly and efficiently met each need.

Special gratitude is due the University of South Carolina Department of History which was generous in its personal and financial support. Drs. George C. Rogers, Jr., James L. Lancaster, Robert D. Ochs, and Walter B. Edgar were always attentive to the study's progress. Especially deserving of thanks are John G. Sproat and John Scott Wilson. Dr. Sproat never failed to encourage; his comments were invariably incisive and correct. Dr. Wilson displayed an unflagging interest in the subject; his broad perspective was essential.

During the various stages of revision, many contributed their comments and immeasurably improved the study. Richard B. Harwell of the University of Georgia Library made several fine suggestions. An outstanding student of the South and especially *Gone With the Wind* as novel and film, his comments were most welcome. An equal debt is owed Jack Temple Kirby of Miami University who graciously contributed his insights; he encouraged much rethinking and the refinement of several ideas. Emory M. Thomas of the University of Georgia also kindly consented to comment on the work.

An extensive program on cinematic images of the South funded by the Virginia Foundation for the Humanities & Public Policy and enthusiastically administered by Robert Vaughan and Judy Dobbs was of considerable benefit. Co-directors of the project, M. Thomas Inge and Melvin I. Urofsky of Virginia Commonwealth University, helped in discarding numerous ideas and bolstering others. Many of the participants, especially Robert A. Armour, corrected errors and added ideas. Thanks also go to: Daniel P. Jordan, George Longest, Walter Coppedge, and

Acknowledgments

James T. Moore of Virginia Commonwealth University; Edgar A. Toppin of Virginia State University; and Roy Proctor of the *Richmond News Leader*.

There are friends as well who exhibited considerable patience and interest; David and Kathleen Beach, who provided a home and company on lengthy research trips, deserve special mention. In addition, without the support and upon occasion the typing and proofreading of my colleagues, the writing would have been far less enjoyable. I am grateful to Mercedes Tromley, Leslie D. Jensen, and Stephanie Lawrence Foltz and to Eleanor S. Brockenbrough and Elizabeth Scott McKemie. The Trustees of the Museum of the Confederacy, in particular Edwina S. Koontz and Penelope H. Eure, generously allowed the time necessary to complete the last revisions.

The staff of the University of Tennesee Press deserves thanks for considerable enthusiastic support. I am particularly grateful to Director Carol Orr and Senior Editor Katherine Holloway for their many good suggestions. Thanks also to Jennifer Siler for putting up with repeated questions and to Lalor Cadley of Atlanta for her welcome help as copyeditor.

Finally, I owe much to the support of my grand and extensive family.

June 1981

The
Celluloid
South

The Growth of a Mythology

THE SOUTH IN FILM

In 1939 the film version of *Gone With the Wind* was eagerly greeted by millions. Rushing to the theatres, the large audiences were fascinated as much by the subject as by the famous cast. The Old South had come alive again. And the film's appeal was not confined to Southerners. Viewers everywhere were moved by the splendor of Tara and Twelve Oaks. Tara was supposedly an upcountry, functional estate, which in its size and landscaping alone suggested much of the image of the small plantations. Owned by the hard-riding Gerald O'Hara, Tara symbolized the robust, sporting, self-made planter ideal. Twelve Oaks, on the other hand, with its huge and ornate staircase, crystal chandeliers, and impressive book-lined study presented a South of culture and refinement. In addition, O'Hara and John Wilkes, the respective owners, displayed a romantic idealism and gentlemanly manner of high degree. The fact that the Wilkes barbecue could have attracted so many quality folk implied much too of the local gentry. It was no surprise that one non-Southern reviewer described the film as showing the "dethronement of the Old South with all its great feudal domains and aristocracy," while another declared that "its treatment of the age of Southern chivalry that was lost with the cause of the Confederacy . . . can be termed nothing less than masterful."[1]

Anyone even mildly interested in the Old South soon encounters the monolithic image of romanticism, of "moonlight and magnolias," so vividly portrayed in the 1939 epic. Where does

[1]*Los Angeles Times*, Jan. 1, 1940; *Portland* (Me.) *Press Herald*, Feb. 9, 1940.

this mythology come from? Certainly modern Southern writers such as Ellen Glasgow, Eudora Welty, Flannery O'Connor, William Faulkner, and Thomas Wolfe have captured a great deal of the region's local color, including its social problems. But for popular culture, the myth's modern development lay elsewhere. For the most part the interpretation has been presented in film —film which makes the antebellum society impressively real to an audience no writer could ever hope to influence. It is a view fostered since 1903 and presented consistently until well into the 1960s.

Such consistency poses numerous questions about popular culture, film, and the role of the South's popular image for the nation as a whole. Why should a modern industrial nation, once torn apart by a war to resolve the fate of the slave-supported plantation system, not only tolerate but enthusiastically support repeated complimentary portrayals of the vanquished? What needs, desires, and assumptions did these films confirm?

At first glance, movies such as *Birth of a Nation*, *Gone With the Wind*, or less-remembered but nonetheless enormously popular pictures of their day such as *Mississippi* seem important by reason of their escapist value alone. After all, movies provide a broad audience with a level of enjoyment few other art forms can match. But the significance of films, and in this case those films depicting the Old South, goes far beyond just a pleasant evening's interlude.

Movies reflect the way we are. *Roots* or *Mandingo* would have been as dismally out of place in the 1930s as say *The Littlest Rebel* would be now. And of course the failure cannot be attributed only to differences in technology. We return to some films because they reveal so much about the society which so avidly supported them. Just as *Uncle Tom's Cabin* of 1903 exposes much of America at the turn of the century, so too does its remake in 1965 reveal vast cultural assumptions. That is why films are important cultural history, for each production was concerned—often intentionally—with lessons for the present viewed through a contemporary interpretation of the past. At the same time, no production company was eager to buck popular approval, and risk financial reverses by unveiling a product too advanced for its time. The film industry accepted

4

beliefs as readily as it created them. The movies of the antebellum South with their increasingly familiar settings and character types reinforced an image shaped cinematically since 1903. However, in the subtle variations and the public responses over seventy years and in the more recent reversals of stereotypes rest many revelations about how Americans perceived themselves and their racial and economic problems: therein lies the importance of a film genre too often remembered only for its luminaries or technical achievements. [2]

The origins of the film mythology of the South are complex and varied, but in large part they can be found in the many instances of fictional exaggeration in the years after Appomattox. Prewar claims that Southern lifestyles bordered on the magnificent were frequent as well, even by Northerners. David Christy of Ohio wrote *Cotton is King* (1855) which did much to foster a concept of the region as dominated by wealthy slave owners and huge cotton plantations. Even Harriet Beecher Stowe's abolitionist novel *Uncle Tom's Cabin* ironically broadened the foundation for a mythology, by depicting a feudal society of faithful workers and kind cavalier planters. The book's evil overseer was, after all, from Vermont.

Other Northerners as well contributed to the image. The prints of Nathaniel Currier and James Merritt Ives were unabashed celebrations of tranquil plantations. Yankee painters also followed the trend; Eastman Johnson's *My Old Kentucky Home* certainly revealed an enchantment with the subject. And of course, Northern minstrel shows and tunes added to the gathering impression. The best remembered of the lyricists, Stephen Foster, wrote "My Old Kentucky Home" in his Pennsylvania residence. His other songs such as "Old Folks at Home," "Massa's in de Cold Ground," and "Old Black Joe" did much to

---

[2]With the exception of Jack T. Kirby's broad study, *Media-Made Dixie: The South in the American Imagination* (Baton Rouge: LSU Press, 1978), other studies are primarily entertaining, specific examinations of casting, production, stunts, and the foibles of actors. See, for example, Gavin Lambert, *GWTW: The Making of Gone With the Wind* (Boston: Atlantic-Little, Brown, 1973); and Roland Flamini, *Scarlett, Rhett and a Cast of Thousands: The Filming of Gone With the Wind* (New York: Macmillan, 1975).

enliven the American stage and planter mystique, as did Daniel Emmett's "Dixie," composed in New York in 1859.

The Civil War of course decreased the popular fascination with matters Southern, and in the first decades after secession each side tried to place the blame for the war upon the other. By 1900, however, the wounds had sufficiently healed so that neither side was tagged with exclusive blame.

The process of literary reconciliation began in the 1870s amidst a new national interest in regional literature. Emerging from the Civil War reunified physically if not yet spiritually, the nation grew more aware of its achievements and potential greatness. The increasing pride in the country generated a curiosity about its myriad elements, including its regional cultures. A fiction of local color developed which described those diverse elements. As a part of the trend, Northern publications became clarions of this nationalism by seeking those writers who could best portray their own local area for a wider readership. *Scribner's Magazine, Century, Cosmopolitan, Harper's Monthly, Lippincott's, Munsey's, McClure's* and *Atlantic Monthly*, all Northern magazines, garnered for regional writers a large and eager public.

As a section long proud of its uniqueness, the South finally had a receptive forum in the postwar years, though with certain conditions. The opportunity was not to be utilized to arouse old animosities but to encourage reconciliation and nationalist sentiment. Articles adhering to any old spirit of truculent provincialism were not satisfactory. Instead, what was desired were portrayals of a locale's picturesque quaintness.

Scribner's Monthly Magazine, which became the *Century Magazine* in 1881, was a forerunner of the new spirit. Under the editorships of J. G. Holland in the 1870s and Robert Underwood Johnson and Clarence C. Buell in the 1880s, the magazine virtually courted Southern authors, eventually publishing the work of such notables as Sidney Lanier, Joel Chandler Harris, Thomas Nelson Page, George Washington Cable, and F. Hopkinson Smith. The pieces were so well received that by the mid-1880s hardly an issue of *Century* lacked a selection by at least one Southern author.

Lippincott's was also an important outlet for Southern writers. Among articles counseling moderation in Reconstruction policies were some of the earliest Confederate reminiscenses published in the North. Occasionally, the editors secured stories by Page or Harris, but the magazine also afforded a chance for lesser known writers. Jennie Woodville contributed dialect poems; so did Sherwood Bonner. The latter's popular "Dialect Tales," depicting the everyday seclusion of life in the South, also appeared in *Harper's Monthly Magazine.*

Harper's was slower to join the trend. Influenced by *Scribner's* "Great South Series" taken from Edward King's 1873 tour, it also began a series on the South. By 1876, John Esten Cooke had provided a piece on Virginia in the Revolution. Then in the 1880s, the publication overflowed with Southern regional writers such as Harris, Page, Ruth McEnery Stuart, Grace King, and Richard Malcolm Johnson.

The *Atlantic Monthly* joined the competition. Sherwood Bonner's dialect tales had helped pave the way by arousing interest in the readership. Mary Noailles Murfree contributed stories of the Appalachians. The magazine aided greatly the careers of Maurice Thompson, who wrote often of the social contacts between the once hostile North and South, and George Cary Eggleston, who frequently used the war as a backdrop to idealize heroes on both sides.

As the writers flourished, so too did a new understanding of old enemies. Newer publications were quick to grasp the theme of regional color and sectional forgiveness. *Scribner's Magazine* reemerged in 1887 and immediately sought the work of Page. Such popularly oriented tabloids as *Cosmopolitan, Munsey's,* and *McClure's* further widened the scope of Southern themes. The ever-growing commercial desire to utilize the stories, evidenced by the rush of newer publications to emulate the older ones, pointed to a confidence that the public's sentiment was changing toward not only the Southen oriented writing, but also the old enemy.

With plots and circumstances established, it was easy for the writers to continue within the popular theme the nation had obviously enjoyed. Thus, the outcropping of local color became in the South a rich vein of nostalgia which grew increasingly exploitable as other sections of the country rapidly changed. After a decade of Northern exposure to the descriptions in magazines, a growing number of regional novelists began to espouse the now respectable planter ideal and to depict wartime Southern heroism with enthusiasm.

John Esten Cooke was one of the best known authors of the school. Having served as a cavalry officer under J.E.B. Stuart, he knew much of the war and chose it rather than the plantation as his most frequent subject. Author of seven books on the conflict, including biographies of Jackson and Lee, he was the first important writer to deal with the war in fiction. His *Surry of Eagle's Nest* (1866) and its sequel *Mohun* (1869) covered Lee's war in Virginia. Several nonfictional accounts, including *Hammer and Rapier* (1869), discussed campaigns of the war. *Hilt to Hilt* (1869) chronicled the exploits of Colonel John S. Mosby's Virginia rangers. As an experienced participant, his accounts of the fighting were often tempered more by reality than romanticism; this in part explains their popularity. In his writings there was seldom bitterness toward the enemy.

He first turned to the agrarian mood in 1870 with *The Heir of Gaymount*, which told of a planter trying to make do with a greatly reduced estate, who in the end finds buried treasure and salvation. But it was only when he treated Virginia in its colonial days that he revealed a strong tendency toward idealization. His novels, *Justin Harley* (1874) and *Canolles* (1877), plus his histories, *Stories of the Old Dominion* (1879) and *Virginia: A History of the People* (1883), viewed the pre-revolutionary society as a revered ideal.

Cooke was a perfect example of the developing literary model in reconciliation writings. His works on the war extolled the new patriotic virtues, as he showed neither rancor toward his foes nor undue favoritism toward his fellows. At the same time, his romanticism emerged in studies of a glorious and bygone revolutionary era in which all, regardless of section, could take pride and in which he could therefore laud native virtues without giving offense. It was an acceptable manner in which to further support the picture of an agrarian and genteel society.

Others, such as George Cary Eggleston, were more enamoured of the plantation world. But like Cooke, Eggleston did not portray the war itself as a righteous crusade. In "A Rebel's Recollections," published in the *Atlantic Monthly* in 1874, he explained that the intolerance and arrogance of the general planter class had contributed to the stress between sections, whereas the Virginia planters had believed secession to be wrong. Those of the Old Dominion had treasured the peaceful prewar contentment and shunned devisive debates.

Eggleston's novel *The Master of Warlock* further explained Virginia's unfortunate duty to stand by her sister states. With the onus of animosity lifted, idealistic backward glances would be more permissible. Eggleston's later work, *The Warrens of Virginia*, outlined the model planter who, significantly, was first an American and only secondly a Virginian.

Far less subtle in his approach to the antebellum society was Thomas Nelson Page. Indeed, Page became the staunchest spokesman for the old regime. Only twelve when the war ended, Page, unlike Cooke, could without difficulty see the 1850s and early 1860s as an epic era. His *In Old Virginia* (1887), a collection of stories previously published in the *Century* and *Harper's*; his *Two Little Confederates* (1888), written for young readers; and his *Burial of the Guns* (1894) all were highly praised in the North.

It was a measure of the growing national mood of forgiveness that the books were so well reviewed. The culture that Page described was a genteel one committed to honor and Southern womanhood and secure in the knowledge that the slaves were devotedly loyal. He also wrote of the "mammy" and the bond between young masters and servants. Rarely did he deal with black fieldhands or white farmers. His elite players therefore served as bastions in a system he described as benign in its race relations.

Like Page, Joel Chandler Harris was a well-known writer whose patriotism was not as obvious as that of many other Southerners who published in the North. His stories of "Uncle Remus," though couched in dialect and incidentally presenting a portrait of the Afro-American cultural heritage, did far more than entertain. They reflected a society. In a wave of articles and books, Harris in the guise of an old Negro spread the mythology of the happy and contented black. In such works as *Free Joe* (1887), Harris appeared to question the race's happy lot, but the majority of his writings painted a joyful existence for the Negro. Most of his outpouring stressed the magnificence of the homes, the vitality of Southern manhood and the charm of the belles, plus the graceful hospitality of the whites assisted by their loyal servants. When Walt Disney in 1946 released his version of the Harris stories, *Song of the South*, the enthusiastic response of the public confirmed the enduring attraction of the fables and their setting.[3]

There were still other literary statements of the glories of a remembered past. Mary McClelland completed several novels for *Lippincott's*. Amelie Rives's novelette "Virginia of Virginia" was printed in *Harper's*. Contributions also came from F. Hopkinson Smith and Harry Stillwell Edwards. The latter in several stories—"De Valley and De Shadow" (1888), for example—blended plantation joy and sorrow. Smith, particularly in his *Colonel Carter of Cartersville* (1891), presented two classic figures often examined in the new school: the colonel and his faithful manservant. His portrait of the cavalier delineated a character proud of his ancestry, appearance, hospitality, and position in society. The personal body servant, always a member of the family, was impeccably capable and dedicated.

Even more a sign of the acceptance of the lost culture was the rise of a band of Northern writers who chose the antebellum world as a theme. John William DeForest, once a Union officer and agent of the Freedmen's Bureau, wrote novels of reconciliation which revolved around love affairs between supposed enemies. Frank R. Stockton added tales of devoted servants; Sarah Orne Jewett contrasted prewar grandeur with postwar ruin; Thomas Bailey Aldrich wrote of the romantic cavalier colonel.

The mythology of the Old south was prevalent in the popular minstrel theatre as well. In the decades after the war, the caricature of the slave as a faithful and contented symbol of stability provided no hint that the institution of bondage had been destroyed. The exaggerated outline of the black character also served as a statement against undue growth. Just as the writers of local color sought to maintain a hold on their region's charms, so

[3] In several rereleases as well as in its original run, *Song of the South* grossed $13,000,000 and ranks 116th among the most profitable films; *Variety*, Jan. 5, 1977.

too did the minstrel companies serve as a force opposed to rapid change. The shows, with their biting humor, were decidedly opposed to urbanization and industrialization. Nostalgia was the norm. Groups such as Lew Johnson's Plantation Minstrels, Haverly's Colored Minstrels, or the McCabe, Young, and Hun Brothers Refined Colored Minstrels provided a steady supply of sentimental escapism.

By 1900 the image of the South put forth in stories, novels, and theatricals had done much to heal the war's wounds and rekindle an interest in the region's ways. In fact the literature and plays drawing upon the newfound spirit of reconciliation were to continue, thus reinforcing the myth.[4] Within this climate of accord, it seemed only natural that the theme would emerge in the new and increasingly wideranging form of popular entertainment, the film.

As first developed in the mid-1890s, the movies were simply short scenes of perhaps a dance, a running horse, or a mother bathing her child, filmed with a single camera. These early attempts appealed to a wide audience, primarily because of the technical novelty of film. But after 1900 the appeal was primarily to the lower classes who were compelled by illiteracy, foreign native tongue, or the sheer drudgery of their everyday lives to shun the printed word and indulge in "nickel madness" at the many arcades in large urban areas. In 1895, Alfred Clark joined film with the past. In several short costume movies, such as *The*

---

[4]For a further analysis of the literary and theatrical phenomenon, see Francis Pendleton Gaines, *The Southern Plantation: A Study in the Development and Accuracy of a Tradition* (Gloucester, Mass.: Smith Reprints, 1962), 62-94; Paul H. Buck, *The Road to Reunion, 1865-1900* (Boston: Little, Brown, 1937), 196-235; Jay B. Hubbell, *The South in American Literature, 1607-1900* (Durham: Duke Univ. Press, 1954), 695-836; Hubbell, *Southern Life in Fiction* (Athens: Univ. of Georgia Press, 1960), 1-30; and Thomas J. Pressly, *Americans Interpret Their Civil War* (New York: Free Press, 1965), 127-226. See also Robert C. Toll, *Blacking Up: The Minstrel Show in Nineteenth-Century America* (New York: Oxford Univ. Press, 1974), 168, 186, 275-80. For another examination of changing perceptions of the region, see Paul Gaston, *New South Creed: A Study in Southern Mythmaking* (New York: Knopf, 1970).

Execution of Mary, Queen of Scots, Clark hit upon one of film's most profound properties: its capability to provide the viewer with access to long-past events, to subject motion and time to the audience's will.[5]

Even more significant was the wedding of film with historical myths that were uniquely American, as in the work of Edwin S. Porter, director of production for Thomas A. Edison's film company. Porter's landmark movies of the early 1900s—*The Great Train Robbery, Capture of the Biddle Brothers*, and *Uncle Tom's Cabin*—contributed greatly to the rise of a wider-based audience, eager for the re-creation of popular, native stories. More importantly, Porter's films heralded two story lines which would rapidly grow to be among the most beloved, the Western and the Old South romance.

The antebellum setting was particularly well suited to the new entertainment medium. Productions had to be brief, which meant the subject matter had to be instantly recognizable and present obvious character types. At the same time, in order to succeed financially the popular pictures had to be escapist entertainment rather than serious fare. Urban and industrial settings were usually avoided in favor of more appealing scenes. Stories of the adventure-filled West would become staples. The plantation tale found its niche as well.

To provide the most appealing image, the film companies drew heavily upon the literature of Southern local color and the minstrel shows so recently prevalent. Though unknown to many of the customers, the body of writing provided just that touch of romance, splendor, and diversion they craved and was in the tradition of the minstrel shows and tunes with which the many lower class viewers were so familiar.

The demand for diversionary melodramas and comedies rather than serious documentary was so paramount that even a harrowing, abolitionist tale such as *Uncle Tom's Cabin* would become—

[5]For a detailed history of early film, see Robert Sklar, *Movie-Made America: A Social History of the American Movies* (New York: Random House, 1975), 3-32; and Garth Jowett, *Film: The Democratic Art* (Boston: Little, Brown, 1976), 35-46.

in the interest of profit and fun—just another short film in the tradition of Page, Harris, and others. Once the middle and upper classes were finally attracted to pictures, a phenomenon in large part brought on by D. W. Griffith's *Birth of a Nation* in 1915, the plantation setting was firmly entrenched. Hollywood could ill afford to ignore the popularity of a plot line originally chosen to meet the early demands of the cinema business. The ramifications of such would later become enormous.

Edwin S. Porter's 1903 version of Harriet Beecher Stowe's abolitionist novel seemed an ironic first step in the development of film's Southern mythology. By 1900 Mrs. Stowe's story was in many respects unrecognizable. Starting as early as the mid-1860s countless white minstrel troupes had blurred the original message by satirizing the story to such a degree that the interpretation strongly implied there had been no need to fight a war over slavery. Moreover, until the rise of black minstrel companies after the Civil War, few Negroes had been allowed to play the lead. Postwar minstrel shows continued to embellish the mystique of the Old South with its "happy darkies" as symbols of plantation simplicity.[6]

Produced for Edison's company, Porter's *Uncle Tom's Cabin* was one of the costliest American movies of that time. Using fourteen settings to carry the tale, the director retained some of the novel's original spirit in his scenes of escape and cruelty. But the film also revealed just how much the Old South mystique had crept into the national psyche. What had before been only imagined or seen in prints or paintings was now visualized in a rapid-paced medium which brought reality to the vision. That Uncle Tom was a white man in blackface said much of the low ebb in race relations at the time; and the influence of the old road shows appeared in a line of cake-walkers in scenes of loading docks and plantations.

More important, a subtle interior scene demonstrated how much of the romantic ideal had become broadly accepted. Outside a large, ornately curtained window, a magnolia branch drooped with blossoms; only a moon was lacking. The most

[6]Toll, *Blacking Up,* 88-97, 127-28, 245-48.

revealing portion of the film was the inclusion of the steamboat race between the *Robert E. Lee* and the *Natchez*. Although it had nothing to do with the plot, it helped to establish the setting and in that context signified the direction in which the film image was headed. Two small and crude wooden models "raced" across a tub of water, the back of which was barely covered by a scene drawn on paper. The setting was one of an impressively large, columned house set on a hilly riverbank and surrounded by precisely furrowed ground and a large warehouse.[7]

The choice of that mansion rather than some more modest house set the tone for the film's romantic Southern hue. Much of the modern misunderstanding of the region, by natives and outsiders alike, was the result of a persistent mythology willingly accepted by countless audiences. This and other films up until 1965 confirmed the predominance of a genteel Southern class of country squires who ruled a well-ordered, contented society devoted to an agrarian ideal and the courtly pursuits, and sustained by a large work force of adoring slaves.

So pervasive was the concept that when a wave of "realistic" film examinations emerged in the late 60s, they were roundly condemned by reviewers. As pictures obviously catering to urban black audiences, the releases were viewed as distortions of fact. It was, however, "fact" built upon equally spurious interpretations in the previous sixty years of cinema. The whole debate was but further evidence of the myth's staying power. Even the opening scenes of the romantic films took on a sameness: a columned mansion surrounded by spacious and well manicured grounds. The slaves were shown diligently at work, frequently singing and seldom supervised by driver or overseer. Films such as *The Fighting Coward* (1924), *Hearts in Dixie* (1929), *So Red the Rose* (1935), *Way Down South* (1939), and *Song of the South* (1946) were all variations on the theme.

The Old South even took on geographic boundaries distinct from those of the Confederacy. The Deep South in film included Virginia, the Carolinas, Georgia, Alabama, Mississippi, Louisiana, Tennessee, plus Kentucky and occasionally Maryland.

[7]*Uncle Tom's Cabin* (Edison, 1903), Library of Congress Motion Picture Section, cited hereafter as LC-MPS.

Other areas—Florida, Arkansas, Texas, and slave Missouri—simply did not fit the mold of the cavalier-planter image.[8]

The ornate repetitions furnished easily recognizable symbols. Characterizations of the Southern herdsmen, mountain people, farmers, town dwellers, and merchants, or the average planter with his few slaves and modest home were entirely absent. When the common folk were portrayed, it was nearly always disparagingly. Even the slaves took on the class consciousness of their masters: Hattie McDaniel as the loyal and strong-willed family servant in both *Gone With the Wind* and *Song of the South* worried about her white charges' associations with nearby "white trash."

The oft repeated image quickly became generally acceptable. The planters, so the scripts declared, were benign, cut handsome figures, and were seldom seen in anything but well tailored attire. Lionel Barrymore with his white suit and planter's hat, white goatee, and cane in *The Little Colonel* (1935) was the epitome of the type. Tyrone Power wore white in almost every advertisement for *The Mississippi Gambler* (1953), as did Clark Gable for *Band of Angels* (1957). It was quite a change when Rex Harrison in *The Foxes of Harrow* (1947) stooped to carrying a whip and wearing a partially opened shirt; but after all, as the movie emphasized, he was an illegitimate Irishman rather than a Southern gentleman.

These movie planters were also exceptionally virile. Their Anglo-Saxon manhood was frequently confirmed by a brief encounter with Creole dandies who scented their handkerchiefs with cologne. The comparison was carried to its extreme in *Drum* (1976) when the homosexual Creole of high society was befriended by the redneck, white-suited planter. Also, any Southern man worth his accent appreciated his mint julep. Gable first appeared in *Gone With the Wind* smiling up the staircase at the ladies and leaning against the bannister with his hand clutching a silver julep cup. The film opened with the Tarleton Twins enjoying their potent refreshment too. When Henry Fonda in *Jezebel* (1938) returned home from the North, he graciously asked

---

[8]See Peter A. Soderbergh, "Hollywood and the South, 1930-1960," *Mississippi Quarterly* 19 (Winter 1965-66), 1-19.

the butler to join him in a homecoming drink—a mint julep. The planter in *The Fighting Coward* (1924) greeted all of his guests with a silver tray laden with the drink.

Military prowess was yet another standard characteristic. In film versions Southern officers were of course gentlemen, for—in pictures, at least—there was no other way than by social position to achieve rank. The young Henry Walthall in D. W. Griffith's *Birth of a Nation* (1915) was "The Little Colonel." Leslie Howard as Ashley Wilkes was a romantic, vascillating idealist; nonetheless he became commander of the local cavalry company and returned home a major. Even Charles Hamilton, the bumbling manchild Scarlett first married, was a second lieutenant. After many months of war, Walter Connolly in *So Red the Rose* finally decided to fight and simply pulled a major's uniform from the closet. Randolph Scott in the same movie shirked his duty until after Shiloh, then tardily departed as a private to come riding back later as a captain.

The code duello also figured prominently. The defense of one's honor became such a stock item that even the musical *Dixiana* (1930) had the required duel. In the musical comedy *Mississippi*, Bing Crosby sought the advice of W. C. Fields and became the feared duellist, "The Notorious Colonel Steel." *The Gambler From Natchez* (1954) and *The Quadroon* (1971) also played heavily on the code in their advertising. Although pistols at dawn were preferred, swords sometimes came into play, as in *The Mississippi Gambler*.

The ladies too were stereotyped. The planter's wife and daughter lived lives of leisure highlighted by duties as hostesses with unlimited wardrobes. Mary Brian in *River of Romance* (1929) favored white and pastel gowns. In *Gone With the Wind*, Scarlett's opening scene was first filmed with her wearing the floral print dress she would wear the next day to the Wilkes's barbecue, then refilmed with her wearing a white gown. Not only did the retake more effectively emphasize her surroundings for the color camera; it also made a statement concerning the quality and variety of her wardrobe. When Bette Davis defiantly donned a blood red gown for a New Orleans ball in *Jezebel*, she committed a glaring social indiscretion for which she paid dearly. As a Southern vixen, Davis was also unique in being a hard horsewoman; most cinematic belles kept demurely to the drawing room and shunned the stables.

The women were all carefully sheltered. That Scarlett did not quite know how to grant a kiss to Rhett after his gift of the Paris bonnet was not unusual. When finally the image of the belles changed after 1965, the ladies made up for lost time. In *Mandingo*, the planter's wife blackmailed her husband's favorite slave into sleeping with her. In *Drum*, the planter's daughter flaunted her charms before the fieldhands. Regardless of the character revisions, the tradition of the refined and strikingly beautiful belle was quite firmly entrenched by then, after almost seventy years of ladylike behavior by such popular starlets as Joan Bennett and Dorothy Lamour. There were some exceptions: Elizabeth Taylor in *Raintree County* (1957) was a bit eager for physical attention, but then again she was driven by madness.

The slave's character was as consistent as his white counterpart's. Despite the contributions of such accomplished black actors as James B. Lowe, Clarence Muse, Noble Johnson, Eddie Anderson, and Hattie McDaniel, the image of the Negro was molded to fit the romantic mythology. It was not until 1969 that Ossie Davis' role in *Slaves* indicated a departure from the norm. Whether as roustabout, fieldhand, or servant, the slave's life in pictures was no more hurried than the white folks' existence in the big house. House servants especially were sympathetic to whatever difficulties the master's family endured, and the whites in turn shared their joys with the servants. Hattie McDaniel's tears over "Capt'n Rhett's" grief at his daughter's death made for a classic bit of acting and adherence to the tradition of the faithful family retainer as well. Teresa Harris, as Marlene Dietrich's maid and confidante in *The Flame of New Orleans* (1941), essentially arranged the courtship of her mistress. Clarence Muse and Bill "Bojangles" Robinson were cast as dedicated servants so often that when they were absent from a production something seemed amiss in the household. When Muse was finally given a chance to play a recalcitrant slave in *So Red the Rose*, he took advantage of the opportunity to give full vent to his anger in a rousing speech of denunciation aimed at the South's system of bondage. Such opportunities were almost nonexistent.

Despite their talents, black actors were doomed to play subservient roles, not only because of their color, but because basic story lines called for the contented pose. Even Sidney Poitier's portrayal of Rau-Ru in *Band of Angels* was closer to the enduring image than to Robert Penn Warren's stalwart character in the novel from which the script was adapted. If in film the slave's life was so pleasantly uncomplicated, it followed that the master must be kind. Filmdom's treatment of the disciplining of slaves was a far cry from reality. The fieldhands in silent film, particularly those of the *Uncle Tom's Cabin* remakes, were punished for real or imagined transgressions; but in the era of sound film the worker remained unwhipped and generally unrebellious until a European version of *Uncle Tom's Cabin* in 1965. The infamous overseer was a rarity, especially in movies after 1927, when the Old South films increased in frequency and in romanticism. When the overseer was present, he was portrayed as a regrettable necessity, or as a foil to point up how gentle and caring "massa" was. Perhaps the best example of an overseer in this mold was Victor Jory as the O'Hara's man Jonas Wilkerson in *Gone With the Wind*.

In the cinema versions the slave quarters and diet were excellent, and the laborers had plenty of time to enjoy both. Within the actual slave system, however, the Negro was viewed as a material investment whose food, clothing, and shelter were only at the subsistence level. The contrary picture in films stressed how powerful the overall impression of Southern beneficence had become and also exposed an attitude towards black bondage itself as an unimportant issue. After all, the cinema implied, slaves were well taken care of and given free rein for pastimes such as religion, dancing, or singing. The quarters were large, had raised floors, and were private, with but one family to a dwelling. And the best servants might earn even more. Walt Disney's "Uncle Remus" lived in a cozy cabin dominated by a cheery fireplace.

Whether in the quarters or in the fields, the workers and the audiences were happiest when the Negroes sang and danced. Music abounded in such early sound film shorts as *Dixie Days* (1928) and *Dixie* (1929). In *Way Down South* (1939) there was joyful harmonizing and heartfelt jubilation in the fields at harvest time. Singing on the riverbank, seventy slaves happily greeted

Gable's return in *Band of Angels*. Ironically those films which included music contributed to a truer image of black culture in one respect. Although sung within the context of the contented slave syndrome, the songs of groups such as the Hall Johnson Choir at least offered authentic spirituals or cleverly styled imitations. They constituted one of the few bright spots in a series of stories otherwise oblivious to the slave's culture. Only in a few films, such as *Song of the South*, was the workers' music a radical departure from the Afro-American laborers' distinctive style.

In film, the economy of the Old South was of course dependent on King Cotton. Although corn dominated in later productions such as *Mandingo* (perhaps dictated by the availability of shooting locales), cotton was still the required subject of at least one conversation or scene in most productions. No river-bank loading area was without a few bales in any movie, regardless of locale. The crop and the re-creation of its handling were so much an integral part of the image of the Old South that David O. Selznick planned to include an introductory scene of cotton being chopped in *Gone With the Wind*. But as the scene was to precede the April barbecue, he was told that the idea would be impossible since the season was incorrect for chopping. Selznick—whose scrupulous attention to detail was legendary—was nonetheless so obsessed with the standard shot of workers in the fields that he hung onto the idea through four months of debate.[9] In the end, he still included a short scene of a few hands tending the plants. Obviously, the producer knew what the people expected.

As Selznick's obsession so effectively demonstrated, American filmmakers failed to create something fresh from already overworked material. Film companies worked within established rules and reflected popular preconceptions. The fact that the film image of the antebellum South was the same throughout seven decades pointed not to the industry's concept alone, but to what the audience came to expect and believe was accurate. The film moguls had only to look at the popularity of novels which nostalgically recaptured the culture, by writers such as Stark Young and Margaret Mitchell, to realize that the trend was not dying. The public wanted more.

[9]Lambert, *GWTW*, 70.

As a result, on one level a film's concept of the South was an attempt to convince the general public of its veracity. On another level, the cinematic portrayal took into account the desires of the audience and played upon the viewer's preconceptions. Hollywood's conceptualization and the public's imagination eventually became mutually supportive. Once caught in the reciprocal exchange of beliefs, did either the film industry or its audience realize that they were reinforcing a myth? Probably not for many decades, as was strongly suggested by the majority of complimentary reviews, by advertising within the industry itself, by the studios' publicity information for threatre operators, and by receipts.

Hence a bizarre twist developed. As one critic remarked, "If you can find the myth, it hasn't been hidden properly, and if it's been hidden properly, you can't find it for sure."[10] Film versions of the slave South functioned far more as agents of reinforcement than as agents for change. The movies tended to confirm, not to lead. Although there were subtle hints in *The Foxes of Harrow* and *Band of Angels* that the mythology of the happy slave was at least wearing thin, overall the movies still succumbed to romanticism's cliches. After 1957, during a period of minority unrest and radical reassessment of racial mores, stories of the prewar society disappeared. Film took the cue, was silent, and did not attempt to capture the new mood until the release of *Slaves* in 1969, the first American depiction of the inherently evil system and a sign that the winds of change were evidently constant.

The new outlook did not inaugurate a new liberal concept, but rather marked a confirmation of the public's new perception of race relations and the South, altered in the previous ten years by the civil rights controversy. And as part of a general new wave of cinema which debunked longstanding and treasured myths, the films attacked the Old South with a vengeance.

In the new movies, represented by the highly successful *Mandingo* and *Roots* and by tasteless productions such as *Drum* and *Passion Plantation*, the interpretation was actually reversed only in certain aspects. The new movies altered the view of slavery

[10]Wilfred Sheed, "Milking the Elk," *New York Review of Books* 23 (April 15, 1976), 35.

without changing the idealization of its trappings; characters were repeatedly examined within traditional settings. Thus, although the slave became by nature noble and the planter lazy and ignorant of his workers, the locale remained the large, white, columned mansion with formal gardens and broad acreage. Perhaps the grandest home, decorated with refinement and impeccable taste, was in *Drum*, yet it was occupied by the lowest, most ignorant planter presented so far. The legend of a South dominated by massive holdings and work forces lingered on.

Even in *Roots*, supposedly a sweeping new interpretation adapted for television, a trace of the old conception existed, particularly in the introduction. For the first segments, spanning the years 1775 to the early 1800s, a voice intoned over a scene of a formal carriage approaching a fine white frame house, "This was the world of the Old South." But as the story moved from Virginia and into the prewar decades and the setting changed to an average North Carolina farm, no such claims were made. Coincidence perhaps, but the term "Old South" had yet to escape its porticoed domain.

The movies had other means beyond mere repetition to make the "vast wealth" of the plantation representative of the entire culture and believeable. It is clear, for example, that films shot on location were furnished with a visual body of documentation: the viewer saw what one commentator has termed a "film museum."[11]

In shooting such movies as *Band of Angels*, for instance, the production staff was careful to find actual mansions such as "Belle Helene." When one added to the authentic setting the proper clothing, furniture, even attitudes, the past certainly came alive. What was so difficult to remember for so many of the antebellum stories, including those of the new view such as *Passion Plantation* (1978), was that the true historical interest lay in the re-creation of that one select portion of society which was by no means representative of the whole.

The enticing details—the houses, ballgowns, fine furnishings,

[11]Marc Ferro, "The Fiction Film and Historical Analysis," *The Historian and Film*, ed. by Paul Smith (New York: Cambridge Univ. Press, 1976), 80-94.

beautiful landscaping—by their very opulence should have revealed the cinematic South as only a fraction of a far wider society. But that is not the case. As advertisements were bandied about so frequently proclaiming a film's accuracy, it is easier to understand how the smallest class became representative. With the required manse pictured in the background, advertisements for the films testified to their adherence to fact. The posters for *Mandingo* cautioned the viewer to "expect the truth."[12] The claims of veracity were an all too common ploy.

In addition, it was easy to become entranced by a story without closely examining it. The surface excitement and realistic detail in *River of Romance* (1929) and *Duel on the Mississippi* (1955), two pictures dealing with duelling, tended to obscure the fact that they placed undue stress on the universal honor in fighting. Though to film an actual prewar setting did not establish it as characteristic of the general society, unfortunately the frequent utilization of similar location scenes finally implied accuracy. This was particularly true for a culture increasingly reliant upon film rather than upon the printed medium.[13] The studios were well equipped to provide authentic touches, many possessing research libraries of tens of thousands of volumes and the staffs devoted solely to such specifics as to how a horse's tail was bobbed in 1860.[14]

[12]*Mandingo* (1975), Poster, LC Prints and Photographs Division, cited hereafter as LC-PPD.

[13]For an overview of the problem of film and reality, see Hortense Powdermaker, *Hollywood, the Dream Factory: An Anthropologist Looks at the Movie Makers* (Boston: Little, Brown, 1950), 13-14; Rachel Reid, "What Historians Want," *Sight and Sound* 11 (Summer 1942), 23-24; Frank D. McConnell, *The Spoken Seen: Film and the Romantic Imagination* (Baltimore: Johns Hopkins Univ. Press, 1975), 14-43; Michael Wood, *America in the Movies, or Santa Maria It Had Slipped My Mind* (New York: Basic Books, 1975), 3-23; and Leo Braudy, *The World in a Frame: What We See in Films* (Garden City, N.Y.: Anchor Press, 1977), 83-94.

[14]See Louis Van Den Ecker, "A Veteran's View of Hollywood Authenticity," *Hollywood Quarterly* 4 (Summer 1950), 323-31; and Mary Field, "Making the Past Live: Inaccuracy in Historical Films," *Sight and Sound* 4 (Fall 1935), 132-34.

The detail was essential, however, as a period's spirit was often captured by the cut of a garment or a piece of furniture. In RKO's *Dixiana* (1930) the studio spent over $100,000 to obtain a wide variety of period furnishings for a Louisiana plantation set. The completed interior included a large ballroom, paneled dining room, hall, verandah, and two bedrooms. The sum was a large amount of money at the time for one set, but the investment proved worth it. One reviewer dubbed the movie, "Radio's opulent tribute to a vanished age of chivalry and passion."[15]

Studios hoped such efforts would improve the potential box office draw when added to the allure of the starring cast. The films of the Old South indeed attracted their share of the film colony's bright lights. In the 1930s, at the peak of cinematic romanticism, stars such as Charles "Buddy" Rogers, Bebe Daniels, Stepin Fetchit, Jackie Coogan, Shirley Temple, Margaret Sullavan, and Donald Crisp contributed their talents to the cause. In the next two decades, Marlene Dietrich, Maureen O'Hara, Tyrone Power, Debra Paget, and Elizabeth Taylor joined the ranks. The production companies poured money, research, and talent into musicals, comedies, and dramas using the Southern theme. Quite simply, plantation stories were good business, attracting Academy Awards and, most importantly, customers. Such movies as *Hearts in Dixie, Mississippi, Jezebel,* and the vehicles for Shirley Temple were enormously successful and encouraged further forays into the genre. As one film historian put it, "Film in America is a collaborative professional activity, a business first and an art second."[16]

As businessmen, the moviemakers continually had to present what was acceptable to the public, and the treatment of such a subject as the slave South supposedly demanded caution. While the myth developed and became accepted, many in the industry worried that the South might dictate the norm established previously in literature, the theatre, and in silent film, that the region

---

[15]*Minneapolis Tribune*, Sept. 6, 1930; see also *San Francisco Chronicle*, July 28, 1930.

[16]Charles Higham, *The Art of American Film* (Garden City, N.Y.: Anchor Press, 1974), ix.

might impose restrictions on a film's content from outside and even from within the industry. There were, in fact, Southerners in executive positions, giving credence to the possibility that the section might exert considerable influence. For example, Sam Katz of Paramount's Publix Theatres chain; Edward Kuykendall, former president of the Motion Picture Producers Association; and directors such as Clarence Brown, W. S. Van Dyke, and King Vidor were all Southerners. But any chance that the Old South themes could or had to be determined by natives simply was unfounded.[17] The mythology was not sustained by Southerners; the area simply lacked the clout to shape a picture's outlook.

For one thing, there was the problem of how to monitor adequately the Southern market. During the 1930s when the most nostalgic films were released, *Variety* used only five Southern cities as gauges of how well a film did financially. Of the five, only Birmingham and New Orleans were of the Deep South; Louisville, Baltimore, and Washington, D.C., made up the balance. The *Motion Picture Herald* used an equally inadequate gauge. As a result, the industry could misperceive what would play successfully in, say, Richmond or Atlanta. Hollywood believed that *Mississippi*, which hewed to the line of antebellum romanticism, would get an excellent response in the region, but the movie was not nearly as well liked there as in the North. *Band of Angels*, on the other hand, which dared to explore lightly the theme of miscegenation, seemed a sure candidate for poor reviews in the South, yet proved to be well received there. Many audiences and critics simply failed to grasp its unique significance. One local reviewer spoke for many, viewing it only as another picture in the traditional mold and enthusiastically exclaiming, "shades of *Uncle Tom's Cabin*, *The Birth of a Nation*, and *Gone With the Wind* and all the other sagas of the Deep South."[18]

[17]For an examination of the degree to which the fear of Southern criticism influenced racial stereotyping, see Thomas J. Cripps, "The Myth of the Southern Box Office, A Factor in Racial Stereotyping in American Movies, 1920-1940," in *The Black Experience in America, Selected Essays,* ed. by James C. Curtis and Louis L. Gould (Austin: Univ. of Texas Press, 1970), 116-44; and Cripps, *Slow Fade to Black: The Negro in American Film, 1900-1942* (New York: Oxford Univ. Press, 1977), 110-11.

[18]*Richmond Times-Dispatch*, Aug. 29, 1957.

Another problem involved the fact that Southern theatres did not have the earning capacity of theatres in other sections. Many movie houses closed from May to September because of the heat. Moreover, the South, including Kentucky and Maryland, could only boast in the late 30s of 3,786 theatres, with a total capacity of under two million. The national total was 17,541 theatres, seating almost eleven million.[19]

The figures raise an interesting point. With less than one-fifth the potential audience, the South could hardly dictate what Hollywood would present. The big profits were to be made elsewhere, and thus no amount of Southern lobbying by area managers or executives could be very persuasive.

However, the movies were consistently well attended and the part of the nation which proved the films' popularity was the non-Southern sector. So much more important were the other areas in determining a release's profitability that movies were shown first outside the South, and the area portryed simply waited its turn. Even after rare premieres in the South, the productions were then quickly ushered off to the more lucrative Northern markets. Following the opening of *Gone With the Wind* in Atlanta in December 1939, for example, the film was shown by the second week of January 1940 or sooner not only in the largest northeastern cities but also in the Midwest. Cities as large as Richmond, Raleigh, and Birmingham waited until February. Frequently, the managers in the South after finally getting a print had to announce shorter runs than preferred as the demand was so heavy in the more profitable North.[20] Southerners alone could never have made such productions viable enterprises.

The plantation epics thrived, then, only with the help of those sections which seemed at first glance the least likely to be enthralled by tales of antebellum wealth, honor, society, and servitude. Actually, the industry was agreeing with, rather than bending to, sectional whim. In the knowledge that large audiences everywhere would welcome the product, there was no inclination to do otherwise.

That the film companies were truly independently swayed by

[19]*Motion Picture Herald*, May 28, 1938.
[20]Based on a survey of ninety newspapers over the period 1927-1976.

Southern mythology in *Uncle Tom's Cabin* (1903). BELOW: Henry Walthall in *Birth of a Nation*.

the legendary quality of the Old South was particularly evident in those movies in which the producers did seem to ignore possible Southern disapproval. Such a picture as *Hearts in Dixie* (1929), with its predominantly Negro cast, was a risky offering for the South. But even if some theatre managers balked, Northern audiences still welcomed what was nonetheless essentially a romantic depiction of the Southland. Amidst the scenes of Negro toil and familial travail were the stock shots of steamboats, race horses, singing cotton pickers, and joyful quarters.

Eventually more serious filmmakers were attracted to the subject, but even their supposedly informative films were far removed from reality. In fact, such pictures pointed out just how firmly the mythology had become rooted in the American mind. In essence the films reflected the spirit of their fictional counterparts. *Dixie* (1924), in the prestigious Yale University *Chronicles of America* series, emphasized slave contentment and loyalty. So too did *The Old South* (1932), omitting any detailed discussion of the profit motive in bondage. Labor scenes were upstaged by those of frolic in the quarters.[21]

This infatuation by both North and South alike with the romantic aspects of prewar life was significant, for the reality was of course quite different and has yet to be appreciated fully in even the most recent films. Actually, the vast majority of homes were of ordinary size; furnishings were more simple than ornate. Massive holdings of slaves were few. Landowners more often than not worked the land themselves, for a life of genteel ease was as rare as in any society. Few women could live as leisured hostesses; men generally were not cultured gentlemen. It was a society of diverse classes and occupations in which the average person was a farmer and a non-slaveholder.

In 1860, almost three-fourths of the population owned no slaves. Of a million and a half white families, a tiny portion could claim membership in the planter aristocracy of wealth, education, and power built upon the labor of others. Only three thousand families could support at least a hundred slaves; fully

---

[21]*The Old South* (Eastman Teaching Films, 1932); *Dixie* (Yale, 1924), LC-MPS and the Museum of Modern Art Film Study Center (New York), cited hereafter as MOMA-FSC.

ninety percent of the "planters" possessed fewer than twenty blacks. But throughout most of their history, the movies presented the mythology of a culture of economic and social units of at least a hundred blacks, an overseer, grand surroundings, and a life of ease.[22]

The South was a section more oriented to dirt farming and land clearing with the help of only the immediate family. The impact of a film mythology accepted by several generations which so completely alters that fact has been enormous. Produced for entertainment, the make-believe became believed. And as the familiar plots were repeated, the common reference point grew ever wider, forming part of the audiences' education. Together, the films were a collection of beliefs which influenced views concerning not just the antebellum South but the economic, cultural, and racial problems of the nation as well.

[22]Though debate continues concerning antebellum Southern society—its culture, profitability, role in secession, intellectual leanings, and system of bondage—there has been little argument about the makeup of the population. The general slaveholder was in a distinct minority, which included an even scarcer planter aristocracy. The census of 1860 provides the statistical data to demonstrate the numerical predominance of farms v. large estates, of common folk v. gentry. Historians have repeatedly raised the point from early studies to the present. A sampling includes William E. Dodd, *The Cotton Kingdom: A Chronicle of the Old South* (New Haven: Yale Univ. Press, 1919), 10; U. B. Phillips, *The Slave Economy of the Old South: Selected Essays in Economic and Social History*, ed. by Eugene D. Genovese (Baton Rouge: LSU Press, 1968), 3-22; Phillips; *Life and Labor in the Old South* (Boston: Little, Brown, 1929), 339; Lewis C. Gray, *History of Agriculture in the Southern United States to 1860* (New York: Peter Smith, 1941), I, 481–83; R. S. Cotterill, *The Old South* (Glendale, Cal.: Arthur Clark, 1936), 265-72; Wilbur J. Cash, *The Mind of the South* (New York: Knopf, 1941), ix-x, 61; Frank I. Owsley, *Plain Folk of the Old South* (Baton Rouge: LSU Press, 1949), vi, 1-2; Avery O. Craven, *The Growth of Southern Nationalism, 1848-1861* (Baton Rouge: LSU Press, 1953), 11-12; Francis B. Simkins, *A History of the Old South* (New York: Knopf, 1953), 133-36; Kenneth M. Stampp, *The Peculiar Institution: Slavery in the Ante-Bellum South* (New York: Knopf, 1956), 29-33; Clement Eaton, *The Growth of Southern Civilization, 1790-1860* (New York: Harper, 1961), 1-24; Leslie H. Owens, *This Species of Property: Slave Life and Culture in the Old South* (New York: Oxford Univ. Press, 1976), 7-9.

For the South itself, reviews and ticket receipts revealed that the movies reinforced a socio-economic and political outlook rooted firmly in the past. Southerners found a modern kindred spirit in film. What postwar romantic literature had so popularly begun, the movies ratified. *Birth of a Nation* and *Gone With the Wind* may well be the most remembered of films, but the theatres presented a steady stream of similar fare which perpetuated the myth of ambience, racial fidelity, and courtly idealism. The movies not only painted the region as the natives wished it to be recalled, but the films also became progressively more attractive as pictures of how many people wished the area would remain.

It was also of no small importance that outsiders produced such a complimentary view of their Southern neighbors. The releases made a white Southerner proud. The influence of the productions upon a politically conservative and at times reactionary philosophy, the survival of a caste system both racial and economic, and a reluctance to embrace fully the present much less the future was assuredly broad. Too many pictures aroused too much nostalgic emotion to be discounted as mere entertainment. Significantly, the pictures were available to all—high and low, literate and unread, white and, in prescribed areas, black as well. All found evidence that their station in life was traditional and also proper. Thus the many releases served as a conservative restraint on the society, confirming the worth of preserving the old social order.

The acceptability of that order was one of the most important ramifications of such films when shown beyond the borders of the old Confederacy. One result was that the cause of the Negro was constantly being hampered within the region traditionally most concerned with his welfare. Naturally, many factors contributed to the nation's long-standing racial outlook. For example, the growing and unwanted black migration from the South to the urban areas was objectionable to many in the North. Another cause of unease among whites was their failure to fathom that the origins of black poverty and ignorance were entrenched in lack of opportunity rather than in inherent characteristics. And the cinema, beginning with the very earliest silent productions, was also very instrumental in bolstering the image of the Negro as a helpless creature whom the script implied had been not only well treated under slavery but saved from his own shortcomings. These films did help make the South's actions in war more understandable, thus helping to heal sectional wounds, but the praise of the region's lifestyle only further obscured a people's plight and perpetuated a mistaken conception of racial inferiority. That the film interpretation was so popular beyond the South confirmed that for millions their introduction to Afro-American history was molded as much by cinematic fiction as by personal contact or knowledge.

In their acquiescence to the racist interpretation, ticket holders of North and South appeared to rationalize that if Clark Gable, Bing Crosby, Henry Fonda, Tyrone Power, and many other popular and respected stars could "own" happy and well-cared-for Negroes, then how difficult or even necessary could the problems of assimilation really be? For decades, these motion pictures sustained a simple rule; all problems could be overcome by artfully obscuring reality. Movies had become the primary form of fiction but were accepted too frequently as fact.

The North could even take great comfort in the fact that the slave had been uniquely Southern. The persistence of conservative films through the production of *Band of Angels* in 1957 allowed one myth to feed upon another in the North. Reviews repeatedly exposed the North's acceptance of the films' premise of Southern paternalism and its underlying implication little had changed. At the same time, others watching the same film could point to the South as the dam against which the surge of equality was thwarted. Quite simply, Hollywood provided a scapegoat which allowed areas beyond the old Confederacy to ignore their own complicity in inequality. As long as the productions presented the South as shouldering so much of the black population, other sections could avoid facing up to their part in the drama.

But blacks were not the only ones to suffer at the hands of Hollywood's stereotyping. The planter and his family and the economy on which they depended were typecast as well. The pictures of refinement were at first pleasing and would remain so for many, many years. The long term result, though, would be radically different. Initially the image paid dividends, for the Southerner was depicted as a man of agrarian persuasion. In the decade of the 20s with its seemingly unrestrained expansion and bustle, it was a welcome contrast. Better yet, in the 30s, when business and industry appeared to have betrayed their promise of prosperity and instead seemed to have wrought nothing but misery, the films of antebellum agricultural stability held forth the relief of an evening's escape from reality and even a fleeting alternative, albeit impractical, to the pell mell rush to modernization.

Ironically though, the typecasting in the very films from 1903 through the 1950s would in the following decades come back to haunt a South trying for economic and social reasons to shed a lingering image of an agrarian folk emmeshed in a memory. The glory of Gable in the 1930s was replaced in the 1970s by an ignorant, racist, and provincial Warren Oates in *Drum*. Once allowed to stand proudly in the past, the South was finally paying the price of the film mythology, and in popular culture found itself at last hobbled by the very character it had once been anxious to label as representative.

But the cinematic view of the section had its advantageous aspects. For so many films, the South had represented much that was good about the nation as a whole. When government faltered and scandal was rampant, when industry caused more hardship than profit, the cinematic South presented an example of American ideals. Amidst a rapidly changing world, the films presented a close family circle, prosperity, respect for authority, and an idealization of the native spirit—characteristics the nation, irrespective of section, could emulate. In that regard, the South was in essence no different from many settings for historical movies.

Like many plot lines drawn from American history, the plantation suffered from being too recent a phenomenon. As one film critic has observed, the nation in movies became "an invented place, where imagined ideals were invoked as a structure for reality."[23] Lacking a lengthy historical tradition and thus a less rose-colored perception of events, it was difficult to be objective. American film makers long sought to preserve a defensive, pristine, and idealistic view which affected not only the charac-

[23]David Thomson, *America in the Dark: Hollywood and the Gift of Unreality* (New York: Morrow, 1977), 37.

terization of cowboys, the wealthy, or G-men but planters as well. Thus Hollywood took an active part in shaping our perceptions of national destiny, unblemished by ugly past realities still too immediate for unbiased scrutiny.

Until the 1950s, the film colony excelled in productions of taste, beauty, and excitement—all adroitly calculated for their undisturbing, pleasant effect. Occasionally, radical changes in plot or setting, as in the screen adaptation of John Steinbeck's *Grapes of Wrath*, challenged the very national character the industry had so laboriously constructed. But overall the films had made conservative theatre goers of us all, for who wanted to deprive Cary Grant of his sophisticated surroundings in high society, or John Wayne of his battles against the fierce plains savages, or Bing Crosby of his dogwood-shaded plantation gardens? The pictures exacerbated the populace's tendency to ignore the problems which productions such as *The Little Colonel* or *Dixie* presented as unimportant. Granted, much of the function of film is to provide an escape in entertainment. It was a tragedy, though, that the Old South genre soft-pedaled so many issues crucial to the maturity of a region and a nation.

II

A Black Defense of a White World

THE SOUTH IN SILENT FILM, 1903-1927

Throughout the silent picture era, American film was fiercely commercial. And no wonder. Film companies had to provide entertaining and profitable stories, to capture wide audiences and keep creditors at bay. Successful plots quickly turned into predictable molds. Serious art or comment in documentaries was rare. Most films dealt either with contemporary life in crime stories, domestic romances, and melodramas, or with a nostalgic past in westerns and historical romances. Both types revealed much about the culture for which they were intended.

In a rapidly industrializing nation, Americans were simultaneously preoccupied with upward mobility and nostalgic about the "idyllic" past. Films captured the mood. Stories were often centered around the successful upper or upper-middle classes, presenting that existence dreamed of by film audiences. *Humoresque* (1920) told of the love affair between a wealthy woman and a violinist. *Happiness* (1923) dealt with a young and ordinary girl under the guidance of a rich society woman who felt compelled to remold the lower classes through one of its members.

Films also pointed out the human price exacted by society's efforts to succeed and grow. D. W. Griffith's *Broken Blossoms* (1919) was a stark glimpse of decaying docks and the people who inhabited them. *Man, Woman and Sin* (1927) provided views into city slums and the attitudes of the fortunate toward the poor. *The Crowd* (1928) revealed the faceless, uncaring nature of urban citizens for one another. *The Beggars of Life* (1927), in following a tramp's and a fugitive's long odyssey, made the point that perhaps everyone was unhappy with his current situation.

With cinema presenting either inaccessible achievement or

depths of failure in modern settings, naturally more escapist fare became both necessary and popular. Costumed romances such as *The Mark of Zorro* (1920) or *The Shiek* (1920) were enjoyable vehicles. Also popular and needed were those stories which looked back on America before the momentous changes wrought by cities, industry, global diplomacy, and power. Films such as Thomas Ince's *Custer's Last Fight* (1912) helped to meet the need. Such western stars as William S. Hart furnished plots filled with action, plus overstated idealism in a simpler, purer existence. Griffith's *America* (1924) made history fascinating and moving.[1]

The tales of the Old South fell between two extremes. Antebellum films, like westerns and other historical stories, were intent on preserving images threatened by a modern world. These movies captured a sense of romantic melancholy. In addition, Southern themes adhered to the credo of upper class ambition. Continually presenting only the planter aristocracy and its willing servants, the stories provided the viewer with a model of achievement devoid of the unfortunate consequences of the rush to the top so evident in the audiences' surroundings.

It was a romantic glance at what at times must have seemed possible: a successful union of idealism and achievement. Occasionally, this idealism even embraced aspects of modernity. In Griffith's *Birth of a Nation*, the lovers—one of the agrarian South, the other of a more modern North—envision a heavenly city of brotherly love, an urban existence combining the best of past and future. In sum, Southern stories depicted a better civilization which still had room for material wealth without the modern repercussions.

The tales of the antebellum South also fulfilled other functions. In the period before the advent of sound, films of the Old South were consistent in their characterizations. What is particularly interesting about these movies is the emphasis on blacks. The stories were centered most frequently not around the planter, his family, and peers, but around the slaves themselves, whereas movies after 1927 and the use of sound would utilize the Negroes as mere secondary participants. It was a bizarre twist of fate that

[1]See Higham, *Art of American Film*, 3-29; Sklar, *Movie-Made America*, 67-103.

the blacks would in the mass culture of cinema be their tormentors' staunchest defenders. Even worse, most of the slaves' parts were acted in blackface. It was not until 1914, for example, that a black was allowed to play the lead in *Uncle Tom's Cabin*.[2]

The infatuation with the Negro was probably due to several factors. The black in movies was generally grossly caricatured. Stories, such as those in the *Rastus* series, presented a fumbling, conniving, lazy, greedy individual whose very fictional existence revealed the animosity of whites. When used within the context of the plantation tale, the depiction of the Negro as a contented servant or laborer was no departure from the accepted contemporary view of the dependent black requiring supervision. From the premise that blacks were no different in any situation, it was an easy step to regard the Old South's labor system as forgiveable.

It should be noted that the Southern literary tradition of earlier years had also leaned heavily on the slave. Local colorists such as Joel Chandler Harris and Thomas Nelson Page had fully developed a stereotyped servant. They were flesh and blood characters, harmless, likeable, and essential in pointing out the benefits of servitude and the antebellum world. The slave represented the simple, old ways. Comfortable in a rural utopia, the Negroes were required by the "blessings" they already possessed to pay no heed to Northern alternatives. It seemed only natural too that the silent films so reliant on the visual and easily recognizable should make use of what had become a stock player.

This acceptance of servility as characteristic of the black race is an important point. Previously so recognizable in literature and light theatre, the black character also came to be conveniently and repeatedly presented in the new medium. And the more often the Negro persona was used, the more often the black's lowly status was confirmed.

The South in its treatment of the Negro became not only more understandable, but even forgiveable for subjugating a race which in movies was so obviously devoid of good sense. The

<hr />

[2]For an overview of early stereotyping, see Daniel J. Leab, "The Gamut from A to B: The Image of the Black in Pre-1915 Movies," *Political Science Quarterly* 88 (March 1973), 53-70; Cripps, *Slow Fade to Black*, 8-40.

films, in essence, had enormous potential for increasing racial misunderstanding and even hatred.

The productions made in the Northeast and eventually the West, therefore, did much to form a popular and simplistic apologia for the South. The vast crowds which would clamor for seats to D. W. Griffith's *Birth of a Nation* were not only a testimony to the director's artistic genius, but also evidence of a lack of interest in solving the nation's racial problems. Nationwide, reviews and advertising made it abundantly clear that the South had experienced a considerable improvement in the perception of outsiders who were beginning to fathom and to embrace the historical passions and fears of the plantation world.

Of course, movies could not take credit for the initial reappraisal. By the beginning of silent film, the non-Southern areas were already far more predisposed to a new viewpoint. Literature had done its part. Historians such as Woodrow Wilson were more likely to view "the late unpleasantness" with a more charitable and balanced perspective now that the passions had subsided. Also, the civil rights policies of Reconstruction had apparently not come to fruition, and the North harbored little desire to go further in altering the relationship between black and white. The Spanish-American War also contributed to a new sense of unity, since the South fought as ably and as patriotically as any region.

For the average citizen, time was another important factor in healing wounds. Even the youngest trooper of the Civil War years was by the turn of the century a man in his fifties. Many veterans were beyond sixty. Veterans' associations such as the Grand Army of the Republic began to hold joint reunions with their Southern counterparts. The reunions were touching evidence of the spirit of forgiveness and recognitions of the opponent's courage.

Film, too, along with literature and the passage of time, contributed to the new feelings of understanding. For Southerners themselves, the productions provided vindication, a source of pride, and a rationale for their forebears' secessionist impulse. By continually harping on the Negro, by emphasizing the plantation grandeur as a means of making movies alluring, film presented the region in a complimentary light to millions of people for whom their only knowledge of the South was through movies. And ironically, the lesson was taught by the black.

The work of Edwin S. Porter and Sigmund Lubin in filming their respective versions of *Uncle Tom's Cabin* provided quite early a model to follow in later productions. Distributed in 1903, both products encouraged other filmmakers to direct further interpretations, which in turn influenced still more to follow similar story lines.

Porter's *Uncle Tom's Cabin* was representative of the emerging silent film. Confined by its staged appearance, lack of modern creative editing, and constant camera range, the Edison Company's production now seems as stilted as any other efforts in the developing media. Located mostly in the northeast, such companies as Edison, Lubin, Kalem, Vitagraph, and Essany were relatively small and often saddled with debt while producing many films in flats or old warehouses. For example, many of Biograph's major releases between 1908 and 1913 were filmed in a house on New York's Fourteenth Street until production facilities were later moved to a Bronx warehouse.

Porter's product was a milestone. Besides his development of narrative movies and his pioneering use of descriptive cards flashed on the screen, his film layed the foundation for the cinematic plantation mythology. In it and in numerous remakes, the myth came to form a justification, a defense, for the South's uniqueness. The vanquished came to be seen as a society once misunderstood but now forgiven, perhaps even revered.

Limited by technology and running time, Porter trimmed considerably his version of the Harriet Beecher Stowe novel. While the story's outline remained the same, there was no doubt that the tone was different. In the Edison Company version, the opening shot of the slave quarters shows the workers to be living quite comfortably. Uncle Tom's house is a sturdy wood frame structure with a stone chimney, surrounded by a fence. The Negroes are well clothed. Uncle Tom's wife wears a white dress and bonnet; the visiting Eliza has a large, flowing white cape.

Several scenes show the blacks brimming over with enthusiasm. Seven males are relaxing on a loading dock, until several others, including women and children, enter. Then the company breaks into "spontaneous" dancing and madcap singing and clapping. Later, when Uncle Tom and his new master arrive at the St. Clair estate, the slaves dance ecstatically, jump in the air, and wave their hats wildly. After he has been established as the household butler, Tom witnesses further revelry. Before a backdrop showing the house's massive white columns, pairs of well dressed slaves enter—the men in dark suits, the women in knee-length dresses and carrying white baskets or parasols.

The whites appear benevolent, almost excessively concerned for the welfare of the blacks. In one scene, Uncle Tom accompanies his master, St. Clair, to a grand bar decorated with marble columns. Grieving over the death of his daughter Little Eva, St. Clair graciously invites his servant to sit with him and share some refreshment. A rowdy fellow arrives (who it turns out is Simon Legree) and insists on buying St. Clair a drink. St. Clair refuses and the drunk angrily throws his whisky in the slave's face. Horrified, St. Clair lunges to his man's defense and is knifed to death for his devoted interest.

After his owner's death, Uncle Tom is to be sold at auction. The situation is made to appear a happy event. Two slave children dance joyfully while adults keep time; other slaves are shooting craps. The buyers, by their apparel at least, are gentlemen. Only Legree looks evil. He seems the sole villain in an exchange otherwise calm and beneficial to both master and slave. The slaves go so far as to display a gratitude at their sale; one smiles broadly at his new gentleman owner.

One of the more revealing aspects of the many productions of Mrs. Stowe's story is how the planter class is portrayed. Early films, without the advantage of extended dialogue for character development, had to make the players obviously hero or scoundrel, leaving no doubt in the viewer's mind where his allegiance should lie. Throughout the first film adaptations of the novel, the typical Southerner is invariably well clothed and well mannered and is kind to his slaves. Humane owners of large estates, such as the Shelby and St. Clair families, in return receive commendable service from their charges. On the other hand, any white guilty of cruelty is made to seem like one of society's outcasts, one who had failed to grasp the region's true way of life. Only the exceptions show disdain for the black's welfare. Therefore, it is not the average slave owner who is attacked by Porter and other directors; it is the few reprobates with their slouched hats, whips, brace of pistols, and bad deportment—all instantly recognizable trappings of villainy.

But finally in the spirit of the original work, Porter's ending serves to place the story on the side of right. As Uncle Tom lies dying, after a brutal beating at Legree's orders, he raises his hands to heaven and sees an image of John Brown. As the abolitionist is being led to the gallows, he embraces a small black child. Then scenes of battle appear, followed by Lincoln shown with a Negro in supplication at his feet. At last the reunion of the nation is personified by two men shaking hands.[3]

In spite of the ending, the plantation lifestyle was presented through most of the film as attractive and benign. And in view of how bluntly stereotyped the grinning, singing blacks were and how satisfied they seemed under Caucasian guidance, it was hard for an audience not only to be proud of the ending, but also charmed by the genteel atmosphere which so strongly implied that the South knew best how to care for the Negro.

With its painted backdrops, dances, and theatrical illusions, the film vividly presented the style of nineteenth-century live theatre, while at the same time it introduced what may be the earliest use of titles. Within his production, Porter popularized the plantation ideal in a new medium. The cinematic myth was born. Like all its followers, the claims of adherence to fact or an original story accompanied advertising. Brochures for theatre operators declared that, "This is the most elaborate effort at telling a story in moving pictures yet attempted," and that "the story of the book is closely followed."[4]

Another version of Stowe's novel appeared in 1903, three months after the Edison/Porter film. The Sigmund Lubin Company also presented a panorama of a grand estate graced by comfortable Negroes, singing and dancing. Moreover, this film attempted more to glorify than to examine critically the Old South. In a publicity booklet, the adaptation was called "one of

[3]*Uncle Tom's Cabin* (Edison, 1903), LC-MPS.
[4]Kleine Optical Co. Advertisement for *Uncle Tom's Cabin* (Edison, 1903), MOMA-FSC.

the prettiest stories ever written." And Uncle Tom's attractive abode was labeled "a typical Southern log cabin." But, again, maintaining a sense of national pride in a film of such regional leanings, a picture of Lincoln adorned the pamphlet's cover.[5]

While neither the Edison nor Lubin releases were intended to hold up the South as a model society, in effect that was the result. As long as the traditional antebellum legend and contemporary Negro stereotyping complemented one another and remained accepted and profitable, the South would continue to be portrayed as a graceful agrarian society, which perhaps did know best not only how to control the black, but how to make him contented with his situation. The movies eventually placed the burden of secession and war not on the Southern system, but on the few who abused it, such as Legree and other radicals.

Both films were sufficiently popular that in 1909 there were two more presentations by the Pathé and Vitagraph companies. The latter promised "the real thing in every respect—real ice, real bloodhounds, real Negroes, real actors, real scenes from the real life as it was in the antebellum days."[6] But the Vitagraph conception was no more "real" than its predecessors' view. Although the company issued lobby cards for their "modern screen version of the everlasting play" with a likeness of "Abraham Lincoln, the Emancipator" included, the film showed little promise of avoiding the cliches of antebellum plots.[7]

One of the film's opening descriptive cards, despite its borders of chains and fastenings, hinted at the view to come. After displaying a verse from "My Ol' Kentucky Home," this statement appeared, "More than a decade before Abraham Lincoln . . . struck the shackles from the slaves, the Shelby Plantation in Kentucky flowered in kindliness." The St. Clair estate would be no different.

The spirit of the original story was captured in only a few shots. For example, when the slave trader Haley arrives at the

[5]Publicity Brochure, *"Uncle Tom's Cabin*: Harriet Beecher Stowe's Famous Story in Life Motion Pictures," for *Uncle Tom's Cabin* (Lubin, 1903), MOMA-FSC. The booklet contains twenty-four stills.

[6]MOMA-FSC Research Files on multiple versions of *Uncle Tom's Cabin.*

[7]Lobby Card, *Uncle Tom's Cabin* (Vitagraph, 1909), LC-MPS Box C-14.

Shelby home and demands slaves in payment of debts, he spies Eliza's young son. The accompanying card states that "most cruel of all the tortures of slavery was the separation of child and mother." The words are emphasized by a drawing of a bound nude female slave leaning to kiss a child. The film even utilized Negroes, though the important roles were still taken by white actors in blackface.

Overall, the image in the Vitagraph story remained one of goodness marred only by a rare demented individual. Shelby and St. Clair are kindly and educated, speak without an accent, and abide in palatial grandeur. Haley and Legree appear as illiterate. Haley likes Eliza's child, Harry, because he is a "smart boy and near white—them kind has brains." Only such outcasts as Haley and Legree drink excessively and carry weapons. Also, in comparison to the several planters, the two are recognizable failures. Besides their lack of learning and deportment, their material surroundings cannot compare to those of masters who treat their slaves well. Even the blacks are shown to be warped by such influences. Legree has two black drivers as sadistic as he, whereas Shelby's fieldhands enjoy a comfortable life, reflecting their owner's goodness and concern.

While laboring for the Shelby family, Uncle Tom lives in a "comfortable cabin" with his wife Chloe, "the best cook for miles around." And "his pickaninnies live in happy ignorance of their fate" at the hands of the interloper Haley. Eliza's Harry has a free rein of the main house and frolics in its large rooms. When Haley later leads Tom away, the slave persuades his compatriots to "Obey the good mas'r—for obedience to Him alone is the first step to the kingdom of Heaven"—an inclusion of the Biblical defense of slavery as ordained by God. Indeed, the kindly whites are once again depicted as knowing best. On the St. Clair holdings, Topsy is given to Little Eva's Aunt Ophelia as she "had her own ideas about the treatment of slaves." The card is bordered by drawings of watermelons.[8]

There were still more repetitions of the story. In 1913 both the Universal and American studios produced new versions of *Uncle Tom's Cabin*. Biograph shortly thereafter released a semi-

[8]*Uncle Tom's Cabin* (Vitagraph, 1909), LC-MPS.

documentary which established a film record of a stage production of the classic. In 1918 Paramount and Famous Players-Lasky produced two more versions.[9] On the whole, these several portrayals adhered to previous generally romantic interpretations. They all had in common the grand view of prewar society. In World Production's 1914 adaptation, the benevolent master provides brick quarters, and gentlemen lament the fate of any black under the charge of a reprobate like Legree.

The films also included those small errors which were so common in cinema's early years but which are now comic relief. Shot on small budgets, with tight schedules and few props, films simply lacked polish. In Vitagraph's 1909 release, a card announced the pursuit of the fleeing Eliza by a pack of bloodhounds. Although the advance billing promised "real hounds," the chase was actually filmed with mastiffs, and uncooperative ones at that. As the dogs and the slave catchers hurriedly round a bend in the road, hot on the trail, one dog pays no attention to the curve and runs headlong into the brush. In the World Production Company's 1914 story, Legree leaves his supposedly antebellum house through a screen door, next to which is a modern weather thermometer emblazoned with a softdrink advertisement.[10]

Regardless of such errors, the films effectively built upon a Southern and racist lore. The process pointed to how strong the antebellum legend had become by the early 1900s, if the best known story with a strongly developed black persona could be so easily warped and remain popular as a defense of the peculiar system.

There were many other productions built upon the Old South mystique, each one a further abandonment of the principles of equality espoused a half-century earlier. Many films went so far as to express the sincerity and righteousness of the plantation world by showing the slave in a sacrificial light, risking his life for his master.[11]

[9]MOMA-FSC Research Files, *Uncle Tom's Cabin*.

[10]*Uncle Tom's Cabin* (Vitagraph, 1909); (World, 1914), LC-MPS.

[11]See Paul Spehr, comp., *The Civil War in Motion Pictures: A Bibliography of Films Produced in the United States Since 1897* (Washington: Govt. Printing Office, 1961).

In *The Confederate Spy* (1910), the prewar atmosphere of peace and contentment served as an introduction. A trade paper described the opening as displaying slaves "happy, contented, and well cared for" in a world of pastoral simplicity. So grateful were the blacks for their good treatment that one, Uncle Daniel, defended the home against Union troops. A reviewer in the same publication touched upon the significance of many similar stories. He wrote that "much good can be done by presenting to those who know nothing about such scenes a reproduction of them," for "in that way a better understanding of the Southern people can be disseminated."[12]

Numerous other films showed the Negro as slavery's militant defender. In *The Informer* (1912), a black family takes it upon itself to save the master's house from being burned by Federal forces.[13] Uncle Wash, in *Hearts and Flags* (1911), protects Colonel Dabney's daughter from Union foragers. The common thread running through *A Special Messenger, Mammy's Ghost,* and *Uncle Peter's Ruse* is the slave's effort to conceal wounded Confederates from Yankee patrols.

Devotion could be carried to even further extremes. In *The Old Oak's Secret* (1914), Old Mose is emotionally unable to leave the plantation, and so hides his master's will which includes a manumission clause. *For Massa's Sake* told of a black so attached to his master that he tried to sell himself to pay off his owner's gambling debts. In such films as *Old Mammy's Charge* (1913), slaves return from freedom in the North to a world they know best and appreciate.

When revolts do occur, they are not against the system itself. A loyal servant in *A Slave's Devotion* flees not from his master but only to escape a cruel overseer. Between 1912 and 1913 such films as *The Debt, In Humanity's Cause,* and *In Slavery Days* were all involved with the gentleness of the Old South, where a black

---

[12]*Moving Picture World*, Feb. 12, 19, 1910; for a summary of the many films on the Civil War and its aftermath, see Cripps, *Slow Fade to Black*, 26-33.

[13]*The Informer* (Biograph, 1912), LC-MPS.

knew his place and never attempted to disturb his caretaker's trust.[14]

When given a choice by even his master, the Negro sided with the South. D. W. Griffith's *In Old Kentucky* (1909) presented a family divided by the Civil War. One son, with the servants looking on, clutches a Union flag and vows to defend it. In reply, his brother, played by Henry Walthall, pledges his life to the Confederacy. At that moment the butler and "mammy" jump and clap for glee, the butler being so bold as to pat the new rebel on the back.[15]

Griffith continued the motif in two other movies, *His Trust* and *His Trust Fulfilled*, which together reinforced the black's satisfaction with slavery. Beginning in 1910, Griffith worked on the two simultaneously in hopes for their release as one story, but the Biograph studios believed that combined the story would be too lengthy. The first film told of the slave Old George, charged by his master to protect the family while the owner served the Confederate cause. When his owner is killed shortly thereafter, the faithful servant abides by the master's wishes. Later when the mansion catches fire, he saves not only his owner's small child but his sword as well. After placing the now destitute family in his own cabin, he stands watch over them.

In the sequel, the war is over. But shunning freedom, the black remains on the estate and with his own savings aids in the education of the daughter. How he had amassed any funds was never explained, but no matter, as the example of devotion appeared more important. Eventually impoverished, the old fellow is helped by the girl's English cousin, who eventually meets and marries the young lady. While witnessing the wedding of the maid for whom he cared so, he stands apart and weeps. His duty done, the man receives a hearty handshake for

[14]See Peter Noble, *The Negro in Films* (New York: Arno, 1970), 29; Donald Bogle, *Toms, Coons, Mulattoes, Mammies and Bucks: An Interpretive History of Blacks in American Films* (New York: Viking, 1973), 9; and Cripps, *Slow Fade to Black*, 32.

[15]*In Old Kentucky* (Biograph, 1909), LC-MPS.

his sacrifices and returns to his cabin to gaze at his master's saber.[16]

That a handshake was the fellow's only reward probably met with no audience disapproval, as films by that time had placed blacks in such a subservient position that the handclasp must have seemed adequate compensation, a boon not to be questioned. Biograph's notices bore out a belief in the total loyalty of slaves to masters. One publicity bulletin stated that "in every Southern home there is an old trusted body servant whose faithful devotion . . . was extreme." Worse, as Old George is watching the marriage ceremony, he is said to be crying— with the tears "streaming down his black *but* honest cheeks" [Italics added].[17]

The implication was significant in forming a popular view of the South and the causes of the Civil War. The public, in continually attending films which praised slavery's missionary and humane aspects and the blacks' contentedness, was increasingly exposed to a thesis that the war must have been fought for the principles of states' rights and the Union rather than over the moral issue of bondage. And with the films also depicting how readily the contrite, newly patriotic defeated had become reunited with the nation, the visual defenses of slavery were not objectionable to most viewers.

For instance, in *A Reconstructed Rebel* an ex-Confederate fights for the Union in a police action in Honduras. *A Flag of Two Wars* tells of a dying rebel who proudly bequeaths his sword to his son, a national hero for his Cuban exploits in the Spanish-American War. Movies such as *Days of War* and *In Old Kentucky* included moving scenes of national reconciliation. In the latter, a Confederate soldier returns home to the delight of the family black butler who had been miffed at the celebration for the Union brother's homecoming. Meeting the waiting victor, the recent

[16]*His Trust* (Biograph, 1911); *His Trust Fulfilled* (Biograph, 1911), LC-MPS.
[17]Eileen Bowser, comp., *Biograph Bulletins, 1908-1912* (New York: Octagon, 1973), Nos. 3778, 3779 of Jan. 11, 1910.

rebel relents and embraces him while an American flag is draped over their hands joined before the smiling Negro's eyes.[18]

By 1915, then, the basic outlines of the cinematic mythology were established. The urban audiences could long for and admire the film's pure Southern pastoral society. One of the most opulent conceptions of the dream was in *Colonel Carter of Cartersville*. Taken from Francis Hopkinson Smith's novel, the 1915 World Production Company's description of the planter's world was grandly detailed. The mansion's interior reflected a life of cultural attainment, statuary and books were strewn everywhere. The various exterior shots showed large, meticulously cared for buildings. While sundry neighboring planters and their families enjoyed a picnic, several fieldhands and a "mammy" tended cotton without supervision. The workers relaxed as the spirit moved them, by dancing to the approval of black youngsters who rolled on the ground in glee. Later scenes showed a grand ball. It was another assurance of a noble, but common, existence.[19]

The South found its greatest champion in David Wark Griffith and his film *Birth of a Nation*. Financed at an astonishing $110,000, rehearsed for six weeks and filmed in nine, edited in three months, and presented as an epic of twelve reels and three hours running time, it altered the methodology of American filmmaking. Griffith developed or refined the close-up, cross cutting, rapid editing, the split screen shot, plus realistic and impressionistic lighting. He also created a spectacle which for decades influenced every cinematic treatment of the South and of Southern Negroes. As cultural illusion, it has no equal. In one momentous stroke, the bigotry and conservatism which had been so strongly suggested in the earlier silent stories was ratified.

Griffith had dealt with the plantation culture in prior films. He directed such movies as *The Planter's Wife* (1909), which addressed the sanctity of the Southern family. He also supervised *The Honor of His Family* (1909) and *The House With the Closed Shutters* (1910), which actually intimated that the legend of the

[18]*In Old Kentucky* (Biograph, 1909), LC-MPS.

[19]Synopsis, *Colonel Carter of Cartersville* (1915), LC-MPS Copyright File LU-9787.

region was in conflict with reality.[20] But any doubts he might have had were soon forgotten. Griffith was ecstatic with this opportunity to present what he deemed the ultimate testament. Working in California in 1914, Griffith had asked Frank Woods, a past associate at Biograph Studios, to seek out new stories suitable for film. Woods and his assistant Russell E. Smith suggested *The Clansman*, a novel and melodramatic play written in 1905 by a Southern clergyman, Thomas Dixon. The story had achieved significant success. Intrigued with the possibilities, the director instructed Henry E. Aitken, a shrewd film distributor and associate, to make the minister an offer. Lacking sufficient cash, Aitken could only deliver $2,500 of a promised $10,000 and an agreement that Dixon if he wished could share in the profits. A clever man, Dixon negotiated not only a share in the profits, but the right to supervise the film's latter half as well; in effect he became another director.[21]

Author Dixon had long been accustomed to the limelight. In 1891 he had been named pastor of the Twenty-Third Street Baptist Church in New York City, and by 1900 his fiery manner was attracting more listeners than any of the city's Protestant ministers. John D. Rockefeller was so impressed that he volunteered to help fund the building of a million dollar "People's Temple" for his activities. In 1902 Dixon had published his novel *The Leopard Spots*, detailing current fears created by the migration of foreigners and Negroes to Northern cities. *The Clansman* had appeared in 1905, with no less virulent a racist tone.[22]

[20]For an analysis of Griffith's earlier work as a director, see Robert M. Henderson, *D. W. Griffith: The Years at Biograph* (New York: Farrar, Straus, 1970), especially 82, 92, 109; and Henderson, *D. W. Griffith: His Life and Work* (New York: Oxford Univ. Press, 1972), 141-65.

[21]Linda Arvidson, "How Griffith Came to Make *Birth of a Nation*," in *Focus on D. W. Griffith*, ed. by Harry Geduld (Englewood Cliffs, N.J.: Prentice-Hall, 1971), 80-83; Henderson, *Griffith: Life*, 143.

[22]Raymond A. Cook, "The Man Behind *Birth of a Nation*," *North Carolina Historical Review* 29 (Oct. 1962), 519-23; Cook, *Fire From the Flint: The Amazing Careers of Thomas Dixon* (Winston-Salem: Blair, 1968); F. Gavin Davenport, Jr., "Thomas Dixon's Mythology of Southern History," *Journal of Southern History* 26 (Aug. 1970), 350-67; Maxwell Bloomfield, "Dixon's

Once Griffith had purchased the story, he could hardly contain his enthusiasm. The director began, even while working on other projects, to study pamphlets, books, and notes. Since his earlier days in New York, working on his unproduced play *War*, Griffith had been obsessed with research. Unfortunately, he was fascinated only by works which bore out his own interpretations. He apparently believed it was unnecessary to weigh evidence. In fact, he established a studio research department to delve into the available sources he needed for his view; the office may well have been a first in the film industry.[23]

Griffith had such firm notions on some aspects of the story that it is more likely he needed little additional reading. As an enthusiastic son of the South, his views on the plantation world especially were firmly entrenched. Born in Kentucky in 1875, he grew up under the guidance of an impoverished, elderly father who claimed he had once wielded considerable clout as a prewar politician and Confederate officer wounded in action. Colonel Jacob Wark Griffith was also a strong romantic, who instilled in his son an idealistic view of the past. Though crippled and poor, the Colonel could still play the role of the aristocratic planter.

Supposedly always suffering from his injuries, "Roaring Jake" Griffith spent his days sipping bourbon on the front porch and supervising his wife Mary's work on the 520-acre farm. The father would also astound his young boy with tales of how, when wounded, he had led a charge from a carriage; of his promotion to brigadier at the side of Jefferson Davis just before the President's capture by Federals; and of his wife's ancestry in the hallowed Carter family of Virginia. The fact that all the tales were untrue the young Griffith either never knew or never admitted.

That Griffith was certainly quite firm in his conceptions is revealed in the research he did conduct. Although careful to read sundry works on the war and Reconstruction, Griffith failed to see the need for further study of the antebellum culture itself. In a

The Leopard Spots: A Study in Popular Racism," *American Quarterly* 16 (Fall 1964), 387-401.

[23]Henderson, *Griffith: Life*, 16-30, 150; Seymour Stern, "Griffith: *The Birth of a Nation*," *Film Culture* No. 36 (Summer 1965), 36.

bibliography he utilized for the 1915 film, there is not one book specifically dealing with the Old South. His reading, instead, included six books on the conflict and a like number on its aftermath.[24]

Ever aware of the symbolic, he began shooting the story on the Fourth of July, 1914. Starting with a budget of $40,000, he was originally convinced he could compact the plot to ten reels. But he became more and more enthralled with the project and determined that every detail should be accurate. It was a problem under which countless films on the prewar South would labor. Inordinate attention to minor details provided authenticity for an interpretation which was itself not accurate. Time was devoted not to the thesis but to its trappings, and the surface detail simply obscured the interpretation's underlying weaknesses.

It was in these details that Griffith conducted his most meticulous research. For the assassination scene in Ford's Theatre, Griffith made sure that the murder occurred at the exact moment in the play *Our American Cousin* as it did at the actual event. He took note, too, of the fact that the temperature on that April night fell suddenly. In the movie, Lincoln changes his position and reaches for a warm cape. With such adherence to fact, plus the utilization of hundreds of extras, Griffith eventually had to

[24]Stern, "Griffith," 34-36; Stern lists the following sources for Griffith's research: Evert A. Duychinck, *National History of the War for the Union, Civil, Military and Naval* (New York, 1861-66); Alfred H. Guernsey and Henry M. Alden, *Harper's Pictorial History of the Great Rebellion* (New York, 1866-68); Paul F. Mottelay, ed., *The Soldier in Our Civil War: A Pictorial History of the Conflict, 1861-1865* (New York, 1884–85); Edward P. Thompson, *History of the Orphan Brigade* (Louisville, 1898); John G. Nicolay and John Hay, *Lincoln: A History* (New York, 1890); plus various issues of *Peterson's Magazine*, Matthew Brady photographs, and eyewitness accounts. For Reconstruction, the bibliography included: Albion Tourgee, *The Invisible Empire* (New York, 1880); John C. Lester and David L. Wilson, *The Ku Klux Klan: Its Origin, Growth and Disbandment* (Nashville, 1884); John S. Reynolds, *Reconstruction in South Carolina, 1865-1877* (Columbia, 1905); plus Elizabeth M. Howe, *A Ku Klux Uniform*; Walter L. Fleming, *The Prescript of the Ku Klux Klan*; and various original Klan documents provided by Dixon.

request additional funds, finally resorting to small individual contributions.[25]

His efforts paid off. On February 8, 1915, *Birth of a Nation* premiered at Los Angeles' Clune Auditorium. It ran there for a record seven months. On March 3, the film had its east coast opening in New York's Liberty Theatre; it reached Boston on April 9 and Chicago on June 4. Griffith was so anxious for the success of his film that he attended each premiere and made a modest introductory speech. He would then retire to the projectionist's booth to view the film and take notes of audience reactions so he could refine the film even more by repeated editing.[26]

Indeed, the film was edited so heavily and frequently that the original is lost forever; yet, the surviving prints still capture the magnitude of the director's craft.[27] Griffith's story focuses on the Camerons of Piedmont, South Carolina. There the population languishes in a locale where, as the introduction puts it, "life runs in a quaintly way that is to be no more." The Camerons and their slaves appear perfectly happy, unspoiled by outside interference or misunderstanding.

If outside advice is unwelcome, there is at least room for friendships beyond the South. The Cameron brothers, Ben and Wade, are close friends of Phil and Tod Stoneman, sons of a Northern member of Congress, Austin Stoneman. War finally comes, though, and the old order and friendships must momentarily change.

Although they form by far the shortest part of the story, the images of the antebellum South in the opening scenes are essential to understanding the remainder of the film. It is an unblemished land; all are at peace. The initial shots of the town of Piedmont show a cart bearing slaves winding its way up a village street. Laughing Negroes are all around; black children play

[25]*Straus Magazine* Theatre Program, New York's Liberty Theatre, LC-MPS Box C-89; Henderson, *Griffith: Life*, 148-50, 152; A. Nicholas Vardac, "Griffith and *The Birth of a Nation*," *Focus on Griffith*, 84-87.

[26]MOMA-FSC Introduction to Research Holdings on *Birth of a Nation*; Henderson, *Griffith: Life*, 156-58.

[27]*The Birth of a Nation* (Epoch, 1915), MOMA-FSC and LC-MPS.

about the cart and some fall only to be pulled with delight back in. Then emerges the portrait of plantation aristocracy, Margaret Cameron, "daughter of the Old South, trained in manners of the old school," is shown being helped into her carriage. Thus the two levels of antebellum reality are quickly set—the blacks in the farm cart and the white maiden in formal carriage with liveried driver.

Then Margaret's parents, Dr. and Mrs. Cameron, appear. A gray haired gentleman, Cameron relaxes on a porch supported by the required white columns. He fondles a cat, while puppies and a slave child—both subservient—play at his feet. A "mammy" looks on the domestic scene with satisfaction. The house itself is surrounded by a white picket fence and flowers. Its interior is dominated by a large entrance hall with a grand staircase, and to either side are large, elaborately furnished rooms.

A visit from the Stoneman brothers provides occasion for a wider tour of the estate. Crossing the fields, the visiting Phil Stoneman waves to the slaves, who with pleasure return the gesture. At the slave quarters the Northerners spy workers in coarse but adequate clothing, who live in cabins of sturdy materials, and are pleased with their condition. Griffith took pains to make the point that the laborers had no more arduous a day than any Northern factory worker; one card explains that the visitors find the blacks in their quarters because it is "the two hour interval given for dinner, out of their working day from six to six." And master and slave alike were preoccupied with providing the proper hospitality. When the Stonemans take their leave, the Negroes wish them well, with the children playfully running behind the departing carriage. The implication was apparent: Northerners had no reason to feel alarmed at the South's ways.

When war finally comes, the South does not appear exceptionally overjoyed, for that would suggest a desire for secession, rather than a mobilization woefully instigated in the face of a threat. There is one celebration, though, a farewell ball in the grand room of Cameron Hall. The men apparently are all gentlemen, since all are of sufficient social and military rank to be dressed in white tie and tails or in officer's dress. The belles, of course, are all alluring and dance resplendent in flowery gowns while clutching bouquets of flowers.

Griffith's intent to portray a refined, cultured populace in comparison to what he viewed as the less cultured North is particularly evident when the celebration scene is compared to a like event in his film *The Battle*. Made in 1911, the earlier movie includes a farewell party in the North. The dance with its almost bacchanalian revelry is in pointed contrast to the polite soiree southward.[28]

When on the next day the local Confederate troop must depart, the entire community turns out to wish its men well. Surprisingly, considering his age, young Ben Cameron is the commander, "the Little Colonel." All about the town are garlands of flowers and bunting. Slaves cheer enthusiastically to see their masters rally to the defense of the system. One old black throws aside his cane to kneel and bow towards the departing minions; another Negro clutches his master's leg in reverence.

Thus was the prewar culture depicted. But did Griffith actually believe it to be true, and to be the norm? He did, and in fact he may have regarded the Camerons not as the peak of a society's hierarchy, but just average participants within it. One Griffith scholar has theorized from research and interviews with the director that the life of the slave South as sketched in *Birth of a Nation* is not that of an aristocracy, but that of a planter middle class. There were in the film "no palatial dwellings; no 'feudal estates'; no glamorized or luxurious interiors . . . , or the magnolia-tree aristocracy of Natchez, Mississippi." Instead, "Cameron Hall is a more representative reproduction than any that has yet appeared on the screen of the typical dwelling place, and with this, the way of life of the Southern people."[29]

Griffith may have believed and hoped that the lifestyle was typical, but typical it certainly was not. To declare so was to claim that the average middle class Southerner could, with all his sons, live a life of ease. It was to declare that the average citizen could maintain a fine carriage and a home with a ballroom and household staff of two exempt from field labor. And if the family was so average, how did such a youthful man without any apparent military talent rise so quickly to regimental command?

[28]*The Battle* (Biograph, 1911), MOMA-FSC.
[29]Stern, "Griffith," 56.

Actually, Griffith's portrayal of antebellum life was the most detailed and pleasant thus far filmed. If the movie seriously was an attempt to capture the spirit of average existence, small wonder that audiences envied the old days.

The director's utopia was decidedly intentional, for he had to make a concerted effort to alter even Dixon's conception. As one who had risen to prominence from the confinement of a small Southern farm, Thomas Dixon had little patience with an aristocracy of leisure, a class without drive. In *The Clansman* he had stated that there were no Cavaliers, no lazy dreamers. His South was peopled with lawyers, doctors, teachers, cotton merchants —men who made their own way. In the original story, Ben Cameron is no indolent planter but a law student; his sister's fiancé seeks to organize a cotton mill. Naturally, Griffith had to remold that view, as it was completely foreign to his own background. Working for a living—whether one was of the middle class or not—was totally contrary to his "reality" of the South. In the film the elder Cameron brother, though facing destitution in 1865, seeks no gainful employment. And though he stoops to offer the now silent rooms of Cameron Hall for rent, young Cameron was never shown by Griffith accepting any boarders into the home, the symbol of so many proud traditions. It would simply have been too demeaning.[30]

The view of the grand South was further accentuated by contrasting it to the North. This culture so alien to the antebellum South was depicted as excessively commercial and equally culpable for any sins of which the South might be accused. For example, Griffith included a scene of hypocritical piety and of monetary lust, in which a New England Puritan minister stands unopposed at the bartering of a frightened African. The director had succinctly passed equal responsibility for slavery to the North.

It was no accident that the nemesis of the South and father of the Cameron brothers' friends was named Austin Stoneman. The stern-faced, club-footed character was a thinly disguised Thaddeus Stevens, the Pennsylvania Congressman so many South-

[30]See Russell Merritt, "Dixon, Griffith, and the Southern Legend," *Cinema Journal* 12 (Fall 1972), 26-45.

erners felt had been responsible for the North's excesses during Reconstruction. The fictional character's name and physical handicap symbolized all that was cold, hard, and deformed in the North, in contrast to Dr. Cameron, a Southerner of pleasant demeanor and appearance. Worse, Stoneman appeared under the evil influence of his mulatto housekeeper, Lydia, a situation reminiscent of Stevens and indicative of the spell under which Griffith thought the prewar North to be under as well, that of abolitionism. In addition, Stoneman's mannerisms and his associates were all mechanical, narrow, and reserved—as Griffith perceived the North to be.[31]

By such methods did D. W. Griffith set the stage and instill in his audiences, both North and South, a sympathy for the defeated. From there he could move to the war itself. In films such as *The Battle* and earlier in his first Civil War movie, *The Guerrilla* (1908), he had begun to develop the techniques he would refine in the action sequences of *Birth of a Nation*. In *The Guerrilla*, Griffith had used forty different shots in a ten-minute span to create a superb sense of immediacy. In his 1915 work, the battle front was even more awe inspiring. In a series of close-ups of the trenches amid sweeping scenes of the Petersburg battlefield in 1865, the movie drives home the intensity of the war. The director also cleverly shaped the confrontation to conform to the tradition in literature so well established by writers such as John Esten Cooke and George Cary Eggleston. Both sides were equally commended for gallantry and compassion. As a result, charges of favoritism were blunted and sympathy gained for the South's efforts.

In the climactic battle Ben Cameron leads his ragtag force in a desperate charge across open ground to the Federal trenches beyond. Hurled against a vastly superior foe, "the Little Colonel's" regiment is decimated, but the Union line is considerably awed by the valiant try. Reaching the enemy alone, Cameron with a last surge of strength stumbles forward, attempting to spike the Yankee cannon with his tattered battle standard.

---

[31]See Everett Carter, "Cultural History Written With Lightning: The Significance of *The Birth of a Nation*," in *Focus on The Birth of a Nation*, ed. by Fred Silva (Englewood Cliffs: Prentice-Hall, 1971), 133-43.

The Klan's victory parade in *Birth of a Nation*. BELOW: *The Fighting Coward*.

Though he collapses outside the enemy's rampart, the Confederate is spared. A Union captain—his old friend Phil Stoneman—exposes himself to fire in order to drag the hero to safety. Enthralled, the troops in both trenches stand and cheer the mutual bravery. The audiences cheered too.

While recuperating in a Northern hospital, Cameron is attended by a nurse whose picture he had seen before. It is the daughter of Congressman Stoneman and sister of his rescuer. Elsie's love affair with the Southerner was also within the postwar literary tradition of sectional reconciliation through romance. To complete the circle, Phil Stoneman is in love with one of the Cameron girls.

The romantic interests were also part of a wider interpretation than just reconciliation. Griffith relied heavily throughout the picture on the concept of the family. The Camerons in their instances of domestic bliss represented the best in human nature and the antebellum South. Obvious efforts were made to relate the image of the family to the North. Too involved with his half-blood housekeeper Lydia, his mulatto protegé Silas Lynch, and his political cronies, Congressman Stoneman cannot see the gulf separating him from his children. The Southern family, on the other hand, has clung closely together through the war and the threat of Ben Cameron's execution. It is only at the end of the story, when Stoneman realizes, almost too late, Lynch's evil designs on his daughter, that he finally reconfirms the sanctity of the family and faces the inequality of the races.

But there were still other lessons in the movie. Returning from the war, Ben Cameron finds his home in ruins and his family impoverished. Blacks roam the streets insulting ladies and forcing gentlemen from the sidewalks. They threaten even that most sacred institution, the Southern family; among placards calling for "Forty acres and a mule" are those demanding "equal rights" and worse, "equal marriage." In the state legislature, now dominated by Negroes, the newcomers guzzle whiskey, eat fried chicken, pass outrageous laws, and spend their time reclining in their new seats of power, bare feet propped on the desks.

Most audiences were at that point in the story as distraught as the vanquished. When a renegade Negro captain forces one of the

Cameron girls to commit suicide rather than submit to a black's lust, the viewers became incensed.

Griffith, left relatively alone by the story's creator, had established the South's agrarian spirit in the first portions of the film, and then turned to Dixon for the ingredients of the racist denouement. Both saw little prejudice in their collaborative ending, however, and made sure that the Southern Negro was as appalled as his white superiors at the unwelcome interference from uppity white and black alike. The Cameron house servant upon seeing a haughty Northern butler exclaimed, "Yo northern low down black trash, don't try no airs on me." The servant added that she believed that "Dem free niggers f'um de N'of am sure crazy."

Finally, driven to the edge of their patience by the excesses of the carpetbaggers and their black partners, the native citizens under "the Little Colonel's" leadership form the Invisible Empire, the Ku Klux Klan, to drive the invaders out. Relying once more on Griffith's symbol of unity, the family, the entire society works together feverishly to guard the plans, sew the hooded uniforms, and bolster enthusiasm. In the stirring finale of events, which even had Northern ticket-holders cheering, the Klan rides into Piedmont and scatters the Negro troops, then moves on to a cabin besieged by other Negro soldiers just in time to rescue the Camerons and several "good" Northern farmers. The act of placing the foreign defenders there was again an effort to show the common bond between sections on the issues of race, family, and preference for a pastoral and racially pure existence.

As crudely as Griffith and Dixon depicted the freedmen, the film ironically has one facet which would not be presented again for over twenty years until *So Red the Rose* (1935) and still later in *Slaves* (1969) and *Drum* (1976). The Negro was portrayed as a disruptive force. For the first time he was a revolutionary. In *Birth of a Nation*, the Negro is shown, however disparagingly, as a figure seeking to alter the laws, economy, and even the social structure of society in order to achieve his fair share. But of course in Griffith's hands, the attempt was only reprehensible. So sustained was the film's case for white supremacy that neither black nor white grasped the significant change the movie represented in finally showing the black as instigator rather than as pawn.

Wildly excited crowds greeted the movie. It was the longest and most expensive film yet made. Tickets sold at an incredible maximum of $2.00. In price, theme, and form, the movie was intended for an elite. Each opening took on the character of a gala premier; 40-100-piece orchestras accompanied the story; ushers were dressed in period costumes.[32] The well-paced direction and advertising paid off: literally millions were exposed to the film's emotional message.

The picture made films a permissible experience for the higher classes as well as a pastime for the masses. *Birth of a Nation* was important not, as is commonly thought, because of its laudatory portrayal of the Old South with applicability for the modern world, for that had been a theme of numerous movies since Porter's *Uncle Tom's Cabin* in 1903. The impact of the 1915 epic lay in the fact that the stereotyped South finally became eminently respectable to many who had before shunned film. A section whose ways and conservatism had long seemed stifling was now defended before a broad constituency. The film pointed to a unity of Northern and Southern whites, joined in an appreciation of the latter's adherence to tradition and in what advertisements termed a "common defense of their Aryan birthright."[33]

Posters and lobby cards proclaimed that the film was "great in historical value," in addition to being "the most realistic and stupendous view of stirring events."[34] The noted social reformer Dorothea Dix in a four-column newspaper article declared it to be "history visualized" and recommended one "go see it for it will make a better American of you."[35] Dixon even persuaded his old college classmate Woodrow Wilson to permit a special White House screening. The President was so impressed that he reportedly remarked, "It is like writing history with lightning,

[32]For accounts of the film's premieres, see "D. W. Griffith Scrapbooks," Microfilm Copy, MOMA-Library.

[33]The white supremacy theme was common to most newspaper advertisements; see for example *New York Dramatic News*, March 6, 1915.

[34]Liberty Theatre advertisement, "Griffith Scrapbooks."

[35]*Boston Globe*, April 9, 1915; see also *Boston Post*, April 4, 6-8, 1915.

and one of my regrets is that it is so horribly true." There was also a special showing in Washington's Raleigh Hotel for members of Congress, the Supreme Court, and the National Press Club.[36] By January 1916 in the New York City area alone the movie had played 6,266 times before an estimated audience of three million. It played for forty-seven weeks at the city's Liberty Theatre; it ran almost a year in Chicago and Boston. It was shown continuously in the South for fifteen years. Each opening was heralded with marching bands; commuter trains brought customers from outlying areas; theatre managers sponsored parades and commissioned huge banner advertisements. A Seattle theatre, instead of the usual orchestra, engaged a Negro quartet to sing "old time songs." Tickets were given as rewards to children for jobs well done or for good behavior. Schools brought entire classes for special showings.[37]

Blacks, of course, were appalled at the film and the backing it received from prominent figures in the North. The NAACP tried to convince police to shut down local showings, distributed copies of the few critical reviews to all who were interested, and published its own rebuttal. In Boston on April 17, 1915, several hundred blacks crowded the lobby of the Tremont Theatre. Soon after the film began, one protestor threw an egg at the screen. In all, it took two hundred police to clear away the demonstrators and another sixty officers to insure that the showing was completed.[38]

[36]*New York Post*, March 4, 1915; Arthur Link, *Wilson: The New Freedom* (Princeton: Princeton Univ. Press, 1956), 253-54. After protests erupted in Boston and elsewhere, Wilson retracted his statement.

[37]"Griffith Scrapbooks"; Carter, "Cultural History," 133; *Seattle Post-Intelligencer*, July 4, 1915; *Brooklyn Eagle*, July 3, 1915; *Portland* (Me.) *Press*, July 8, 1915; *Manchester* (N.H.) *Mirror*, July 10, 1915; *Spokane Chronicle*, July 20, 1915; *St. Louis Times*, Aug. 14, 1915; *Pittsburgh Chronicle-Telegraph*, Aug. 21, 1915; *Providence* (R.I.) *Evening Tribune*, Aug. 17, 1915; *Columbia* (S.C.) *State*, Aug. 22, 1915; *Portland Oregonian*, Aug. 29, 1915; *Scranton Times*, June 1, 1916; *Scranton Republican*, June 1, 1916; *Steaton* (Ill.) *Independent Times*, May 14, 1916.

[38]Andrew Sarris, "*The Birth of a Nation*: or White Power Back When," *Village Voice*, July 17, 1969; Thomas J. Cripps, "The Reaction of the Negro

Some Northern whites were inclined to agree that the tale was grossly biased. Boston's Mayor James Curley banned Sunday performances in an attempt to quiet displeasure. Charles W. Eliot, president of Harvard University, charged that the picture perverted white ideals. Oswald Garrison Villard in *The Nation* wrote that it was a "deliberate attempt to humiliate ten million American citizens." In Chicago, police were needed to control protestors, and anyone under eighteen was barred from admission. The movie was banned at various times in Kansas, West Virginia, and in Atlantic City, Newark, and St. Louis.[39] A reviewer in Milwaukee warned that the picture fomented race hatred and added, "the fact that this film represents the 'last word' in motion picture production . . . makes its menace all the more potent."[40]

But the efforts were to no avail; the protests failed to dent the film's popularity. For every noted Northern white the black cause could enlist, the backers of the movie could point to even more who supported the work, individuals such as novelist Booth Tarkington, philanthropist George Foster Peabody, California governor Hiram Johnson, explorer Richard Harding Davis, and critic Burns Mantle. Even the demonstrations were used to boost ticket sales. In some cities theatre managers actually hired Negroes to carry placards and hopefully draw interested onlookers and potential customers.[41]

Quite simply, the vast majority of non-Southern whites were enraptured with the production. In a New York movie palace, "people were moved to cheers, hisses, laughter, and tears, apparently unconscious, and subdued by the intense interest of the play." They "clapped when the masked riders took vengeance on

to the Motion Picture *Birth of a Nation*," *The Historian* 25 (May 1963), 244-62; "Griffith Scrapbooks"; see also NAACP, *Fighting a Vicious Film: Protest Against The Birth of a Nation* (Boston: NAACP, 1915).

[39]Milton Mackaye, *"The Birth of a Nation,"* *Scribner's* 102 (Nov. 1937), 40-46; Bosley Crowther, *"Birth of a Nation,"* *New York Times Magazine*, Feb. 7, 1965.

[40]*Milwaukee Free Press*, March 11, 1915.

[41]"Griffith Scrapbooks."

the Negroes" and "when the hero refused to shake the hand of a mulatto."[42]

Most Northern reviewers were as impressed as the audiences. One dubbed the production "altogether American." Others praised the historic realism; Griffith was viewed as "engaged in the telling of history." A trade journal reported the movie accurately revealed that "the slaves had easy hours, plenty of time for recreation, comfortable quarters, and kind masters." Another preceived the Old South as "resting in the soft, leaf-flecked light of the rosy days before the war." As for its overall importance, many reviewers found that "historically it is magnificent; it is a great, true, artistic photograph."[43]

As for the Southern response, it was predictably enthusiastic. Indeed, the South saw the picture as a godsend. In a Spartanburg, South Carolina, movie house men whooped and screamed with delight or anger. Some brought weapons and shot at the screen in efforts to save Flora Cameron from the embraces of Gus, the Negro soldier. New Orleans citizens saw attendance as an act of patriotism and closed public schools to give children an opportunity for this unique educational experience. Southern reviewers heaped praise on the picture. One North Carolina columnist believed the film best showed "the fun and frolic of plantation days as well as the heartache and pathos of the stricken South." Another critic exclaimed that "it took a southern man to furnish the text . . . ; it took a southern boy . . . to play the leading role . . . ; and it took southern courage to provide the real dramatic events which counted for so much."[44]

Despite the enormous success of the project, Griffith was infuriated by the protests generated in some quarters. He wrote his own defenses against NAACP attacks.[45] He took his profits

[42]*New York Evening Post*, March 4, 1915; *Billboard*, March 20, 1915.

[43]*Brooklyn Times*, March 4, 1915; *Motography*, March 20, 1915; *Moving Picture World*, March 13, 1915; *Motion Picture Magazine*, April 3, 1915; *Motion Picture News*, March 13, 1915.

[44]"Griffith Scrapbooks," *New Orleans Daily Statesman*, March 13, 1916; *New Bern* (N.C.) *Sun Journal*, March 18, 1916; *Birmingham Herald*, June 16, 1915.

[45]For example, see *Boston Journal*, April 26, 1915.

and invested them in another movie, *Intolerance* (1916), a gigantic effort, costing many times more than his 1915 release, which was to record a history of bigotry—not his of course, but that of all those who had criticized his masterpiece *Birth of a Nation*. But the best defense of his 1915 production was certainly its massive popularity, which assured the continuing mystique of the South, a theme he would return to periodically.[46]

In *The White Rose* (1923), a tale of the modern South, Griffith tried to show that the aura and quality of antebellum life still survived. The hauntingly beautiful opening scenes were of a country still populated by servile blacks: a massive, porticoed home, surrounded by peaceful rivers, placid swamps, and trees laden with Spanish moss. Filmed in the Bayou Teche country, at the "St. Martinsville, La., estate of the Carringtons, wealthiest planters in the South," it centered around the director's familiar preoccupation: "the family came of European nobility, taking great care in marriages to preserve the pure strain of aristocracy."[47]

After 1915, rare was the film which failed to build on the foundation laid by the romantic tales produced since 1903 and so efficiently reinforced in *Birth of a Nation*. There were a few exceptions in the silent era. One, *The Coward* (1915), was different from the majority in that it admitted the possibility of an ungallant Southerner. The son of a wealthy planter refuses to enlist in the Confederate army until forced to do so by his pistol-wielding father. He quickly deserts, and in disgrace sulks in his room, comforted by the household servants. But courage and the Southern spirit win out in the end. Overhearing Union

---

[46]In rerelease, protest always occurred, but the film's popularity survived into the early 1960's. *Variety* in 1931 reported that "the *Nation* is not dead," for "its subject is too vital to ever let it die." See *Variety*, Jan. n.d., 1931 (MOMA Files); June 1, 1938; June 7, 1961; Nov. 8, 1961; Dec. 16, 1970. Plans were once made to remake the story or adapt it for television; see *Film Daily*, Dec. 2, 1954; *Variety*, April 13, 1960. And despite continued protests, the film in recent years has played in such diverse areas as Atlanta, Dallas, East Lansing, and Ann Arbor. See *Film and Television Daily*, Sept. 30, 1968; *Variety*, April 13, 1970.

[47]*The White Rose* (United Artists, 1923), MOMA-FSC.

plans of attack and with his escape covered by a slave who has to shoot a Federal, he rushes to warn his compatriots and thus redeems his character.[48]

Several pictures, instead of maintaining the romantic outlook of the agrarian and happy blacks, began to lean more heavily on the racist bitterness engendered by *Birth of a Nation*. Most, such as *Broken Chains* (1916), failed because they relied too extensively on the theme of race without the usual rural, benevolent motif. *The Bride of Hate* (1916) told of a Southern doctor who wreaks revenge by encouraging a love affair between his enemy and a light-skinned slave he had won at cards. When the gentleman discovers the ruse, he is driven to drink and eventual death. Another, *Free and Equal,* was easily as bad. Filmed in 1915 but not released until 1925, the plot involved a Northern liberal judge who believed a black to be the equal of any man. A Southern colonel, feeling otherwise, wagered the judge could not keep a Negro in his own house. The result was predictable. The chosen black tried to force himself on his host's daughter, and not succeeding, he then raped and murdered the family's maid.[49]

As horrid overstatements, such productions were doomed to fail financially. But the question arises as to whether the stories were unpopular because they were overwhelmingly pro-Southern and anti-Negro, or more probably because of something else entirely: that their hoary, disturbing revelations involving black characters and the fate of those whites who crossed the color line were too frightening to tolerate as entertainment. Actually, far from attacking the South's beliefs, the films further proved its position.

There were a few films which did present a land of disenchantment. In *True to Their Colors*, a melodrama, the planter's boy, a "little son of the South," is disturbed at the overseer's treatment of a favorite slave and decides to run away to the North, "where the black people were not ill treated."[50] But such views

[48]*The Coward* (Ince, 1915), LC-MPS.

[49]Bogle, *Toms*, 24-25; Noble, *Negro in Films*, 47; Cripps, *Slow Fade to Black*, 124.

[50]Synopsis, *True to Their Colors*, LC-MPS Copyright File LP-10627.

reflected far more a desire for a heart-rending melodramatic vehicle than any attack on the South.

Another film spoofed the region in a plot taken from Booth Tarkington's novel and play *Magnolia*. A story of both comedy and drama, *The Fighting Coward* (1924) revolved around the concept of Southern honor. Primarily a satire, it had every stock ingredient jammed into the tale, providing an excellent inventory of assumptions which had taken hold a decade after Griffith's film.[51] But as even one non-Southern reviewer admitted, it was regrettably overdone in places. The silent film's extended use of an accent, and incidentally the difficulty of deciphering printed conversation in dialect, was especially noted.[52] For example, central to the plot was a "mattah of honah" which raised "angah" from the planter, "Suh" or "Shuah," whose many visiting "neighbahs" often "weah heah" at the estate.

It is a story of "the old time South, before mint juleps were imbibed surreptitiously and economically." The stage is set by introductory shots of the grand "Magnolia Mansion," family seat of General Rumford and his lady, who sit sipping mint juleps while surveying their holdings. Slave children play about; a steamer plies up the river, its decks full of lazy Negroes. Worried about his ward Tom's Northern habits, the General remarks— while helping himself to another drink—that the lad "has one serious problem that worries me, he doesn't drink." It appears the master tolerates little misbehavior. He has a rather ragged manservant who follows him about with a silver tray of refreshment and instructs him "that houn' dog flinched undah fire yestahday, take her out and shoot her."

The film abounds in caricatures. The stock blackguard is a "Majuh Pattuhson," once jailed "just for shooting his brother." The hero is a rather naive fellow who tips his hat to saloon girls and is admonished, "you all don' have to take yo' hat off to me honey, I'se black." Our hero, however, is trained in the ways of the proper Southern gentleman by engaging "Massa Gen'l" Orlando Jackson, who fashions his charge into a passable rake and

[51]*The Fighting Coward* (Paramount, 1924), International Museum of Photography/George Eastman House (Rochester), cited hereafter as GEH.
[52]*New York Times*, March 17, 1924.

duellist. With his new bravado, the young man is at last attractive to the belles, one of whom gushes, "I adore a man who is brave, reckless, and romantic—a killer."

The Fighting Coward was the first film which playfully caricatured the South's aristocratic class. Major Patterson had a standing as a gruff gentleman, but little else. The pompous General was a delightful portrait of the planter ideal, and his daughter Elvira a lady of fickle charms. But even within this comedy, the hero in order to gain recognition had to add to his innocent idealism and manners a concept of honor so strong that he would willingly fight for it, especially when a lady and a plantation were at stake. As a result, he would make the perfect Southern gentleman—in the mold of all the Shelbys, St. Clairs, Carters, and Camerons before him. The movie was sufficiently well received that it was remade twice, in 1929 as *The River of Romance* and in 1935 as *Mississippi*.

The Fighting Coward was but a rare departure; films quickly returned to the old formula. In *The Love Mart* (1927) Antoinette Frobelle, "reigning queen belle of the South," is accused by the scandalous Captain Remy of supposedly the worse social stigma, Negro blood. She is quickly sold into slavery to Victor Jallot, a young gentleman fencing master. Believing the lady's protestations, he frees her and restores the woman's reputation by exposing Remy for the scoundrel he really is. Once cleared, Antoinette weds her rescuer.[53]

In light of films since *Birth of a Nation*, this story taken from Edward Charles Carpenter's 1907 work, *The Code of Victor Jallot*, is significant. Without the overwrought excesses of a *Broken Chains* or *The Bride of Hate*, the movie nonetheless managed once again to strike out at the image of blackness, and like such earlier films as *Colonel Carter of Cartersville*, it captured the mythical charm of the South without becoming a burlesque, as in *The Fighting Coward*. Gay New Orleans, gracious homes, the planter aristocracy of honor and bravery, the beautiful belles in need of an

---

[53]Synopsis, *The Love Mart* (1927), in Kenneth Munden, ed., *The American Film Institute Catalogue of Motion Pictures Produced in the United States: Feature Films, 1921-1930* (New York: AFI, 1971), 458; see also *New York Times*, Dec. 26, 1927.

able sword were to be the standard mixture in many another film based on the traits evolved in the three decades of silent movies.

Within this body of mythology in cinema there was yet another occasional view of the antebellum section, that of the non-planter. In 1917 the first of many versions of Mark Twain's Southern stories was produced. *Tom Sawyer* was a very brief exploration of the familiar tale; it was followed quickly by *Huck and Tom, or the Further Adventures of Tom Sawyer* (1918) and *Huckleberry Finn* (1920).[54] In their scenes of childhood, small river villages, and a non-slaveholding middle class, the tales were unique.

The river town in these movies is alive with boys at play on a street dominated by white fences, comfortable homes, and large shade trees. But even in the stories of innocent youth, vestiges of the recently established myth are found, particularly concerning the Negro. Inserted into Tom's clever fence whitewashing scene, in which he tricks his friends into doing the work, is the ubiquitous smiling simpleton slave.[55] And in *Huckleberry Finn* the character of the unhappy slave Jim, escaping sale and separation from his family, is played down considerably.

In that vein, the stories of slave humility and appreciation persisted and were still the mainstay, represented best by the repeated adaptations of *Uncle Tom's Cabin*, radically reinterpreted from the original. In characterizations little had changed from the first films.

Although a black played the lead in 1914, by 1918 blackface was predominant again; Marguerite Clark played the dual role of Little Eva and Topsy. The same nostalgia so evident earlier prevailed in several productions. *When Do We Eat?* (1918), *Little Eva Ascends* (1922), and *Uncle Tom's Gal* (1925) were all based on the travels of threatre companies and their predictable reading

---

[54]*New York Times*, Dec. 3, 1917; Feb. 3, 1920; Synopsis, *Huck and Tom, or the Further Adventures of Tom Sawyer* (1918), LC-MPS Copyright File LP-12003; Synopsis, *Huckleberry Finn* (1920), LC-MPS Copyright File LP-14604.

[55] *Tom Sawyer* (Paramount, 1917), LC-MPS.

of the story. *Uncle Tom's Uncle* (1926) was a comedy for the *Our Gang* series.[56]

The most ambitious of all the interpretations, serious and otherwise, was the *Uncle Tom's Cabin* of 1927. Directed by Harry Pollard for Universal Studios and begun in the spring of 1926 with location shooting in Plattsburg, New York, the film starred the Negro actor Charles Gilpin as Uncle Tom. But there were objections to Gilpin's overly aggressive reading of the script, so a more pliable James B. Lowe was signed. Lowe, an athletic actor who had broken into films as the black sidekick of a cowboy hero in Universal's *Blue Streak* series, brought a measure of dignity to the part.[57]

Compared to previous interpretations, the story did expose certain plantation evils. In one shot a brutally beaten Uncle Tom appears in a crucifixion pose, after which a likeness of Christ is visible. Legree is grotesque, stumbling about with food drooling from his mouth and blood trickling from his forehead. In a revised conclusion Legree receives his just retribution at the hands of William T. Sherman's troops.

However, when contrasted to the rest of the picture these scenes did little to counteract what had become a standard view of the plantation. One Northerner termed the morbid shots only "distasteful."[58]

In the final analysis the story was overall another rose-colored bit of Southern lore. Pollard, the director, had made a version twelve years earlier which at the time he thought would be the last. He admitted in 1926 to wanting to direct a "super picture of the great American drama," but his true purpose was suspect. He was a Southerner and saw the film as an opportunity, not for an anti-slavery statement attacking racism in the Old South, but

[56]MOMA-FSC Research File, *Uncle Tom's Cabin*; Jim Pines, *Blacks in Films: A Survey of Racial Themes and Images in the American Film* (London: Studio Vista, 1975), 11, 11n.

[57]MOMA-FSC Research File, *Uncle Tom's Cabin*; Cripps, *Slow Fade to Black*, 159-61.

[58]Synopsis, *Uncle Tom's Cabin* (1927), LC-MPS Copyright File LP-24673; *New York Times*, Nov. 5, 1927.

James B. Lowe in *Uncle Tom's Cabin* (1927). BELOW: Robert Young and Lionel Barrymore in *Carolina*.

instead as a comment on "the gallantry, charm, hospitality, and gentility of the antebellum days in the most aristocratic section of the United States." It was to be a portrayal in the epic manner of "the most beautiful pictures of courtly life the world had ever seen." It was hardly the stuff of which exposés were made. To accentuate the South's innocence, he made sure that the harshness of bondage was due to a Legree whom Pollard declared "must not be a typical Southerner" but "an unscrupulous cruel Northern capitalist."[59]

It was but another perversion of the original work. Although Mrs. Stowe's immigrant Legree had symbolized the deplorable universality of improper emotions and the corrupting influence of the Old South's system, Pollard reshaped the gambit as a commentary on the damaging interference of outsiders, unappreciative and uncomprehending of the ideal.

The film was regarded as a major production, as was shown in local advertising and reviews, and was still in first run distribution in 1929.[60] Some Southern theatres had delayed requesting prints as managers feared patrons would object to the inserted scenes of Sherman's "March to the Sea."

Nonetheless, in Montgomery, Alabama, the production was hailed as "in every way an epic picture of the most romantic and colorful period of American life." In Nashville, the film was held over, and instead of the usual musical accompaniment the theatre used "numerous old-time cotton-field ballads." The local advertising, though showing Eliza escaping a pack of hounds literally nipping at her feet, in reality was more in tune with the idyllic aspect of the story, using every opportunity to deemphasize the original message. One bulletin exhorted, "Do not—we beg of you—let anything you have ever heard—thought—or seen—of any form of production of *Uncle Tom's Cabin* prevent your see-

[59]*Montgomery Advertiser*, April 21, 1929; *Salt Lake Tribune*, May 16, 1929.

[60]Ironically, Pollard's 1927 version of *Uncle Tom's Cabin* was rereleased in 1958 as a countermeasure to the repeated revivals of *Birth of a Nation*. With an added introduction by Raymond Massey, discussing the significance of the story, the film's perspective changed. See *Variety*, Dec. 10, 1958; *New York Times*, Oct. 5, 1958.

ing the first *real* presentation." Another advertisement added that "lavish expense made possible the rebirth for the screen of the glorious days of the Old South—old plantation days—old steamboatin' days—the glamour and the romance and the thrills . . . ."[61]

Areas outside the South also stressed the nostalgic at the expense of the novel's intent. In Topeka "the greatest human drama ever filmed" was preceded by a live performance of the Dixie Jubilee Singers, to put the audience in a pleasant retrospective mood. For the showing in Manchester, New Hampshire, the billing promised that "you will cry with Little Eva—you will hate Simon Legree—you will pity Uncle Tom—you will shudder at the stark realism of Eliza crossing the ice" in what was locally viewed, however, not as an attack but as Pollard's great romantic picture. Theatres in Seattle and Salt Lake claimed the film was a "screen miracle." Posters, though showing Lincoln, were equally dominated by dancing plantation Negroes and such captions as, "a magnificence never before achieved—thrill after thrill—picturesque plantation days—the feudal glories of the beloved Old South."[62] Such plaudits were yet another measure of the extent to which the image of the section had been redeemed nationally and of how the South's ideals and racial conservatism had become inoffensive if not attractive.

A further gauge of the degree to which the Stowe novel had been warped to conform to the region's mythology was *Topsy and Eva* (1927). In production at the same time as Pollard's film, it was by far the worst of the numerous adaptations. Based on a play by Catherine Chisholm Cutting, the picture starred the Duncan Sisters, Rosetta and Vivian, who had long performed as a blackface minstrel act. It was a hackneyed film, directed by Del Lord, who would later direct many of the Three Stooges shorts. Even D. W. Griffith, long eager to do a "Tom show," worked ten days at reshooting and editing. But to no avail. The film was

[61]*Montgomery Advertiser*, April 21, 1929; *Nashville Banner*, April 21, 1929.

[62]*Topeka Daily Capital*, May 5, 1929; *Manchester* (N.H.) *Union*, March 11, 1929; *Seattle Post-Intelligencer*, April 21, 1929; *Salt Lake Tribune*, May 16, 1929.

relegated to second billing, and the Duncan Sisters went back to their vaudeville routine.[63]

From the start, the story's racist tone was apparent. On a beautiful moonlit night a doctor races a white stork to the St. Clair estate to attend the birth of Little Eva on St. Valentine's Day. In pointed contrast, a black stork, fighting a gusting rainstorm, bears its awkward bundle to a rude cabin. A huge "mammy" shoos the bird away. Topsy is eventually left in the trash can. Above—in "Heaven, Colored Department"—two black angels roll dice while another registers Topsy's birthdate, April Fool's Day.

The publicity for the film was as disrespectful as the plot. One publicity release revealed that "the money paid for the huge amounts of burned cork bought for the use of Rosetta Duncan . . . would buy four dozen pairs of ladies' silk stockings of a very fair grade."[64]

Thus on the eve of the Great Depression, the silent films' conception of the South ended as it had begun nearly thirty years earlier, with an interpretation of *Uncle Tom's Cabin*. Influenced by a national conservative mood, racial fears, and the Southern local colorists, the early filmmakers had established a far more widely disseminated view of the romantic antebellum South.

The first decades of the 1900s had been a period of increasing conservatism. By the 1920s, for example, the Klan with its anti-black and anti-foreign dictates had experienced a resurgence as strong in the North as anywhere. Other emotional crises, such as the Russian Revolution and the Red Scare following World War I, only added to a fear of strange people and thoughts. By the end of the 20's, Americans felt a strong attraction toward "normalcy." In film, the South especially appeared as a region of similar desires, staunch conservatism, and white, Protestant isolationism.

In fact, of course, the South was considerably different from the delicately shaded society film made it out to be. As one of the section's sharpest critics, H. L. Mencken pointed out that the

[63]*Topsy and Eva* (United Artists, 1927), LC-MPS; *New York Times*, Aug. 8, 1927.
[64]Studio Bulletin, *Topsy and Eva*, LC-MPS Copyright File LP-24175.

contemporary South was but a "Sahara," a wasteland devoid of culture, manners, or other refinements of civilization. In fact, the South then harbored savage tendencies which manifested themselves in racial lynchings, reactionary fundamentalist religion, and narrow puritanical thinking. The South of the 1920s was in stark opposition to the Old South of the imagination. The appeal of the plantation society, therefore, could rest for many on the simple fact that it existed no longer and was a challenge to the more recent South and all its intellectual, political, and economic failings.[65]

The escapist films so reliant on the lowly slave and his place in the antebellum world furnished a pleasant view for a public increasingly cognizant of the region's past charms and motives. Ironically, the new respectability was built upon the very characteristics and defended by the very subjugated race which had helped bring the section to ruin some sixty years earlier.

The unfortunate ramification was that the films' emphasis was as much and often more on the region's manner of race control and its romanticized wealth than on its simple and predominantly working-class, agrarian lifestyle. The section became locked within a film mythology, became a celluloid South. It was an artificial image which would make reality and eventual change all the harder for natives, and a true understanding of the South ever more difficult for outsiders. Even more regrettable, what the South gained in self-esteem and the nation achieved in reunification was diminished by the step backward in race relations, a situation the films were in large part responsible for confirming and approving.

[65]See George B. Tindall, *The Emergence of the New South, 1913-1945* (Baton Rouge: LSU Press, 1967), 184-218; Fred C. Hobson, Jr., *Serpent in Eden: H. L. Mencken and the South* (Chapel Hill: Univ. of North Carolina Press, 1974), esp. 11-32.

III

The South and Hollywood's Golden Era

ENTERPRISE AND ENTERTAINMENT, 1928-1939

The cinema of the Depression was considerably different from earlier film efforts, and not just because of the advent of the "talkies." During the 30s the studios were ever more aware of their power to mold popular culture and of the monetary potential involved with it. Studios such as RKO, Columbia, Paramount, Warner Brothers, and MGM became far larger than had seemed possible only a decade earlier. With contract players, huge sound stages, eager backers, and ambitious executives, the companies developed a system of enterprise and entertainment the likes of which had never been seen.

Publicity departments issued reams of information each day to a public craving insights into productions and the actors' private lives. Studio heads became as well known as their stars. Front office moguls such as Jack Warner, Louis B. Mayer, and David O. Selznick wielded enormous power and their productions are stamped with their own inimitable style. Film was increasingly an enterprise, a business whose commercial demands superceded those of art. And the product most demanded by the studios' well manipulated public was entertainment, entertainment pure and simple with little room for social comment.

The reasons why audiences sought escape and not probing criticism were simple. The people in the decade beginning with the Great Crash of 1929 experienced terrific shocks to past perceptions of cultural stability, including long-held beliefs that hard work and continued industrial growth would bring eventual success. Morale was abysmal and frustrations severe. Movies did much to recognize the disheartened attitude and bolstered the public's sagging spirits. The productions had to appeal to both the audience's ideals and its problems. To do so was to support a faith in eventual recovery and in the immutability of at least the viewer's ambitions if not his job. A film on the Old South, such as *Jezebel*, set as it was in magnificent surroundings, provided a sense of wealth and ease which was vicariously experienced and eagerly accepted as proof that the nation had its moments of prosperity. It was important that the Depression be considered as only an interruption.

The movies which revolved around plantation life did, however, contain more than a pleasant glance at someone else's better fortune. As with many productions from the period, ancillary meanings lurked just beneath the surface. The movies of the antebellum era setting were but one genre of many which addressed the economic crisis.

In crime stories, for example, the crooks were no longer presented merely as bad. They were poor, often of foreign extraction, and frequently bent on striking out in revenge rather than simply for monetary gain. Their very existence was a blow against society. And their desire to improve their place within it was one many could comprehend. Such classic period films as *Little Caesar* (1930), *The Public Enemy* (1931), and *Scarface* (1932), depicting individuals attacking "the system," were extremely popular. The public was equally fascinated with the exploits of real criminals, such as John Dillinger and Clyde Barrow.

Even musicals reflected the hard times and the need for a better period. Behind the glitter often lurked the threat of destitution. The chorines of the well-remembered *Gold Diggers of 1933* had to present a smash hit or face unemployment. Succeeding, their song seemed almost a taunt: "We're in the Money." Horror stories also sometimes carried a message. *King Kong* (1933) included a fear of an urban society's destruction by the unknown.

Comedy too played its role in dealing with the problems of the Depression. *Horse Feathers* (1932) poked fun at higher education; another Marx Brothers film, *Duck Soup* (1933), went further and satirized nationalism and politics. In *Modern Times* (1935) Charlie Chaplin was at the mercy of society's vast technology, as was the audience. A family of poor but happy eccentrics in *You Can't Take*

It With You (1938) comically battled the forces of sophistication, money, and industrialization. Gary Cooper, as the wealthy hayseed of *Mr. Deeds Goes to Town* (1936), discovered the best way to spend his money was by helping the poor, starving city dwellers. Other more innocent pictures captured the ticket holder's desires for an escape from recurring tensions and insecurities. Such movies as *The Wizard of Oz* (1939) and *The Big Broadcast* (of 1932, 1936, 1937, and 1938) were entertaining interludes.

There were also those retrospective films which recalled a better time; the stories of the South fell easily into this category. Productions involving the plantation became increasingly lavish from the release of *Dixiana* in 1930 to the later *Mississippi* in 1935, and of course *Gone With the Wind* in 1939.

By the beginning of sound movies, the South's emergence as a popular cinematic subject had practically guaranteed the topic's continued exploration. In silent film the South had been viewed as a section no different from the rest of the nation in its racial conservatism and its desires for material achievement. And in the 1930s, if many blamed big, urban business for the failure of the American economy, the region's rural conservatism took on yet another meaning.

In the cinema, the prewar agrarian culture staunchly resisted industrialization and urbanization and economic hard times in general. The pressures of everyday life in an industrial society were simply not evident. The overseer in *Way Down South* (1939) was more interested in his workers' welfare than in the day's quota of cotton. Wanting to raise a house for a slave couple, the blacks were released from labor with the admonition, "Give 'em a nice wedding."[1] Also, the urban poor were unheard of in the Old South romances. In *Dixiana* and *Jezebel*, New Orleans was but a delightful seat of aristocracy.

Here was a society apparently unsusceptible to the modern economic upheaval. That the image was historically untrue or that the contemporary agricultural South suffered miserably throughout the Depression could be momentarily forgotten amid

[1]Dialogue and Cutting Continuity, *Way Down South* (1939), LC-MPS Copyright File LP-9176.

the splendor of *Gone With the Wind*'s counterargument. The movie furnished "proof" that the ruination of the old way constituted the destruction of much that was good. Men such as Frank Kennedy could no longer remain gentlemen planters but had to stoop to mercentile pursuits; young women such as Scarlett had to sully their hands in business. It was a crisis, an upheaval, of the simple, predictable, and pleasant way of life which seemed at the moment alien to contemporary audiences. It was no idle statement of Rhett's, that he wished to return to Charleston, where "charm and grace" must still survive.[2]

By World War II the cinematic South had fully emerged as a pristine society, secure in its class and economic systems. In fact, the Confederacy's failure and the accompanying destruction of the plantation system served to keep the region's image intact, relieved from any exposure to economic blight. Responding to films such as *So Red the Rose* (1935), the South took pride in those remaining vestiges of its uniqueness—its class, racial, and agrarian consciousness. Audiences could marvel at a culture so reliant on the land and the seasons rather than on the city and business trends.

But also of paramount importance in the 1930s was the sheer fun of such movies. The romance, the *joie de vivre*, of these films furnished a tonic to a population beset by reality. Crowds flocked to hear Bing Crosby croon in *Mississippi* and to see Shirley Temple and Bill "Bojangles" Robinson hoof through their stair routine in *The Littlest Rebel*. The comedy of Bert Wheeler and Robert Woolsey in *Dixiana* was infectious. Bobby Breen in *Way Down South* was the perfect movie orphan, smiling and singing his way into the audience's heart. A vivacious Bette Davis in *Jezebel* and Charles "Buddy" Rogers—"America's Boy Friend"—in *River of Romance* provided plenty of romantic interest for viewers.

In fact, the region became such a stock source of stylish escape that the postwar South as well took on the attractiveness of its earlier period. The war appeared to have changed nothing in *The Little Colonel* (1935), a vehicle for the talents of Shirley Temple, Bill Robinson, Hattie McDaniel, and Lionel Barrymore. Colonel

[2]Dialogue and Cutting Continuity, *Gone With the Wind* (1939), LC-MPS Copyright File LP-9390.

Lloyd (Barrymore) ruled over a magnificent estate tended by devoted servants. Blacks still gathered on the front lawn to sing "Carry Me Back to Ol' Virginia," and the Colonel still raised his glass to "the South and confusion to all her enemies."[3] It was as if the war had never occurred.

The appreciation of things Southern could be carried to even further extremes, as in *Carolina* (1934), set in the Depression era. Janet Gaynor and Robert Young fall in love in the memory-filled plantation resided in by the usual master and servant, Lionel Barrymore and Stepin Fetchit. A grand ball is hauntingly re-created, with the Confederacy's noblest heroes in attendance— basking in adulation after the victory at First Bull Run. Beauregard, Jackson, and even the silver-haired Robert E. Lee, mistakenly identified as the commander responsible for the glorious victory, all appeared.[4]

Even when the New South appeared in film without the trappings of wealth, it was nonetheless often an enchanting place. Will Rogers and Irvin S. Cobb cavorted through *Steamboat 'Round the Bend* (1935), which captured much of the style of Mark Twain's humor in a tale of riverboat racing.[5] Rogers joined the riotous Stepin Fetchit in John Ford's *Judge Priest*, a delightful verbal rematch of the Civil War.[6]

[3]*The Little Colonel* (Twentieth Century-Fox, 1935), MOMA-FSC. See also Dialogue Continuity, LC-MPS Copyright File LP-5464. With its cast and theme, the picture was quite successful; for commercial reaction to the film, see *Motion Picture Herald*, Feb. 23; March 2, 9, 16, 23, 30; April 6, 20; May 4, 18, 25; July 6, 13, 1935. The critical reactions, however, were somewhat mixed; see, for example, *New York Times*, March 22, 1935; *Variety*, March 27, 1935; *New York World Telegram*, March 22, 1935.

[4]*Carolina* (Twentieth Century-Fox, 1934), GEH. See also Dialogue Continuity, LC-MPS Copyright File LP-4468. Despite its outspoken romanticism, the film was critically well received; see, for example, *New York Times*, Feb. 16, 1934; *New York Herald Tribune*, Feb. 16, 1934; *New York World Telegram*, Feb. 16, 1934; *Variety*, Feb. 20, 1934.

[5]*Steamboat 'Round the Bend* (Twentieth Century-Fox, 1935), MOMA-FSC; see also Dialogue Continuity, LC-MPS Copyright File LP-5971. For representative reviews, see *New York Times*, Sept. 20, 1935; *Motion Picture Herald*, Nov. 16, 1935.

[6]See *New York Times*, Oct. 12, 1934; *Motion Picture Herald*, Feb. 9, 16, 23; March 16, 30; April 20, 1935.

Will Rogers and Stepin Fetchit in *Judge Priest*. BELOW: Jane Withers in *Can This Be Dixie?*.

Music in a Southern setting was also popular, as evident in such successes as *Showboat* (1936), hailed by critics as possessing "all the color and panoply of river days."[7] Tunes joined comedy in *Can This Be Dixie?*, highlighted by such forgettable songs as "Pick, Pick Pickaninny."[8] Other bits of regional lore, racehorses and gamblers, also had their share of films. George Raft and Louise Beavers played for high stakes throughout *The Lady's From Kentucky* (1939).[9] Will Rogers contributed his talents to yet another "glorious romance under Southern skies," *In Old Kentucky* (1935).[10] Similarly, *Kentucky* (1938) lovingly explored the "core of gentleness and strong moral fiber" in a tale of thoroughbreds.[11] In *My Old Kentucky Home*, the Hall Johnson Choir hummed Stephen Foster melodies.[12] *Maryland* (1940) included scenes of scarlet-coated hunters riding to the hounds and spirited Negro church meetings graced by the familiar Clarence Muse and Hattie McDaniel.[13]

Such romantic films readily offset those few explorations of the area's seamier side. Warner Brothers' *I Am a Fugitive From a Chain Gang* (1932) aroused a storm of protest from the South, especially from Georgia, where the true story was set. Without the comic relief of the later *Cool Hand Luke* (1967), the production's revelations of the cruelties and injustices of the section's penal system were certainly upsetting. But the nation was seemingly as interested in the suits and countersuits involving the author and onetime prisoner, Robert E. Burns, as in the images the autobiographical film conveyed.[14]

[7] *New York Times*, May 15, 1936; see also Synopsis, *Showboat* (1936), LC-MPS Copyright File LP-6347.

[8] Dialogue Continuity, *Can This Be Dixie?* (1936), LC-MPS Copyright File LP-7093; see also *Variety*, Nov. 18, 1936.

[9] *New York World Telegram*, April 27, 1939; *Variety*, April 12, 1939.

[10] A top money-maker the fall of 1935, *In Old Kentucky* was well received in diverse areas; see *Motion Picture Herald*, Dec. 28, 1935; Jan. 25, 1936; *Birmingham News*, Nov. 14, 1935; *Phoenix Arizona Republic*, Dec. 1, 1935.

[11] *New York Herald Tribune*, Dec. 24, 1938; *Variety*, Dec. 21, 1938.

[12] *Variety*, Feb. 9, 1938.

[13] For a typical review, see *New York Post*, July 13, 1940.

[14] The horrors of the Southern chain gangs shocked many reviewers; see, for example, *New York Sun*, Nov. 11, 1932; *Variety*, Nov. 15, 1932; *New*

Banjo on My Knee (1936) with Joel McCrae purported to be a drama of Southern low life. But Buddy Ebsen's dance steps and Walter Brennan's one-man band detracted from any merit the picture may have had as a portrait of Mississippi River shanty folk.[15] Pictures such as *Cabin in the Cotton* (1932), which explored the problems of the tenant farmer in a persistently deferential society, were just not popular enough to diminish the audience's obsession with the other celluloid South.[16]

Hollywood's preoccupation with the old South as an alternative to present hard times was not the theme of Southern literature, however. In fact, while the films presented a region of beaux and belles, the writings of natives dealt with the far more common folk who resided in poverty and ignorance, and who were depicted in what nearly became a literary genre known as Southern Gothic. At first glance, the Hollywood Southern romance and the literary New South appear as two entirely different interpretations vying for public acceptance. In fact, the cinematic image was far stronger, though both could thrive and even support one another.

The more seriously inclined could shun the cimena and seek deeper social comment in literature. By the 30s writings on the South were awash with scathing examinations. It had been a slow process, but in the early 1900s, as the works of Thomas Nelson Page and others began to grow too predictable, readers sought other commentaries on the region. One of Page's friends, John

York Herald Tribune, Nov. 17, 1932. However, subsequent charges lodged by the Georgia Prison Commission against both Warner Brothers and Burns for alleged falsification of the facts soon diverted attention. Eventually the courts ruled against the Commission, and in its statutes the state substituted the term "public works camps" for the more onerous "chain gang." See *New York Herald Tribune*, Dec. 16, 19, 22, 23, 28, 1932; May 25, 1934; *New York World Telegram*, Dec. 22, 1932; Oct. 7, 1938; *Variety*, May 29, 1934; June 16, 1937; *New York Times*, Jan. 27, 1934.

[15]Critics were usually unappreciative of the film; see *Variety*, Dec. 16, 1936; *New York World Telegram*, Dec. 12, 1936.

[16]At least a few reviewers were impressed with the film's stark realism in contrast to so many other Southern pictures; see, for example, *The Stage*, Nov. 1932; *New York Herald Tribune*, Sept. 30, 1932.

Fox, Jr., served as a transitional writer, bridging the gap between the plantation romances and the stark realism to come. Fox's writings, *Crittenden* (1898) and *The Little Shepherd of Kingdom Come* (1903), were still heavy with neo-Confederate implications, but his later works—*A Mountain Europa* or *Heart of the Hills*, for example—dealt more with pastoral scenes of an upland South peopled by forthright, humble folk of simple tastes.

Ellen Glasgow, ironically a Richmonder of social position, wrote not only of the yeoman farmer but of "white trash" as well, and displayed a remarkable understanding of ordinary folk whom she believed held the South's future. In *The Miller of the Old Church* (1911) and *Barren Ground* (1925), the ordinary citizen was sympathetically explored; the planter was relegated to a secondary role.

Many writers were even more outspoken when presenting the small farmer. Henry Kroll's *Cabin in the Cotton* (1931), from which the 1932 film was made, reflected much of his own upbringing as the son of a Tennessee sharecropper. Edith Summers Kelley's *Weeds* (1923), Dorothy Scarborough's *In the Land of Cotton* (1924), Elizabeth Maddox Roberts' *The Time of Man* (1926), and Jack Bethea's *Cotton* (1928) were equally hard-hitting novels of social comment, advocating a reexamination of traditions and beliefs previously so grandly praised by Page and others.

Some writers were more gentle, while still evoking sympathy for the lower classes. Caroline Miller won a Pulitzer Prize for *Lamb in His Bosom*, the story of an independent antebellum frontiersman. Enthralled by Florida, Marjorie Rawlings wrote two bestsellers set in her adopted state. *The Yearling* (1938), a Pulitzer Prize winner, and *Cross Creek* (1942) were both full of nostalgia for the area's back-country environs.

There was yet another stream of local color fiction in the 1930s which highlighted the region in frightening hues. T. S. Stribling's *Teeftallow* (1926) and *Bright Metal* (1928) and his trilogy of the early 30s—*The Forge, The Store,* and *The Unfinished Cathedral*—all attacked the section's low life. In it the people were detestably ignorant, stubborn, violent, and staunchly fundamentalist. The characterizations would be echoed in the enormously popular works of Erskine Caldwell and those of the lesser known William Faulkner.

Faulkner's dozen books, such as *The Hamlet* (1940) or *Sartoris* (1929), did not present Southerners in harmony with the land. Those of his characters who had to survive off the land, notably the Snopes family, were pathetic, greedy, and lacking in scruples. Caldwell's *Tobacco Road* (1932) and *God's Little Acre* (1933) forged unforgettably grotesque characters such as Jeeter Lester, far removed from the protagonists of the regional novels of the late 1800s.

Southern writers such as Glasgow and Faulkner were sincere in their efforts to reassess their region's history and significance. The authors represented a new generation, born long after the Civil War and thus less encumbered by the romanticism of the Lost Cause. Faulkner was born in 1897, Caldwell in 1893. Growing to maturity in a postwar South aware of the past while facing a present of emerging industry, world war, and agricultural hard times, the writers described their South as they knew it. No longer was it the land of Tidewater aristocracy but one of inland farms and towns peopled by individuals the earlier writers never outlined.

While authors like Caldwell often depicted the South as backward, there were other writers who saw the region in a far different light. True, authors as a whole sought to relieve the region of its "moonlight and magnolia" image, but few desired that the section lose all its distinctiveness. Some labored harder than others to maintain unique characteristics.

In the late 1920s, a group of Vanderbilt University scholars and sympathetic cohorts published a critique of the headlong rush away from the old ways that writers such as Caldwell found so offensive. The group was made up of twelve men of letters including poets John Crowe Ransom, Allen Tate, and Robert Penn Warren, the critic and novelist Stark Young, and the historian Frank L. Owsley. The group's writings are best remembered by the collection of essays, *I'll Take My Stand: The South and the American Tradition* (1930) in which they argued that what was wrong with the South was not its rural poverty and backwardness, but rather its haste to obliterate all of its pastoral traditions in order to enter the industrial age.

In essence, these writers held up for examination some of the basic assumptions of the period. The "Vanderbilt Agrarians" perceived the South as an alternative to the excesses of a mass materialist culture devoid of grace and leisure. They pointed out that to worship progress for its own sake was to blind one to life's aesthetic, humanistic values, values persisting in the South.[17]

But what was the influence of the revisionists and their opponents upon the image of the South, particularly when contrasted to the region as Hollywood presented it? Despite the number of Pulitzer awards, the large sales, and even lurid plots by Caldwell and others, the revisionist writings held surprisingly little influence over the broad, popular conception of the South.

Coincidentally, the movies adhered in part to the spirit of the Agrarians. Whereas the dozen scholars sought solace from an all-encompassing modern society, so too did the movies happen to offer the viewers a reprieve from the encroachments of the outside world. For economic rather than intellectual reasons, Hollywood served up generous portions of captivating Southern lore which restored to the harried Depression ticket holder's imagination some semblance of uncomplicated order. What the essayists tried so hard to disseminate and then only to a select

[17]Sheldon Van Auken, "The Southern Historical Novel in the Early Twentieth Century," *Journal of Southern History* 14 (May 1948), 157-91; Louis D. Rubin, Jr., "The Historical Image of Modern Southern Writing," *Journal of Southern History* 12 (May 1956), 147-66; Rubin, "Southern Literature: A Piedmont Art," *Mississippi Quarterly* 23 (Winter 1969-70), 1-18; Rubin, ed., *I'll Take My Stand: The South and the Agrarian Tradition* (New York: Harper, 1962), vi-xviii; Alexander Karanikas, *Tillers of a Myth: Southern Agrarians as Social and Literary Critics* (Madison: Univ. of Wisconsin Press, 1966), 3-32; John L. Steward, *The Burden of Time: The Fugitives and Agrarians* (Princeton: Princeton Univ. Press, 1965), 91-205; and Richard Gray, *The Literature of Memory: Modern Writers of the American South* (Baltimore: Johns Hopkins Univ. Press, 1977), 150-256; see also Rubin and Robert D. Jacobs, ed., *Southern Renascence: The Literature of the Modern South* (Baltimore: Johns Hopkins Univ. Press, 1953); Rubin, *The Faraway Country, Writers of the Modern South* (Seattle: Univ. of Washington Press, 1963); Rubin, *The Wary Fugitives: Four Poets and the South* (Baton Rouge: LSU Press, 1978); and Louise Cowan, *The Fugitive Group: A Literary History* (Baton Rouge: LSU Press, 1959).

readership, motion pictures did within a popular culture. It was an audience perhaps not cognizant of the philosophical shadings in the debate between tradition and modernity, but it was at least as attracted as the Agrarians to the dream. The trade publications bore evidence of the theme's drawing power, and ticket sales were too high to alter what was a business bonanza.

Indeed, movies as mundane as the antebellum tale *River of Romance* or the postwar *The Little Colonel* were a far more persuasive and widely recognized answer to, say, Caldwell's *Tobacco Road*, than any literary effort. *Tobacco Road*, for instance, played on Broadway for seven and a half years, and Caldwell's *God's Little Acre* had sold over eight million copies by 1966, far more than even *Gone With the Wind*.[18] But film was simply a more widespread medium. Even the total sales of *God's Little Acre* over a thirty-five year period could not match one film's ticket sales for a single night in each of the nation's theatres, seating approximately eleven million. The success of such early Depression movies as *Hearts in Dixie* and *Dixiana* provided hard commercial evidence that the money was in romance not realism.

Not until the 1940s, and particularly the postwar period, would large numbers of films based on the work of Caldwell, Faulkner, and Tennessee Williams emerge. And even then the considerations were primarily economic rather than artistic. The releases were not regarded as a needed reinterpretation, but instead as an investment in titilating stories aimed at restoring prewar audiences which by the early 1950s found the attractions of television and suburbia more alluring than downtown theatres.

For those devotees of both the cinema and revisionist Southern literature, they were not necessarily torn between two extremes. The novels of the 1930s did in fact bolster the image of the Old South. For example, many newspapers in the 30s employed one critic to handle both film and book reviews, and the great majority of these critics saw no conflict between the image in, say, Henry Kroll's novel *Cabin in the Cotton* and RKO Studio's *Dixiana*. The lamentable state of Southern society in fiction was

---

[18]See Alice P. Hackett, comp., *Seventy Years of Best Sellers, 1895-1965* (New York: Bowker, 1967), 12-30.

taken either as evidence that the Civil War had indeed caused the demise of something to be treasured, or at worst was viewed as an overstated exposé of a problem not in itself very different from the rest of a suffering nation.[19]

In the late 1920s, as Hollywood production companies realized the potential of the Old South as a vehicle of escapist entertainment, the silent era's emphasis on the black was no longer necessary. There was a greater need after the Depression began for distracting pictures of planter wealth and comfort. In the first sound films, however, the central role of the Negro survived, albeit for an interesting reason.

In October 1927, Warner Brothers' *The Jazz Singer* had displayed the intriguing possibilities of sound productions in a story which revolved around jazz and sentimental melodies born of the South and the Afro-American experience. Studios, quick to perceive potential successes, experimented with shorter two-reel productions using blacks and their music. The primary reason was profit, of course, but also many believed the Negro voice to be ideally suited to sound releases. Indicative of the belief were Robert Benchley's comments in a 1929 issue of *Opportunity*. He wrote, it "may be that the talking movies must be participated in exclusively by Negroes," because of "a quality in the Negro voice, an ease in its delivery, and a sense of timing in reading the lines that makes it the ideal medium for the talking picture."[20]

Using the black voice might have paved the way to numerous serious roles, but such was not the case. To be sure, Negroes could get work, but the story lines changed little. The plantation was still presented as a place of leisure for slaves. The Forbes Randolph Kentucky Jubilee Singers in *Slave Days* (1929) har-

---

[19]Non-Southern reviewers perceived *Dixiana* as a "music haunted Southern paradise" which possessed both a "brilliant theme and glamorous locale" outlining a "glowing life" when contrasted to the hard times of the 1930s; see, for example, *Boise Idaho Daily Statesman*, Sept 7, 1930; *Chicago Daily Tribune*, Sept. 1, 1930; *Indianapolis News*, Sept. 27, 1930; *Des Moines Register*, Sept. 7, 1930; *Seattle Post-Intelligencer*, Aug. 9, 1930.

[20]Quoted from reprint, Robert Benchley, "*Hearts in Dixie*, The First Real Talking Picture," in *The Black Man on Film: Racial Stereotyping*, ed. by Richard A. Maynard (Rochelle Park, N.J.: Hayden, 1974), 46-48.

monized around the slave quarters. In *Cotton Pickin' Days* (1930), the Randolph voices gathered around the fire and cabins to sing "Give Me That Ol' Time Religion" and "Camptown Races."[21] The films were important in sustaining the image of the antebellum society; those short movies such as *Night in Dixie* reestablished the existence of a tranquil slave life, free of white interruption most of the time.[22]

When the whites deigned to visit, as in *The Melody Makers* series, it was only to enjoy the music; the quarters resounded with "My Ol' Kentucky Home" and "Ol' Black Joe." Films such as *Dixie Days* (1928) and *Dixie* (1929) followed the same themes. Vitaphone's production of *Dixie Days*, using yet another cabin set, presented again spirituals of the prewar culture, "sung by a group of native Southern darkies." The "thrilling" choruses of "All God's Chillun' Got Shoes" emphasized the increasingly romantic view.[23]

King Vidor's *Hallelujah* contained shadings of the postwar pastoral South alongside scenes of Negro town life. But its predecessor, *Hearts in Dixie* (1929), captured best an antebellum spirit in a picture actually of the New South. It began originally as another two reels of musical entertainment, but the rough cuts were impressive enough to add a connecting story. Walter Weems—once a Southern minstrel man known as "The Boy From Dixie"—wrote the script, which included only two whites. The full-length production was unique among major Depression era films in showing rural black joys, sorrows, and ambitions without constant white influence. But the film still made the old ideal attractive, and the complimentary picture was all the more powerful as the blacks provided the proof. What made the idyllic South appear even more appealing was the story's postwar setting. The picture gave few signs of any significant changes from the antebellum culture, thus implying strongly how persevering

[21]For a discussion of the utilization of the Negro voice in early sound films, see Cripps, *Slow Fade to Black*, 219-35.

[22]*Night in Dixie* (DeForest Phonofilm, n.d.), fragment, LC-MPS.

[23]Synopsis, *Dixie Days* (1928), LC-MPS Copyright File MP-5263.

the system was.[24] In fact, many reviewers were confused and indeed regarded the movie as a tale of the Old South. The film was thus representative of the fascination with the delights of both the prewar and postwar South and how the two periods in fact blended in the public's imagination.

So reminiscent was its tone that commentators saw it as an "epic of the South befo' de war."[25] Advertising boosted that assumption. Bulletins encouraged customers to "hear the Old South talk and sing" or to become involved in "this intensely human drama of the Old South before the war." *Hearts in Dixie*, "the screen's first singing, dancing, and talking comedy of the Old South," invoked numerous devices to transpose a bygone era's tenets to a more modern setting.[26]

The film opens with a gentleman expressing his hope that the story will help one "to forget the cares and troubles of everyday life" and that this "life of a race of humans" will prove entertaining. Certainly the dancing and music were rousing. The Billbrew Chorus of sixty, the forty Fanchon Steppers, and the Four Emperors of Harmony provided fast-paced interludes in scenes of joyful work and recreation. The numbers effectively carried on the spirit of the contented worker created in silent film.

The principal character is Nappus, played by Clarence Muse, an old man devoted to his son Chinquapin, his daughter Chloe, and his granddaughter. But whatever nobility was found in his role was more than offset by Stepin Fetchit's comic performance as Gummy, his son-in-law. He is, as Nappus put it, just "naturally hopeless," as he passes the time complaining of "feet trou-

[24]*Hearts in Dixie* (Fox, 1929), MOMA-FSC; see also Cutting Continuity, LC-MPS Copyright File LP-234.

[25]*Des Moines Register*, April 14, 1929; see also *Portland* (Me.) *Sunday Telegram and Press Herald*, June 16, 1929; *Detroit Free Press*, March 30, 1929; *Omaha World Herald*, May 26, 1929.

[26]Many reviewers were enthralled with the film's traditional spirit. See, for example, *Washington Post*, March 31, 1929; *Hartford* (Conn.) *Daily Times*, April 27, 1929; *Des Moines Register*, April 15, 1929; *Louisville Courier-Journal*, April 28, 1929; *Cleveland Plain Dealer*, March 16, 1929; *Newark Star-Eagle*, April 24, 1929.

Clarence Muse in *Hearts in Dixie*.

ble" and looking for spareribs. When his wife Chloe and daughter die, his only interest is in finding another mate and cook. Once remarried, he discovers that his new wife does not appreciate his meager talents and sees him only as a "good for nothin' hunk o' licorice" or a "two-legged bottle of ink."

There was pathos, however. When Chloe and her babe grow ill, they are treated by a Negro voodoo priestess who insists that Nappus refrain from fetching a white doctor. All present agree. The old fellow alone realizes that what he viewed as his race's primitive ignorance will cause the death of his loved ones. In a scene of maudlin adherence to the tradition of black subservience, Nappus goes hat-in-hand to the doctor. At first, the white wants no part of the dilemma. But he relents when Nappus adds, "I know you ain't got much time to be messin' aroun' me and mine, an' somethin' tells me that if we believe mo' in the white folks and less in chants and charms, we'd all be better off." But they are too late; mother and child are dead. Finally, Nappus decides that he must sell all his worldly goods to afford sending his beloved Chinquapin north to school to overcome his people's ignorance.

Despite the ending's presentation of a black's ambitions for his son, the film fairly overflowed with antebellum romanticism. For example, while Chinquapin awaits the river steamer *Nelly Bly*, the boat's captain asks a dock worker what cargo he has. His reply reflects the region's mythology and racial conservatism. His answer comes, "Oh, about the same—three of Colonel Potter's race horses for St. Louis" and "just a pickaninny." The title *Hearts in Dixie* said much too. Though the young boy was to go elsewhere for his education, his heart, family, and heritage lay southward.

That the picture was intended to capture a blend of Southern charm and Negro happiness and gratitude was obvious in local advertising. Many theatres chose to announce their bookings by emphasizing the section's mystique of aristocracy rather than the story's black cast. On one hand, the bulletins leaned heavily on popular preconceptions of the planter ideal and thus encouraged attendance. The practice also forestalled any adverse reaction to a nearly all-Negro company until the viewer could see for himself how traditional the interpretation actually was. In Richmond and Louisville, posters were accented by a mansion surrounded by trees covered with Spanish moss; the movie included no such scene. In Hartford, Connecticut, an advertisement featured another nonexistent shot of planter gentry and their ladies greeting an arriving steamer. Many other Northern areas used similar pictures, presenting well-to-do whites.[27]

On the other hand, even in those areas which stressed the film's cast, there was no mistaking the romanticism involved in the picture's view of black workers. Posters were sometimes bordered in cotton balls and centered with blacks highstepping at the approach of a sternwheeler. Other advertisements showed joyous Negroes dancing in the fields and on the riverbank. In Washington, patrons were encouraged to attend a "musical drama of the real Dixieland" and to "hear and see . . . the crooning workers in the cotton fields." A Phoenix theatre boasted that the production was "a slice of life from the very heart of the country that gave you the mammy songs." The region's general happiness and agricultural stereotyping were stressed in advertising touting that the players were from "the cotton fields and levees of Dixie" and that the audiences were "goin' South—All ado'd fo' Vicksburg, Natchez, N'Awlins—Bound for the fields of cotton and the land of song." There were "cotton field capers, shufflin' feet, levee lyrics" which displayed the "soul, the loves of mammyland." It was a picture that the theatre managers assured "has everything —banjo strummin', singers hummin', fiddlers thumbin', barbeques crumbin', wide grins gummin'."[28]

---

[27]*Richmond Times-Dispatch*, April 28, 1929; *Louisville Courier-Journal*, April 28, 1929; *Hartford* (Conn.) *Daily Times*, April 27, 1929; *Boise Idaho Daily Statesman*, April 7, 1929; *Indianapolis News*, April 19, 1929; *Boston Daily Globe*, March 30, 1929; *Milwaukee Journal*, May 6, 1929; *Houston Post-Dispatch*, March 29, 1929.

[28]*Washington Post*, March 31, 1929; *Phoenix Arizona Republic*, April 10, 1929; *Little Rock Arkansas Democrat*, May 12, 1929; *Boise Idaho Daily Statesman*, April 7, 1929; *Topeka Daily Capital*, July 14, 1929; *Baltimore Sun*, March 31, 1929; *Boston Daily Globe*, March 30, 1929; *Minneapolis Morning Tribune*, May 16, 1929; *Butte Montana Standard*, May 12, 1929; *Manchester* (N.H.) *Union*, June 16, 1929; *Seattle Post-Intelligencer*, May 19, 1929; *Los Angeles Times*, March 6, 1929; *Povidence* (R.I.) *Journal*, May 10, 1929.

Reviews also embraced the mythology. A Western paper labeled the release excellent, "as if the very heart of Dixie had been transplanted to the silver sheet, to the accompaniment of banjo strumming, characteristic dancing, spiritual crooning, fascinating dialect, romantic environment, and accurate background." The commentator also added that the story's "close adherence to the legend and lore of Dixie makes it utterly inescapable in its influence on the reviewer." In San Francisco, a reporter dubbed the tale of "the lives of these primitive people" as "educational as well as entertaining," since it reflected "in realistic fashion the home life of the Negro in the South."[29]

In the Northeast, *Hearts in Dixie* was perceived as "eloquent and impressive in its reproduction of those days" of blissful existence. In the Midwest, the film was held over in Chicago, as it was a delight "to lean back lazily and look into the hearts, homes, and manners . . . of the real Southern Negro." A Topeka writer described it as a "vision of the Southern Negro in his happy-go-lucky outlook upon life." Just how far racial stereotyping had come was apparent in an article which supported the contention that the biased image was correct: "Its characters are all true to type and bring the fresh spontaneity and enthusiasm for which the race is known." Worse, in Cleveland a critic wrote that the story "is like the entire colored race, light-hearted, ready with its songs, dances and laughter."[30] Those few who found fault with the film criticized its portrayal of blacks as individuals who "prance and warble and kick up dust in the clear spaces in front of the old, old Southern cabins."[31]

Hearts in Dixie, its roots in the earlier romantic black pictures, was a transitional film; it, and such short productions as *Dixie Days,* were soon rarities. Emphasis turned to wealthy whites, thereby perpetuating the mythology while providing the com-

---

[29]*Phoenix Arizona Republic*, April 10, 1929; *San Francisco Chronicle*, April 25, 26, 1929.

[30]*Hartford* (Conn.) *Daily Times*, April 27, 1929; *Chicago Daily Tribune*, May 13, 1929; *Topeka Daily Capital*, July 14, 1929; *Portland* (Me.) *Sunday Telegram and Press Herald*, June 16, 1929; *Cleveland Plain Dealer*, March 18, 1929.

[31]*New York Post*, Feb. 28, 1929.

fortable, predictable image the white audiences craved. In rapid succession, studios released *River of Romance* (1929), *The Mississippi Gambler* (1929), and the musical comedy *Dixiana* (1930).

An even more popular musical comedy was Paramount's *Mississippi* (1935), with Bing Crosby, W. C. Fields, and Joan Bennett. The final adaptation of Booth Tarkington's *Magnolia*, it was far more spectacular than either of its predecessors, *The Fighting Coward* or *River of Romance*. This delightful film was so successful that a month after its release it was tied with Will Roger's *Life Begins at Forty* and Jeanette MacDonald and Nelson Eddy's *Naughty Marietta* as box-office leaders. Beyond the South, the picture played to full houses in such diverse areas as New York, Washington, Los Angeles, Chicago, Indianapolis, Baltimore, St. Louis, and Newark.[32] The overwhelming majority of movie house managers were pleased and impressed.[33]

The extravaganza was so well received that other musicals borrowed heavily on the spirit. The two film biographies of Stephen Foster, *Harmony Lane* (1935) and *Swanee River* (1939), though dealing with a career spent primarily in the North, took pains to stress that the composer's attachment to the South was not only musical but emotional as well.[34] Don Ameche and Al Jolson in the latter film sung the praises of a charming, hospitable South, a region several critics regarded as "warm, gracious, and lovely" in comparison to the "rough and rowdy" urban North.[35]

The antebellum scenery was even more enthusiastically presented in Paramount's 1935 production of *So Red the Rose*. Adapted from Stark Young's best-selling novel of 1934, the

[32]*Motion Picture Herald*, May 11, 18, 1935; *Washington Post*, April 18, 1935; *Los Angeles Times*, April 10, 1935; *Chicago Daily Tribune*, April 25, 1935; *Indianapolis News*, April 18, 1935; *Baltimore Sun*, April 19, 1935; *St. Louis Post-Dispatch*, April 7, 1935; *Newark Star-Eagle*, April 30, 1935.

[33]See, for example, *Motion Picture Herald*, May 18; June 15, 22, 29; July 6, 20, 1935.

[34]Studio Press Book, *Harmony Lane* (1935), LC-MPS Copyright File LP-5752; and Dialogue Continuity, *Swanee River* (1939), LC-MPS Copyright File LP-9693.

[35]See, for example, *Motion Picture Herald*, Jan. 13, 1940; *Miami Herald*, Jan. 6, 1940; *Richmond Times-Dispatch*, Dec. 29, 1939; *New York World Telegram*, Dec. 30, 1939.

movie praised the South as no picture had since *Birth of a Nation*. In fact, the release too vehemently attacked the conduct of Union troops in the war, at the expense of ticket sales beyond the South.

But such a mistake still could not dim the public's desires for repetitions of the prewar themes. Warner Brothers' 1938 release of *Jezebel* was no less outspoken in its defense of the plantation lifestyle. It met not only with audience approval, but also garnered an Academy Award for Bette Davis in the title role. The film was cleverly made to benefit from the publicity already generated by David O. Selznick for his unfilmed script of *Gone With the Wind*. But *Jezebel* made it on its own merits. Besides Davis, the studio marshalled a fine cast for director William Wyler, including Henry Fonda, George Brent, Margaret Lindsay, and Donald Crisp. Lesser stars contracted for the film were Spring Byington and the increasingly familiar black performers Teresa Harris and Eddie "Rochester" Anderson.

Way Down South was also in the traditional mold, which was somewhat surprising considering that Clarence Muse, the fine actor long relegated to playing subservient slaves, and Langston Hughes, a noted black author, together wrote the screenplay. With the often used Hall Johnson Choir providing the standard musical interludes, the 1939 release was a vehicle for Shirley Temple's less popular male counterpart, Bobby Breen, who had performed in an earlier Southern romance, *Rainbow on the River* (1936). That film, reminiscent of *Old Mammy's Charge* (1913), involved a "mammy," played by Louise Beavers, and her efforts to keep the young "massa" she had faithfully protected throughout the war.

A measure of the lengths to which the mythology had grown was also revealed in the cinematic versions of Mark Twain's tales of boyhood on the Mississippi River. Though the *Tom Sawyer* of 1930 was almost Western in theme, with its sound track of "Oh Susanna" and with the exploits of Jackie Coogan and Junior Durkin failing to capture a distinct Southern setting, the other adaptations showed the influence of antebellum productions.[36]

[36]*Tom Sawyer* (Paramount, 1930), MCA Corp. Universal/16 (New York), cited hereafter as U/16; see also Studio Press Book, LC-MPS Copyright File LP-1736.

Al Jolson in *Swanee River*. BELOW: Bebe Daniels in *Dixiana*.

Produced by David O. Selznick and starring Tommy Kelly, Jackie Moran, Victor Jory, and Walter Brennan, *The Adventures of Tom Sawyer* (1938) evoked a far stronger nostalgic spirit.[37]

But the myth of a happy land was especially obvious in the 1931 picture *Huckleberry Finn*. With Coogan and Durkin again, and with Clarence Muse as Jim, *Huckleberry Finn* avoided the issue of slavery and Jim's need to escape sale and separation from his family. His travels were simply explained as his desire to care for the boys.[38]

Worse, Muse's role was characterized as "a jovial old Negro of the type common to the unspoiled South." Advertisements spoke of "banjo darkies." To gain the attention of potential customers, the film company recommended that theatre managers employ a black minstrel; "in almost every town, you can pick up a colored fellow or two to pick a mean tune out of a banjo." For the best results, the publicity department urged that "he should be of good character, an old pappy with odd cotton side feathers on chin and head, the latter topped shiny bald."[39]

What was unfortunate about these versions of Twain's work, besides the racism, was the lack of awareness of the differences between the stories of Tom and Huck. The latter tale was a far more serious affair of personal decision and growth, involving a youth's discovery of his culture's flaws and its inhumanity. The maturing was largely lost in *Huck and Tom* (1918) and in *Huckleberry Finn* (1920 and 1931). Finally, in the 1939 production of *Huckleberry Finn* some of the original novel's intent was presented. Mickey Rooney as Huck had become an abolitionist of sorts by the end and had convinced the Widow Douglas to free his slave friend, played by Rex Ingram. Interestingly enough, many reviewers felt that the picture failed to present well the "boyhood" story captured in previous productions.[40]

[37]Synopsis, *The Adventures of Tom Sawyer* (1938), LC-MPS Copyright File LP-7894; see also *New York Daily News*, Feb. 18, 1938; *Variety*, Feb. 16, 1938.

[38]*Huckleberry Finn* (Paramount, 1931), U/16.

[39]Studio Press Book, *Huckleberry Finn* (1931), LC-MPS Copyright File LP-2400.

[40]See, for example, *New York Times*, March 3, 1939; *New York World Telegram*, March 3, 1939; *Variety*, Feb. 15, 1939.

It was certainly not for lack of effort that a studio occasionally fell short in its attempts to please critic and public alike. If a film company's advertising was grand enough to draw attention, and if the picture delivered the entertainment that the publicity promised, the reviewers and audiences were pleasantly satisfied; Hollywood's enterprise had succeeded. The films of the Old South merited some of the most outlandish publicity, romantic and escapist plots, and contented patrons of any genre.

Released the same year as *Hearts in Dixie*, *River of Romance* attracted both reviewers and audiences, and was held over in numerous areas. A New Jersey critic admired the romantic plot, with its "lovely old-time settings, and some charming old-time darkies, who sing their heart-piercing folk songs in a minor key." Impressed with Buddy Rogers' performance as a Southern gentleman, Western theatre owners declared the protagonist "loved like he fought—and he fought like h____!" Rogers' character, Tom Rumford, was a "gambler, adventurer, gay terror of the Mississippi—fascinating and mysterious." The plot was viewed as depicting "the heyday of the Old South when mint juleps, cotton, chivalry, and Mississippi River gambling held sway."[41]

Though a Seattle writer believed some of its aspects were "flagrantly sentimental," he had to admit that the tale would be popular as it was "simply drenched in 'atmosphere,' with its picturesque gamblers, its boastful killers, its feuds, singing darkies, cotton fields, and social functions in which men quarrel for the favor of lovely, drawling belles and so forth." An Eastern commentator came closer to the mark in recognizing that the movie captured a spirit, a way of life "which has not been affected by the changing standards of the metropolitan North." A

---

[41]Synopsis, *River of Romance* (1929), *American Film Institute Catalogue*, 657; see also *New York Times*, July 29, 1929. For representative Southern reviews, see *Charlotte Observor*, July 21, 1929; *Memphis Commercial Appeal*, July 28, 1929; *Nashville Banner*, Aug. 11, 1929; *Houston Post-Dispatch*, July 26, 1929. Beyond the South, advertising and reviews were in agreement on the film's attraction; see *Newark Star-Eagle*, July 22, 1929; *Portland Oregon Daily Journal*, July 17-19, 1929; see also *Cleveland Plain Dealer*, July 22, 1929; *Sioux Falls Daily Argus-Leader*, July 21, 1929; *Milwaukee Journal*, July 18, 21, 1929.

Westerner agreed; "it breathes the very odor of the magnolias and jasmines."[42]

The Mississippi Gambler, released in 1929 as well, also dealt with honor and riverboat gambling. As yet another story of a "bold, handsome gentleman gamester who'll win everything you've got," the production added more to the image of the manly planter obsessed with manners. In this case, the gentleman gladly contrived to "lose" his money to a lady in distress.[43]

To the steadily progressing regional spirit was added RKO's *Dixiana*. The 1930 romance starred Bebe Daniels, the comedy team of Bert Wheeler and Robert Woolsey, and Bill "Bojangles" Robinson. It included the first original music ever commissioned for a film, plus a few scenes of color photography. But despite the efforts of Robinson, "the dusky hoofer," and Hall's Negro Chorus, the music scores were part of the production's problem. Tunes such as "I'm Your Baby Now" and "Mr. and Mrs. Ippi" too closely mirrored modern tastes at the expense of grasping the period's mood. Also, dialogue and humor was obviously often contemporary, and several members of the cast wore current hairstyles and glasses. The story line, taken from the book by Anne Caldwell, was of little help in redeeming the picture. As was the case with many early musicals, the story was only a skeleton on which to hang modern comedy routines and song and dance numbers.[44]

With all its shortcomings, however, *Dixiana* played to substantial audiences in several areas. It was touted by RKO as a major film and publicized accordingly. Many newspapers carried full-page advertisements.[45] Advertising posters were dominated by

[42]*Seattle Post-Intelligencer*, July 20, 1929; *Providence* (R.I.) *Sunday Journal*, Aug. 11, 1929; *Salt Lake Tribune*, July 19, 1929.

[43]Synopsis, *The Mississippi Gambler* (1929), LC-MPS Copyright File LP-778; see also *Sioux Falls Daily Argus-Leader*, Aug. 20, 1930; *New York Times*, Oct. 26, 28, 1929.

[44]Synopsis, *Dixiana* (1930), LC-MPS Copyright File LP-1530.

[45]See, for example, *Los Angeles Times*, July 21, 1930; *Chicago Daily Tribune*, Sept. 1, 1930; *Portland* (Me.) *Sunday Telegram and Press Herald*, Sept. 14, 1930; *Boston Daily Globe*, Sept. 5, 1930; *Detroit Free Press*, Aug. 22, 1930; *St. Louis Post-Dispatch*, Aug. 21, 1930; *Cleveland Plain Dealer*, Sept. 5, 1930; *Newark Star-Eagle*, Sept. 12, 1930; *Portland Oregon Daily*

scenes of gambling, fist and knife fights, duelling, romantic encounters—all set among pictures of excessive revelry. Los Angeles premiere audiences were promised an authentic bit of the antebellum society, "Old New Orleans—playground of passions—its spirit and its splendors . . . captured in all reality." In the South itself, theatre managers spoke of the production as "fired with the hot blood of the Old South." It was a story "every true Southerner should see," for it was "poured from the very life blood" of the region. The usual announcements held out the attraction of "unbridled love in the sweeping inferno of a city gone mad with revelry and carnival pleasure." Added to that was the interest in a plot "lashed into frenzied passion—a city drunk with debauchery—two men—pistols drawn—in a torrent of hatred—jealous for a Southern belle."[46]

To spur curiosity, the studios usually distributed articles to the local press. RKO was no exception. Newspapers informed readers that the movie of "fashion, gaiety, and unbridled amusements" included a cast of five thousand and six detailed sets built at a cost of $500,000. Reviews provided by the studios bragged that the release depicted "streets aflame with frenzied lovers and fervent kisses." It was a society in which men were "toasting life and love at midnight and calling for duelling pistols for two at dawn." The cult of honor and beauty was made a cornerstone of the plantation world, where "imperious maidenhood reigns supreme, and the slap of a glove across the cheek sounds the signal for swords and seconds."[47]

All the publicity efforts paid off. *Dixiana* was held over in cities such as Washington, Los Angeles, San Francisco, and Philadelphia. The mayor opened the film in Portland, Oregon. Impressed, Westerners praised the "music-haunted Southern

---

Journal, Aug. 8, 1930; *Providence* (R.I.) *Journal*, Sept. 4, 1930; *Sioux Falls Daily Argus-Leader*, Sept. 28, 1930; *Salt Lake Tribune*, Sept. 10, 1930.

[46]*Los Angeles Times*, July 21, 1930; *Atlanta Constitution*, Aug. 31, 1930; for instances of the most commonly used advertisements, see *Detroit Free Press*, Aug. 22, 1930; *Albuquerque Journal*, Oct. 12, 1930; *Philadelphia Inquirer*, Sept. 13, 1930.

[47]*Minneapolis Tribune*, Sept. 7, 1930; *Washington Post*, Aug. 17, 1930; *San Francisco Chronicle*, July 28, 1930.

paradise." The production's "brilliant theme and glamorous locale" had outlined "the glowing life of the Old South." The ornate settings and costumes captivated ticket holders in Chicago, Indianapolis, Des Moines; in Seattle a writer heralded the release as "a gorgeous affair." It played to record crowds in Detroit. Southward, in Little Rock, thousands lined up for the first day's features; demand was so heavy in Memphis that crowds had to be turned away. The film was even cheered by audiences for its "faithful detail" and was purported by the studio and Southerners alike to be "historically important in the American parade."[48]

Together, *Hearts in Dixie, River of Romance, The Mississippi Gambler,* and *Dixiana* ushered in the sound film's romantic outlook. The Old South offered a model society—rural, contented, and free from current ills. And the agrarian ideal was presented in not so subtle a fashion to the industrial North. In *River of Romance*, for example, the protagonist despaired of his sedate Northern ways and became the perfect gentleman—brave, honorable, and Southern. *Dixiana*'s wealthy planter was actually a transplanted Easterner, a Quaker who sought the South's refined setting.

A later musical comedy carried the legend further. *Mississippi* (1935) was set "amid an atmosphere of magnolia, crinoline, and Kentucky whiskey." In the opening scenes, General Rumford's "Magnolia Plantation" was magnificent, dominated by an eight-columned portico. Flowers were everywhere, and young maidens strolled quietly through the garden. The home's interior was no less appealing; crystal chandeliers highlighted the decor's

---

[48]*Washington Post*, Aug. 24, 1930; *Los Angeles Times*, Aug. 12, 1930; *San Francisco Chronicle*, Aug. 8, 1930; *Portland Oregon Daily Journal*, Aug. 3, 1930; *Detroit Free Press*, Aug. 31, Sept. 5, 1930; *Philadelphia Inquirer*, Sept. 19, 26, 1930; *Boise Idaho Daily Statesman*, Sept. 7, 1930; *Chicago Daily Tribune*, Sept. 1, 1930; *Indianapolis News*, Sept. 27, 1930; *Des Moines Register*, Sept. 7, 1930; *Seattle Post-Intelligencer*, Aug. 9, 1930; *Little Rock Arkansas Democrat*, Aug. 18, 1930; *Atlanta Constitution*, Aug. 31, 1930; *Atlanta Journal*, Aug. 31, 1930; *New Orleans Times-Picayune*, Sept. 6, 1930; *Charlotte Observer*, Oct. 12, 1930. Reviews generally critical were in fact a rarity; see *Cleveland Plain Dealer*, Sept. 7, 1930.

splendor. Constantly attended by two house servants, the General was an eager host who thought that "nothing but a tall mint julep will ever make my old bones tingle."[49]

Paramount Studios played upon the film's romantic aura in particular for advertising. Publicity brochures for theatre managers suggested that costumed ushers, wearing hoop skirts with lights around the hem, be used for handing out notices announcing the coming film. For the opening itself, it was suggested that a Negro be hired to lie on a cotton bale in the lobby and play banjo tunes. Repeatedly, the studio encouraged the public to "come on down South—see the romantic old Dixie of crinoline days—dashing blades and pretty belles—moonlight and magnolias." The audiences were to be captivated by a story set "in the days when ladies swooned and men duelled for entertainment." In a trade magazine, the company advertised that "with the fragrance of magnolias scenting the moonlit night, Bing Crosby sings his way into the heart of Joan Bennett, the loveliest lass in the Mint Julep Belt."[50]

Local advertising also relied heavily on the romantic images. Posters dominated by steamboats and banjos encouraged the public to come and "hear Marse Bing sing."[51] Many advertisements issued in the North included cotton bales, strutting blacks, and grinning caricatures of the Five Cabin Kids, a singing group of Negro youngsters who were variously called "darkie" children, "those Ethiopian quintuplets," the "suntanned, rhythm-shouting scamps," or the "most entertaining bits of chocolate candy sweetness."[52]

[49]*Mississippi* (Paramount, 1935), U/16; see also *New York Times*, April 18, 1935.

[50]Studio Press Book, *Mississippi* (1935), LC-MPS Copyright File LP-5417; *Motion Picture Herald*, March 2, 1935.

[51]See, for example, *Birmingham News*, April 12, 1935; *New Orleans Times-Picayune*, March 29, 1935; *Minneapolis Tribune*, March 28, 1935; *Philadelphia Inquirer*, April 6, 1935.

[52]*Hartford* (Conn.) *Daily Times*, March 28, 1935; *Topeka Daily Capital*, April 13, 1935; *Washington Post*, April 5, 1935; see also *New Orleans Times-Picayune*, March 29, 1935; *Portland* (Me.) *Press Herald*, April 3, 1935; *Boston Daily Globe*, March 23, 1935; *Omaha World Herald*, March 28, 1935; *Providence* (R.I.) *Journal*, April 3, 1935.

In Baltimore, citizens were told that "if you could see but one picture this year, *this* would be the one to see." A Boston manager stated that it was "the one big event of a decade." In Butte, Montana, the story was described as one in which "the ladies wore crinoline and the gentlemen didn't enjoy their morning coffee unless it had been preceded by a duel." One New Hampshire theatre operator cautioned the public, "don't you all miss dem da folks from Dixie."[53]

Promotional efforts in the South were not nearly as excessive, though there were exceptions. The manager of the Rialto Theatre in Kingsville, Texas, hired a "team of darkies" for a publicity stunt. Wearing overalls and standing on a small platform in front of the movie house, one played the harmonica while the "other colored boy" stood before a cutout of a steamboat and "tapped for the entertainment of passersby." In Nashville one could come to "hear those darkies humming, banjos strumming"; a Charlotte bulletin invited patrons to "flirt with all the lovely Southern belles."[54]

A few reviewers were not impressed with either the publicity or the picture. A San Francisco critic complained that the release was "verging on unintentional satire" with "its humorous depictions of proud kunnels and fire-eating Southern bloods." One St. Louis reporter found the story mediocre, and a reviewer in Louisville, Kentucky, commented that the film was "dated and dull" chiefly because it was "so artificial."[55]

High praise, however, was far more common. Most believed *Mississippi* was "delicately flavored with the Old South" rather than excessively done. A Pierre, South Dakota, manager found that the production did much to improve his area's conception of the South. A small Idaho operator declared that it drew extra

[53]*Baltimore Sun*, April 6, 1935; *Boston Daily Globe*, March 23, 1935; *Butte Montana Standard*, April 7, 1935; *Manchester* (N.H.) *Union*, May 3, 1935; see also *Seattle Post-Intelligencer*, April 10, 1935; *Salt Lake Tribune*, April 1, 1935; *Philadelphia Inquirer*, April 5, 1935.

[54]*Motion Picture Herald*, June 15, 1935; *Nashville Banner*, March 28, 1935; *Charlotte Observor*, April 28, 1935.

[55]*San Francisco Chronicle*, April 12, 1935; *St. Louis Post-Dispatch*, March 31, 1935; *Louisville Courier-Journal*, March 16, 1935; see also *Variety*, April 24, 1935.

numbers and "pleased 100 percent." "The customers just naturally like songs and scenes of the South" reported a manager in Kansas. Managers in Oklahoma and Washington were impressed too with the "beautiful story of the Southland." An Arizona writer reported large, enthusiastic audiences as did a Detroit reporter. In Omaha and in Minneapolis audiences viewed a production one critic believed was "staged with reticence and taste, often with beauty."[56]

One film which could lay claim to little reticence was *So Red the Rose*. Regarded by Paramount as its "great emotional and history revealing story of the South," the production premiered simultaneously in the eleven capitals of the old Confederacy. In the studio's publicity bulletins, the film's cast and crew boasted of the movie's magnificence and accuracy. The actor Walter Connolly believed the picture to be of significant historical importance in revealing the deep motivation of North and South. Explaining that the rebels "fought gallantly with their hearts breaking," he added that seeing the emotional effort in *So Red the Rose* made one "realize more vividly than ever before that the war was inevitable because both sides believed so ardently in the justice of their own cause."[57]

Paramount also stressed the sincerity of both sides. The studio suggested advertising techniques which would create national rather than just Southern interest and pride in the production. As a "great glowing picture of the Old South," it nonetheless concerned "one of *America's* proudest generations in all its brave beauty and chivalry." But there were also advertising banner lines furnished particularly for the Southern market, such as "under the Bonnie Blue Flag the Old South rides again."[58]

[56]*Motion Picture Herald*, May 18; June 15, 22, 29; July 6, 20, 1935; *San Francisco Chronicle*, April 12, 1935; *St. Louis Post-Dispatch*, March 31, 1935; *Louisville Courier-Journal*, March 16, 1935; *Washington Post*, April 6, 1935; *Phoenix Arizona Republic*, April 7, 1935; *Detroit Free Press*, March 29, 1935; *Omaha World Herald*, March 29, 1935; *Minneapolis Tribune*, March 28, 1935.

[57]Studio Press Book, *So Red the Rose* (1935), LC-MPS Copyright File LP-5970.

[58]Numerous newspapers utilized the national theme in advertising; see,

The publicity releases in addition pointed out the antebellum heritage of the players. Director King Vidor and actress Elizabeth Patterson were Southerners. Leading man Randolph Scott and heroine Margaret Sullavan had family roots in Virginia. The studio commented that Sullavan was in fact related to Robert E. Lee and claimed that she had made the Confederate battle standard carried by cavalry in the picture. In an interview, she remarked on the story's importance as one of the few "authentic films." Scott concurred that it was "the absolute accurate impression."

To insure the desired realism, production was supervised by a "noted authority on 1860 Southern life," William G. Beymer. Professors from Louisiana were brought in to help with the actors' accents. Property master Russell Pierce gathered the necessary decorative pieces, which he termed "probably the greatest massing of geniune antiques in the history of Hollywood." Seventy-five men labored three weeks to construct the set of a beautiful mansion and quarters for two hundred slaves.[59]

Unfortunately, the film was poorly adapted from Stark Young's novel and simply lacked much of the book's force. Nonetheless, the picture contained numerous portraits of the belle, the ideal planter, and black-white relationships.

Margaret Sullavan as the planter's charming daughter Vallette was certainly the most romantic heroine portrayed thus far. Even her practical and business-like cousin Duncan (Randolph Scott) is overcome by her charm and is moved to call her "a flower of the Old South." One wonders how he knew it was as yet "old." He pointedly added, "you represent all its virtues and what's more you embody all its faults"—tempting him to forget work and responsibility.

She has ample opportunity to exhibit her flirtatious nature during a visit of her brother Edward's companion, Pendleton (Robert Cummings). A handsome young Texan, the visitor is

for example, *Santa Fe New Mexican*, Nov. 22, 1935; *Phoenix Arizona Republic*, Nov. 21, 1935; *Boise Idaho Daily Statesman*, Jan. 23, 1936; *St. Louis Post-Dispatch*, Nov. 28, 1935; *Providence* (R.I.), *Journal*, Dec. 25, 1935; *Sioux Falls Daily Argus-Leader*, Jan. 8, 1936; *Houston Post*, Nov. 29, 1935.

[59]Studio Press Book, *So Red the Rose*.

overcome upon spying Vallette. Actually Edward had instructed his sister earlier to "spread her fan" and entertain his friend. And Vallette filled the role of the cultured Southern lady to perfection. She talks of reading Byron and speaks of Pendleton as "youth and poetry." At dinner, she eats demurely, undaunted by her unappreciative little brother Middleton's taunts that afterwards she will probably sneak a bone to her room. The merciless Middleton also informs the guest that his sister is "a heartless flirt" and rather flighty.

Vallette like her followers was spoiled and strong-willed, easily a match for the character of Julie in *Jezebel* and Scarlett in *Gone With the Wind*. And like Bette Davis and Vivien Leigh, she stomped her foot when displeased, dressed to distract a man from his original designs, and imperiously ruled over social events with a clever smile or glance. Also played to perfection by Bebe Daniels in *Dixiana* and Joan Bennett in *Mississippi*, the role was no satiric caricature but a carefully cultivated Hollywood ideal, dating back to *Birth of a Nation*.

Equally mythological was the character of the planter, Malcolm Bedford (Walter Connolly). Lord of "the proudest plantation in Mississippi," he owned a massive estate. Unsupervised slaves harvest cotton, while the master reclines on his porch, sampling various mint julep recipes. Attended by his faithful servant William, Mr. Bedford adds yet more bourbon to the glasses while lamenting Edward's conduct in a line strongly reminiscent of *The Fighting Coward* and *Mississippi*, "He's a good son, but he drinks too little."

His relationship to his workers was also a familiar characterization. In a vastly overdone scene of which Griffith would have been proud, the master prepares to leave for war. Standing in his carriage, Bedford charges his "folks to guard and protect this plantation," as he had "never been a bad master to you and you've never been bad slaves." Appreciative, the blacks doff their hats, sing spirituals, and watch the master's departure with sadness. With the ever-loyal William holding an umbrella over him, Bedford waves farewell as seven field hands run alongside, crying "I'll be waitin' for you master."

The message of black subservience grew even more pointed when the slaves, hearing that Union troops are nearby, finally

Claude Gillingwater, Gail Patrick, Bing Crosby, and Joan Bennett in *Mississippi*. BELOW: Elizabeth Patterson, Randolph Scott, Janet Beecher, Margaret Sullavan, Daniel Haynes, and Walter Connolly in *So Red the Rose*.

decide the time has come for freedom. In what seems a complete personality change, the blacks under the leadership of a field hand, Cato, begin grabbing chickens, pigs, anything of value, while screaming "I got mine!" Their only concept of freedom is one of no work and no rules. The blacks are seen only as looters and not revolutionaries. Their leader, played by Clarence Muse, says little of liberation but "Oh Lord, we all be settin' in dem golden chairs in de' big house."

Vallette appears in the midst of all this to find the slaves whipped into a frenzy. But white supremacy is only momentarily endangered. Confronting a young laborer, she forces him to step down from a cotton bale which she then takes for her own position, thus standing above him physically and racially.

She tells them the Federals will not free them from work—which, she assumes, is all they desire—and the deposed worker calls her a liar. (It was a line Muse originally had, but refused to deliver, as Vallette's answer was a hard slap across the slave's face.) Furious, she cries out, "Why you wretched, ungrateful scoundrel!" Turning on a now subdued Cato, she continues, "You don't know these Yankee people—this is your home; why do you want to destroy your home?" She reminds Cato of his caring for her as a child, and the worker and his followers pledge to go back to the fields faithfully.

The old order reconfirmed would thus endure, despite the Confederacy's defeat, symbolized by Malcolm Bedford's rather overdone demise. Hearing his still loyal workers singing to him, the planter struggles toward the window to acknowledge their fidelity. Outside, the blacks are on their knees, waving and harmonizing. But Bedford collapses. Limp on the floor, his hand rests beside his belt buckle, stamped "C.S.A."; by it flows what signified that planter's and the South's life blood, his spilled bourbon.[60]

Though immensely overdrawn, that and other scenes were hailed in the South as superb, the best since Griffith's epic. And in premieres which rivalled later openings for *Gone With the Wind*, people flocked to the theatres. The studio made considerable efforts to insure that. Margaret Sullavan and Randolph Scott

---

[60]*So Red the Rose* (Paramount, 1935), U/16.

ordered bouquets of roses to be placed on the Confederate memorials of the capital cities. The company arranged special showings of the film for a convention of the United Daughters of the Confederacy. Annie G. Massey, the organization's President-General, wrote that she found the film "in every way historically correct." Her quote was reprinted in all the studio's brochures. In addition, she corresponded with all the chapters and urged them to "lend our influence to making pictures of this type a success."[61]

In Richmond, local advertisements praised "the flower of Southern chivalry dewed with the shining glory of a woman's tears." The premiere festivities included carriages bearing local dignitaries to the showing. The Montgomery opening was preceded by a concert of wartime ballads. For the Little Rock showing, all surviving veterans of the war were invited guests. "The New South's tribute to the Old South" was occasion for pageantry in Atlanta, where the film's first scenes of cotton picking and architectural splendor were staged by local citizens who promised that it was "so real in appearance that one can get a whiff of the famous mint julep that is served." Jackson, Mississippi, citizens were eager to see the picture "no son or daughter of the South will ever forget, a picture that will rank among the truly important pictures of our time." In Raleigh and other cities, the ceremonies attracted local politicians and were broadcast over area radio stations. A Columbia, South Carolina, theatre employed "a Negro of the war days" to serve as doorman and greet the arriving costumed dignitaries and uniformed veterans. In the background, a chorus sang "Old Folks at Home" and "Dixie."[62]

[61]*Motion Picture Herald*, Nov. 16, 1935; Studio Press Book, *So Red the Rose*.

[62]*Richmond Times-Dispatch*, Nov. 14, 15, 1935; *Montgomery Advertiser*, Nov. 14, 1935; *Little Rock Arkansas Democrat*, Nov. 10, 1935; *Atlanta Constitution*, Nov. 10, 15, 1935; *Jackson Daily Clarion-Ledger*, Nov. 14, 1935; *Raleigh News and Observor*, Nov. 10, 15, 1935; *Columbia State*, Nov. 15, 1935. For representative Southern reviews, see *Charlotte Observor*, Jan. 19, 1936; *Memphis Commercial Appeal*, Nov. 27, 1935; *Houston Post*, Nov. 29, 1935; *Dallas Morning News*, Dec. 7, 1935; *Charleston* (S.C.) *News and Courier*, Dec. 8, 1935.

Rare was the disparaging Southern voice. One of the few was a New Orleans commentator who admitted that every character was "true to type," but questioned "whether all or any of them are true to life." He went on to raise the issue that "the gray of '61-'65 has turned white, sight is dim and hearing is uncertain" but "there's always 'Dixie.'"[63]

But single voices had little effect on the wave of customers eager for a bit of sectional self-congratulation and reinforcement of beliefs. Some audiences cheered after each performance. In many theatres across Dixie the film produced outbursts of tears.[64]

The Northern response was more intriguing. Was the picture believeable to non-Southerners? A cursory examination of play dates would imply that the release failed miserably. In Boston and Buffalo the film did not gross half of the previous top return. The same was true of Philadelphia and New York. The production ran six days in Denver and Kansas City; it lasted a week in Indianapolis, Chicago, Seattle, Cleveland, Los Angeles, and Minneapolis.[65] Certainly the record suggests a lack of faith in the message, but a closer analysis shows otherwise and delineates the specific problem.

The film actually was among the top four grossers for December, a holiday season in which competition was always keen. Considering the small number of Southern movie houses relative to the national total, theatres beyond the South thus had to have been responsible for a large part of that success. In fact, the film in diverse locales was popular, particularly for its romantic view. An industry periodical saw the movie as "graphically reflecting the traditional happy family life and hospitality of the South," and hence found it would appeal to any type of audience. Indeed, a Washington critic found the production "authentic," and a Phoenix reporter admired its "subtle vitality" as did a reviewer in Wilmington, Delaware. Writers in Boston and Detroit were equally touched by "the charm of life on a big plantation ruled by

[63]*New Orleans Times-Picayune*, Nov. 24, 1935.

[64]See, for example, *Birmingham News*, Dec. 1, 1935; *Richmond Times-Dispatch*, Nov. 15, 1935.

[65]*Motion Picture Herald*, Dec. 7, 14, 21, 28, 1935; Jan. 4, 18, 1936.

a humane, kindly master," as were writers in Utah, Oregon, Pennsylvania, Indiana, and South Dakota.[66]

What was objectionable about the film for many was not its outline of aristocratic and conservative society per se, but its attack on the Union as solely responsible for the war. That was the rub with Northern audiences. Typical was the comment of an upset New York reviewer who thought it difficult to share the release's rage "against the uncouth legions of Mr. Lincoln as they dash about the lovely Southern landscapes putting crazy notions in the heads of the plantation slaves."[67]

Therefore, it was not the agrarian ideal or race control that was so objectionable. If that had been the case, it would have affected the financial and critical response to earlier films such as *Mississippi* or later ones as *Jezebel*, both enormously popular. It was simply that King Vidor in directing the picture had failed to do what even the biased D. W. Griffith had done in *Birth of a Nation*. Whatever the view of Southern society, the war itself had to be shown as between two equally sincere and honorable opponents. Not to do so only rekindled animosities which detracted from the antebellum romanticism.

The best evidence of the continuing acceptance of the Old South mystique and its attendant racial conservatism was the repetition of the theme in *Jezebel*. So good was Warner Brothers' 1938 product that several reviewers suggested the filming of *Gone With the Wind* be delayed as *Jezebel* was bound to diminish the

[66]*Motion Picture Herald*, Aug. 7; Nov. 16, 1935; Jan. 4, 18, 25; Feb. 1, 22, 1936. For representative favorable reviews, see *Washington Post*, Nov. 29, 1935; *Phoenix Arizona Republic*, Nov. 24, 1935; *Hartford* (Conn.) *Daily Times*, Dec. 6, 1935; *Wilmington* (Del.) *Journal-Every Evening*, Dec. 12, 1935; *Chicago Daily Tribune*, Dec. 17, 1935; *Indianapolis News*, Nov. 23, 1935; *Baltimore Sun*, Dec. 8, 1935; *Providence* (R.I.)*Journal*, Dec. 26, 1935; *Boston Daily Globe*, Nov. 16, 1935; *Detroit Free Press*, Nov. 23, 1935; *Minneapolis Tribune*, Dec. 8, 1935; *Omaha World Herald*, Dec. 20, 1935; *Philadelphia Inquirer*, Nov. 23, 1935; *Pittsburgh Press*, Dec. 15, 1935; *Sioux Falls Daily Argus-Leader*, Jan. 8, 1936; *Dallas Morning News*, Dec. 8, 1935.

[67]*New York Times*, Nov. 28, 1935; see also *Variety*, Dec. 4, 1935. Some newspapers, however, thought the North was treated sympathetically; see, for example, *Louisville Courier-Journal*, Nov. 23, 1935.

impact of Mitchell's bestseller. It was ironic, since Jack Warner had proposed that producer David O. Selznick use Bette Davis and another Warner contract player, Errol Flynn, for the parts of Scarlett and Rhett. But neither Selznick nor Davis wanted the familiar swashbuckler in the lead. Consequently, Warner Brothers filmed *Jezebel* in less than two months and accompanying publicity mercilessly referred to Selznick's tardiness in filming his own Old South romance. Davis was so effective that critics thought she took "the wind out of the sails of any prospective Scarlett O'Hara" and that the film itself stole "quite a bit of the thunder of *Gone With the Wind*, still uncast." As success became more obvious, the Warner studio became ever bolder in its references. One frequently used advertisement, drawing from both the new film's red costuming and the unfilmed Mitchell plot, declared that Davis was "Scarlet—Siren of the South—Her lips were a challenge to any man—Her Heart beat only for one."[68]

The film contained many aspects of the by then thoroughly familiar Southern mythology. Set in the New Orleans of 1852, the picture was particularly interesting in its revelations of antebellum urban life and social customs. The film began with a street scene: Black vendors stroll about hawking flowers and festival masks. All around them walk whites of obvious social distinction. Some of the aristocracy pass by in carriages attended by Negro footmen. Nearby a bar resounds with gentlemanly comraderie, facilitated by the always present julep. Again, all present are well attired.

In earlier films such as *Dixiana*, the public saw an urban South with its street scenes. And in later films too, such as *Flame of New Orleans* (1941), *The Foxes of Harrow* (1947), *Band of Angels* (1957),

[68]See *Wilmington* (Del.) *Journal-Every Evening*, April 22, 1938; *Boston Daily Globe*, April 1, 1938; *Detroit Free Press*, April 2, 1938; *St. Louis Post-Dispatch*, April 24, 1938; *Butte Montana Standard*, Jan. 7, 1940; *Charlotte Observor*, May 29, 1938; *Newark Star-Eagle*, April 2, 1938; *Seattle Post-Intelligencer*, April 16, 1938; *New York Sun*, March 11, 1938; *Memphis Commercial Appeal*, March 27, 1938; *Houston Post*, April 10, 1938; *Burlington* (Vt.) *Free Press*, April 1, 1938; *Pittsburgh Press*, April 16, 1938; *Portland Oregon Daily Journal*, April 8, 1938.

Mandingo (1975), and *Drum* (1976), the black vendors and city dwellers were present. But this segment of the population was never examined closely. Were the blacks slave or free; how did the system permit their free access to such sections; were they craftsmen who made their own goods? Minor points perhaps, but the frequent use of the pleasant urban settings as in *Jezebel* pointed to a strong stereotyping of slavery. Never were the participants developed or explained in contrast to the field workers or house servants so often given speaking parts. An audience could only assume in light of all the other Negroes in similar films that all blacks were slaves and relatively unskilled. In addition, that these workers had such free run of the streets and an opportunity to earn money only lent more credence to the concept of bondage as benign, well-meant, and with few restraints.

Such scenes also said much about Southern whites. The urban society appeared devoid of any white class beneath the aristocracy—no merchants, craftsmen, not even a middle class. Everyone seems well to do, and cared for by a devoted slave class. Passersby give slight hint of being workingmen or tradesmen. In film after film, as in *The Mississippi Gambler* (1953), *The Gambler From Natchez* (1954), and particularly *Jezebel* with its frequent shots of large gatherings and balls, there was no sign of the diversity of the region's population and customs. Even the site was repeatedly duplicated; New Orleans was invariably the antebellum city preferred by most filmmakers. Only *Gone With the Wind* depicted another, Atlanta.

Jezebel was also stereotypical in its presentation of social mores. The norm dictated that any meeting of gentlemen called for a drink and certain types of conversation. In an ornate hotel bar, Negroes circulated with trays laden with juleps. The men gambled or talked of thoroughbreds, refraining from discussions of the fairer sex as "a gentleman doesn't mention a lady's name in a bar." When in a lady's home, the gentlemen merely consumed their bourbon in more formal glasses. The men also took pride in their drinking ability. One fellow waged his own fight against a spreading yellow fever plague by a simple expedient, "every time I see an ol' dead wagon, I pour four fingers of bourbon; yesterday I drunk nigh on to two quarts."

Women too had their social conventions, and men were expected to hold their women to the proper code. After all, a Southern belle was "a chalice, a frail, delicate chalice to be cherished and protected." When a woman forgot her place, though, the man had to react predictably—"He'd cut him a hickory, sir—a hickory, and he'd've flailed the livin' daylights out of her, then put lard on her whelps and bought her a diamond broach, . . . and she'd a' loved it."

With all her faults, Julie (Bette Davis) was enough a product of her culture to go only so far. Though she upset society with her red ball gown and curt manners, her original intent was to prod her stodgy, businesslike suitor into an affair of honor to prove his love. She told him almost with delight that "you'll find it necessary to defend me." She fully knew that she was "just supposed to flutter around in white," greet her guests with aplomb, and sing with the slaves who appeared to have little to do but harmonize at the approach of every carriage and at all social functions.

Her intended, Preston Dillard (Henry Fonda), made easily as many social mistakes as his fiancé. First, he upsets the master-slave relationship which makes even the usually unflappable Uncle Cato uncomfortable. Arriving at Julie's plantation, Dillard picks up a mint julep and asks, "Uncle Cato, we've known each other a long time; I'm back home now—will you join me in one?" Visibly shaken, the servant is only able to reply, "Why, why Mr. Pres, it ain't hardly proper, but I'll kind of take one out to the pantry an' bless you an' Miss Julie."[69]

The film's mythology was as undiluted as the bourbon. But whether the public saw it as such was another matter entirely. Definitely as outspoken as *So Red the Rose*, Warner Brothers' answer to *Gone With the Wind* was not only popular but taken seriously as well. A trade magazine told potential exhibitors that *Jezebel* "gives full scope to the historical background . . . and draws substantial color therefrom." Too, the reproduced New Orleans society was "convincing and interesting." Another industry paper agreed that the picture dealt with all aspects of

---

[69]*Jezebel* (Warner Brothers, 1938), LC-MPS; see also Studio Press Book, *Jezebel*, MOMA-FSC.

Bette Davis and Henry Fonda in *Jezebel*. BELOW: Bette Davis and George Brent in *Jezebel*.

prewar society. The culture presented was not restricted, but was "an engrossing cross-section of all Southern manners and customs," a comment which revealed how regimented the myth of a wealthy culture had become. If the film business itself believed the film to be "undoubtedly faithful," then indeed the legend was regarded by many as reality.[70]

Jezebel immediately attracted large crowds and earned extended runs. For the South, there were extra performances in New Orleans of course and in other areas such as Louisville.[71] Western areas such as Seattle and Portland held over the film of the "Scarlet Sweetheart of the South." Eastward, a Philadelphia house extended the movie's run three times. Other cities such as Indianapolis, St. Louis, Cleveland, and Newark also lengthened their show dates.[72]

A theatre manager in Maine believed it was a "nice picture" for any area. Managers in Nebraska assented. When complaints arose, they usually concerned not the romantic interpretation but the Southern accents, which they complained were either poorly duplicated or incomprehensible.[73]

For example, a Washington, D.C., reviewer perceived *Jezebel* as "set off by a background of opulent life . . . redolent of the days when gentlemen faced each other with pistols . . . and ladies observed the proprieties with punctilious regard for tradition and great charm." Critics in Phoenix and Los Angeles and San Francisco marvelled at the "great care" taken in accurately recreating the era of "the white-pillars-and-mint-julep civilization." Commentators of Boston, Newark, and Detroit responded

---

[70]*Motion Picture Herald*, March 12, 1938; *Variety*, March 16, 1938.

[71]See, for example, *New Orleans Times-Picayune*, May 7, 1938; *Louisville Courier-Journal*, April 14, 1938; *Montgomery Advertiser*, June 12, 1938; *Little Rock Arkansas Democrat*, March 29, 1938; *Meridian Star*, May 29, 1938; *Charlotte Observor*, May 29; June 4, 1938; *Richmond Times-Dispatch*, March 24, 1938; *Atlanta Journal*, March 24, 1938; *Raleigh News and Observor*, April 17, 1938.

[72]*Los Angeles Times*, March 25; April 6, 1938; *Seattle Post-Intelligencer*, April 28, 1938; *Portland Oregon Daily Journal*, April 18, 1938; *Philadelphia Inquirer*, April 30, 1938; *Indianapolis News*, April 14, 1938; *St. Louis Post-Dispatch*, April 28, 1938; *Cleveland Plain Dealer*, April 15, 1938.

[73]*Motion Picture Herald*, May 7, 14, 21, 28; June 4, 11, 25, 1938.

similarly. Writers in Cleveland, Hartford, and Wilmington "urgently recommended" the great film during which "audiences actually cheered." In a Portland, Oregon, article the writer found the movie "sound" and "completely free of hokum."[74] With such agreement on the legend, the South's comments were almost superfluous.[75]

Perhaps the best evidence that the legend was firmly entrenched was found in *Way Down South*, a romantic script by two well known blacks. It was hardly an angry black statement by its writers, Clarence Muse and Langston Hughes, and the story clearly revealed the futility of attempting to alter the traditional plots. Regardless of insight or talent, while on studio's payroll, one wrote what the studio wanted, i.e., what was popular and profitable. The story was set in prewar Louisiana, where "on vast estates . . . dwelt the aristocratic plantation owners and, under the system of slavery, their faithful Negro retainers."[76]

The advertising was no less traditional. Bulletins stressed banjo-strumming, grinning, and dancing slaves. And captions promised "a loveable, thrilling show of plantation life resplendent with magic and songs," or "happiness from ringing Dixieland" with its "jungle-born dances." Studio-supplied publicity articles repeatedly claimed that the picture of the "land the Lord

[74]*Washington Post*, March 26, 1938; *Phoenix Arizona Republic*, March 27, 1938; *Los Angeles Times*, March 25, 1938; *San Francisco Chronicle*, April 2, 1938; *Boston Daily Globe*, March 31, 1938; *Newark Star-Eagle*, April 12, 1938; *Detroit Free Press*, April 2, 1938; *Cleveland Plain Dealer*, March 28, 1938; *Hartford* (Conn.) *Times*, April 21, 1938; *Wilmington* (Del.) *Journal-Every Evening*, April 23, 1938; *Portland Oregon Daily Journal*, April 8, 1938; see also *Topeka Daily Capital*, May 1, 1938; *Portland* (Me.) *Press Herald*, April 6, 1938; *Providence* (R.I.) *Journal*, April 2, 1938; *Milwaukee Journal*, April 21, 1938.

[75]For representative Southern reviews, see *Richmond Times-Dispatch*, March 24, 1938; *New Orleans Times-Picayune*, April 30, 1938; *Houston Post*, April 10, 1938. For a critical response, see *Louisville Courier-Journal*, March 26, 1938.

[76]Dialogue and Cutting Continuity, *Way Down South* (1939), LC-MPS Copyright File LP-9176. A few critics expressed surprise at the film's overdone romanticism; see *Variety*, Aug. 23, 1939; *Motion Picture Herald*, July 22, 1939; *New York Post*, Aug. 17, 1939.

shakes hands with" was "realistically held together" by the plot which with its estate of four hundred slaves presented "all the charms of easy-going life."[77]

By the end of the 1930s, then, there was no doubt that the theme begun so simply in 1903 had achieved enormous success. An ever enterprising Hollywood, seeking popular story lines, seized upon the Old South romance repeatedly as a proven moneymaker. And the utility of the genre could not be denied, for it did improve morale during the Depression era. The plantation stories fell into the industry's pattern of providing film fare which let one escape into another existence, if only for a moment.

The plot's ingredients were repeated often enough so they became perfectly believeable and acceptable. What was of significant social importance, though, was the manner in which the cultural tenets were presented. In the rush to produce and enjoy the films was submerged the damage such pictures inflicted. Without the strident animosities of the silent era—the virulent racism of say *Birth of a Nation*—and lacking any organized or vocal protest from critic or fan, the releases often appeared as innocent theatre offerings. Yet the stories still contained within them racist sentiments and a strong social and economic conservatism as well.

In stories such as *Mississippi* or *Dixiana* or *The Little Colonel* which seemed so much more well meant than many pointed silent films such as *His Trust* or *His Trust Fulfilled*, the same arguments did survive. But the emphasis was on entertainment rather than on social theory, as in the work of Griffith and Pollard; thus film companies and their patrons ingested the same beliefs, but did so almost unknowingly. The films of Bing Crosby or Henry Fonda in their often unconscious subtlety were far stronger arguments than the silent era's patently obvious Henry Walthall as "The Little Colonel." And because the propaganda was so frequently presented as secondary to the music, comedy, and drama and therefore not the major thrust of any

egment
[77]See, for example, *Boise Idaho Daily Statesman*, Feb. 21, 1940; *Portland* (Me.) *Press Herald*, July 27, 1939; *Charlotte Observer*, Aug. 6, 1939; *Sioux Falls Daily Argus-Leader*, Aug. 8, 1939; *Memphis Commercial Appeal*, Aug. 27, 1939; *Nashville Banner*, July 27, 1939.

story, the precepts of the Old South were becoming increasingly accepted assumptions, all the more unshakeable because of their facile presentation in escapist films.

Even if widespread sentiment for more liberal scripts had existed, there was little cause to expect anything other than films like *Hearts in Dixie, Mississippi*, or *Way Down South*. Since Hollywood reflected rather than guided popular opinion, the industry was hardly prepared to embark on what would have been a radical change in racial perceptions. During the Depression, enough perceptions of contemporary America were being assaulted without adding another in the form of exposés of the injustices of white supremacy. Probing productions, while they were justified, were simply not acceptable, as Clarence Muse and Langston Hughes discovered. It would have been catastrophic economically for the film business, whose function was not reality but enterprise and entertainment in the face of hard times.

IV

The South as
National Epic, 1939-1941

GONE WITH THE WIND

It was "a bigger and better *Birth of a Nation*—a kindred triumph for this day and time" exclaimed a trade paper reviewer.[1] But *Gone With the Wind* was far more than that. The film was a broad reflection of the times. When Margaret Mitchell's novel was published in 1936, the United States was still in the midst of the Great Depression. And by the film's premiere in December of 1939 and the winter of 1940, the nation was fully aware of the political and military ravages in Europe. The world and domestic scene was no better during the picture's second distribution in 1941.

For the nation as a whole, the plot captured the past in a gripping manner and set it before the public as an example of the fortitude and ideals of another civilization which had also faced monumental uncertainties and had survived. Though the South was the only part of the country which had experienced devastating defeat, the lesson was applicable to all. And although the plot revolved around Hollywood's romanticized South, the film presented an example few could ignore. As a result, the image of the once vanquished took on a new luster.

As an instance of American strength in the face of social upheaval similar to that facing Europe, the film was a graphic instance of the threat looming abroad and a warning of the sacrifices necessary to preserve a society. As a recounting of previous economic blight more severe than even that of the 30s,

[1] *Motion Picture Herald*, Dec. 16, 1939.

the production was also prime evidence that survival and recovery were not only possible but probable, given the regenerative strength of the native American character. The picture, therefore, was a national epic of contemporary meaning.

The United States was not alone in perceiving the film's power and significance. In war-torn London, the tale of suffering played there for almost the entire Second World War, enthralling audiences with its encouraging message of a society's emergence from the ashes of war. In 1945 the liberated areas of Europe were wildly excited to view a film of spiritual survival at any cost. Even though many of the prints were still in English without subtitles, the movie was nonetheless a broadly popular tale to which the people could relate with ease.

And as the culmination of the antebellum pictures of the 1930s, the film was no less ornately produced, no less romantic in its praise of the prewar South than its predecessors. *Gone With the Wind* pointed better than any previous movie to the utility of the plantation theme as more than mere entertainment. And the film was eagerly awaited. A Gallup Poll of December 1939 estimated that 56.5 million people planned to attend the release.[2]

Earlier such films as *So Red the Rose* had presented a similar message, pointing to the supposed superiority of Southern civilization and its will to survive. But such films had also done much to destroy any relevancy in unjust, even superfluous, attacks upon the conquerors. On the other hand, movies such as *Jezebel* had succeeded critically and financially as examples of the plantation culture. Though admittedly relying on *Gone With the Wind*'s pre-release publicity, the movie also utilized a plot which only by comparative example rather than by direct confrontation criticized areas beyond the South. The trick was to present the comparison in such a way as not to insult the eventual victors or losers—which explained in large part why films focusing only on the war itself have often been box-office disasters. Pictures such as *Way Down South* or *Mississippi* were perfect, with their light drama and absence of overly pointed contrasts. A cinematic argument without insults was far easier to heed.

Gone With the Wind certainly reflected an effort not to offend.

[2]*New York Times*, Dec. 20, 1939.

For example, the soldier Scarlett must kill in the last days of the war was in the novel one of William T. Sherman's crack Union cavalry raiders. But in the film, the character actor Paul Hurst played a Federal deserter and looter so as not to portray disparagingly the average trooper. Also, direct references to the Ku Klux Klan were omitted, in order not to arouse the animosity Griffith's production had engendered.

With difficult issues soft-pedaled and the valiant story line, it was no wonder the South was viewed as never before as an example of the American spirit incarnate for its fortitude, respect of tradition, and determination to weather defeat. Far more than just Southerners, countless millions could take heart from the film's message. As one Eastern reviewer stated, "the story of the Old South with its Cavaliers and cotton has given America its most eloquent and grandest film narrative." A Midwestern critic remarked that the drama of the planter culture was for all, since it was a "story of great events in American history," not merely Southern.[3]

Producer David Selznick of Selznick International was at first hesitant about securing the film rights to the novel; he feared the plot might be too similar to that of the mildly successful *So Red the Rose*.[4] But it was too hard to pass up a property which would at one point sell a million copies in six months—an amazing success for a book composed to combat ennui. The story of the book's creation was as interesting as the plot.

Margaret Mitchell—Mrs. John Marsh—was in 1926 recuperating from an injury to a chronically weak ankle. She was confined to bed with nothing to do until the frequent encouragement of her husband influenced her to write. She had some previous writing experience. She had written for the *Atlanta Journal*; she had completed several unpublished short stories; and she had once attempted a novel of the Jazz Age. But a novel of the South reflected far better her Atlanta upbringing.

Born in 1900, she spent her childhood eagerly listening to

[3]*Wilmington* (Del.) *Journal-Every Evening*, Jan. 27, 1940; *St. Louis Post-Dispatch,* Jan. 28, 1940.

[4]Rudy Behlmer, ed., *Memo from David O. Selznick* (New York: Viking, 1972), 143.

tales of her hometown and the Civil War. The young girl spent many Sunday afternoons learning of the South's fight for independence from those who had survived the war. As a child of six, she rode each afternoon with several Confederate veterans, eager to tell tales of the war. In later life the author would laughingly remark that until she was ten she had no idea the Confederacy had even lost the Civil War. It was hardly surprising then that she chose the South as the setting for the writing effort she perceived as only therapeutic and entertaining.

The work continued long after her convalescence, strictly as a pastime. When Miss Mitchell first began, she knew only the opening and conclusion of her story; indeed she wrote the last chapter first. Thereafter, she seldom wrote a chapter in its proper sequence. When each portion was completed, she would simply put it away in a manila envelope to be forgotten, sometimes for years. Despite her considerable efforts, she treated the work quite casually and was never very confident of its appeal. Her carelessness was evident on many envelopes. She scribbled messages or grocery lists on some; others were covered with coffee stains. And throughout it all, only her husband John was permitted to read any of the work, though occasionally a friend discerned that Peggy Marsh was working on something rather mysterious.

At times the manuscript was mysterious to even the author. There were alternative chapters so that the story could proceed along several plot lines. One chapter was redone seventy times; numerous others were rewritten thirty times. Other sections remained untouched or only roughly sketched. Characters' names were in some instances not even determined. Scarlett was first conceived of as Pansy O'Hara. Melanie at times was either Permelia or Melisande. It was quite some time before Tara was found preferable over its original name, Fontenoy Hall. Titles varied also; she considered *Tote the Weary Load, Another Day, Bugles Sang True,* and *Not in Our Stars*.

In 1930, four years after its beginning, the book was still only two-thirds complete, with even its first chapter incomplete. In fact, hidden in the Marsh closet were at least a thousand typed pages which had only slowly increased and only at the encouragement of Mr. Marsh. For a variety of reasons, she did comparatively little work after 1930; at times she was simply tired of the project, and in 1934 she could do little as she was confined by a neck brace after an automobile accident.

By the spring of 1935, however, encouragement was to come from another quarter. One of Mrs. Marsh's close friends in whom she had confided her efforts had gone to work for the New York publishing firm of Macmillan. Then an associate editor, Lois Cole had told her colleague Harold Latham of the volume. Intrigued, Latham while visiting Atlanta pointedly asked Mrs. Marsh if he could examine her work. She replied that no such manuscript even existed. But upon hearing of the encounter, an incredulous John Marsh convinced his wife to turn the book over for Latham's perusal. Soon after, the editor was called to his hotel lobby and quickly given a huge stack of envelopes. So lengthy was the manuscript, he had to purchase a suitcase to transport it all.

On the train to New Orleans, Latham labored through soiled, yellowed, and hastily corrected pages filled with a variety of almost indecipherable penciled, penned, and typed revisions. Arriving at his destination, he immediately received a telegram insisting that he return the novel to Atlanta as the author had changed her mind. But it was too late. Latham was enchanted and refused the demand. Though poorly written in spots, and incomplete in others, the book was nonetheless well worth publishing. A surprised Margaret Mitchell Marsh finally relented. After a furious pace of rewrites and additional research to insure the book's historical accuracy, Macmillan scheduled publication for May 1936 with an initial printing of 10,000 copies.

Almost immediately, the novel captivated the imagination of reviewers. Pre-publication copies quickly ran out, and the publication was postponed so that more copies could be printed. The Book-of-the-Month Club decided to offer *Gone With the Wind* for its July selection, and 50,000 additional volumes were printed. And the enthusiasm was not ill founded—the book would eventually reach domestic sales of more than 7,000,000. In 1937 the Atlanta author received the Pulitzer Prize. All this attention completely stunned the new novelist. Almost equally as surprising to her was the attention the book received as a possible film script.

Early in 1936, before the work's publication, David O. Selznick's story editor in the East, Kay Brown, sent her employer an extended synopsis. Though she admitted that no one knew the writer, she saw great possibilities for the story. Selznick hesitated at first. He fretted over the problems of the plot's Civil War setting, the difficulty of casting, and also the asking price of $65,000. Undaunted, Kay Brown delivered a copy of her outline to Selznick International Studio's board chairman, Jock Whitney, who replied that if Selznick did not purchase the film rights, he would. Prodded into action, the producer bid $50,000.[5]

The project was his. Little did he know how enormously successful the book would become, or how difficult it would be to capture the legendary story on film. The movie was becoming an obsession, made all the worse by the delays and frustrations of filming. Because of contractural arrangements, casting problems, script revisions, and research, it was not until November 1938 that shooting began—two years and three months after the bestseller's publication.

But Selznick in his determination to have the best refused to hurry. Sidney Howard provided much of the screenplay, but Selznick himself was forever tinkering with the script. Never satisfied, he enlisted the talents of numerous well known Hollywood writers, including Oliver H. P. Garrett, Ben Hecht, Jo Swerling, and F. Scott Fitzgerald. The original director George Cukor was replaced well into the shooting by Victor Fleming. To satisfy overwhelming public preference, Selznick had to bargain with his father-in-law and former employer Louis B. Mayer for the loan of MGM's foremost contract player, Clark Gable. In return, MGM received worldwide distribution rights and half the total profits.[6]

Once he had embarked on the project, Selznick committed himself wholeheartedly to a magnificent portrayal of the South, accurate in every detail. Camera crews were sent throughout the

[5]For an overview of Miss Mitchell's work, see Finis Farr, *Margaret Mitchell of Atlanta* (New York: Morrow, 1965), esp. 25-56, 99-147; see also Richard B. Harwell, ed., *Margaret Mitchell's Gone With the Wind Letters, 1936-1949* (New York: Macmillan, 1976), especially 1-2, 5-6, 61-62, 111, 299-300.

[6]Lambert, *GWTW*, 16-17, 31-36; Flamini, *Scarlett*, 3-5, 8-9, 12-13, 16; Behlmer, *Memo*, 142-44; see also Bob Thomas, *Selznick* (New York: Doubleday, 1970).

region to film authentic settings and scenes such as Negroes returning from the fields. Ironically, only a shot of the gaily lit steamboat on a dark river was used to introduce Scarlett and Rhett's honeymoon trip. (Some of the footage appeared in later movies such as *Show Boat* and *Raintree County*). The effort, however, was a prime example of the expense to which Selznick was willing to go to make his film a masterpiece.

The producer was particularly exacting in the small details. The California soil where outdoor scenes were filmed was colored to match the red Georgia terrain. For Scarlett's postwar dress in which she worked the fields, actual thorns were used in place of buttons, exact simulations of those used as substitute buttons in 1865. Similar care was taken in Scarlett's wedding dress. The gown was supposedly once worn by her mother, so the dress was originally made to fit Barbara O'Neill, who played Mrs. O'Hara, and then discolored slightly to simulate aging and then finally taken in to Vivien Leigh's measurements.

There were other equally detailed precautions taken to insure authenticity. Many marvelled at Scarlett's ersatz dress made from velvet curtains, but more remarkable still was her hat made also from items close at hand. The bonnet sported chicken feathers and even hen's feet as clasps. Vivien Leigh wore one calico print dress throughout a third of the film; to represent the disintegration of her social position and of the Confederacy, twenty-seven copies of the garment were made in various stages of wear.[7]

At the recommendation of Margaret Mitchell herself, Selznick hired various technical advisers to oversee production details. Will A. Price checked the cast's Southern accents. A noted expert on antebellum social customs, Susan Myrick, was employed. The Georgian "Emily Post of the South" was a columnist for the *Macon Telegraph*. Her grandfather, a rebel general, had owned one of the state's grandest plantations; her father was also a Confederate veteran. Raised in rural Georgia after the family

[7]The anecdotes regarding the film's exactness of detail are many; see, for example, Studio Press Book, *Gone With the Wind* (1954 rerelease), MOMA-FSC; Studio Press Book (1961 rerelease), LC-MPS Box C-109; Souvenir Booklet (1967 rerelease), LC-MPS Box C-41; Studio Press Book (1967 rerelease), LC-MPS Box C-19.

fortune had waned, she possessed a wide knowledge of area customs and manners of rich and poor, white and black alike. In addition, an artist and historian, Wilbur G. Kurtz, aided in verifying historical details. He had a phenomenal grasp of Atlanta's past and had learned the area at first hand during extended walks over the battlefields and farms.[8]

The problem—and one common to pictures of the Old South—was that the studio's obsession with detail extended only so far. Whether or not oral thermometers could be used for the hospital scene had to be carefully verified, but Selznick's sweeping conception of the Old South was accepted without question. And few could interfere with his perceptions. Margaret Mitchell had stipulated, much to the producer's chagrin, that she wanted no part of the film adaptation once she had granted the rights to her story. She was determined to remain detached in case the production disappointed her fellow Southerners. More importantly, sudden fame and the accompanying attention had altered her life so considerably that she did not wish to encounter further interruptions by working for Hollywood. As a result, Selznick had relatively free rein over the general romanticism of the picture, despite the criticism of his advisers.

The producer's overwhelmingly romantic concept of the antebellum region was particularly evident in his instructions for the Tara set. Though researchers would study period photographs, sketches, and other documents to achieve the right architecture for the forty acre set for the Atlanta of 1864, the prewar O'Hara mansion owed more to imagination than to research. Consequently, it reflected the mythology built up for so long by previous films and accepted seemingly without question by a filmmaker whose preciseness of detail had helped establish his reputation.

In the novel Tara was not the grand seat of plantation power, but the upcountry Georgia home of a not particularly wealthy

[8]Harwell, *Letters*, 71-72, 118-20, 132, 219, 298, 357-58, 406; Behlmer, *Memo*, 159, 206, 235; Thomas, *Selznick*, 155. For an account of Kurtz's efforts to achieve accuracy, see Richard B. Harwell, ed., "Technical Adviser: The Making of *Gone With the Wind*, The Hollywood Journals of Wilbur G. Kurtz," *Atlanta Historical Journal* 22 (Summer 1978), 7-131.

planter. The house was a rambling and functional structure of no particular architecture, a fairly ordinary house in other words, especially in light of the cinematic presentations of Southern homes. Selznick realized that such a structure comported neither with his idealization of the section nor—more importantly—with the public's.

The movie version of Tara was hardly representative of the class of which Miss Mitchell wrote, though she had admittedly given the O'Hara estate an avenue of cedars and neatly ordered, whitewashed slave quarters. But by the writer's own admission, it was quite "hard to make people understand that North Georgia wasn't all white columns and singing darkies and magnolias. . . ." Even Southerners questioned her as to why the novel's setting was not the mansion they had come to expect. At least in the picture people could count on that romantic splendor.

Selznick, his production designer William Cameron Menzies, and art director Lyle Wheeler presented a grand house of white columns, handsome vistas, and blossoming dogwoods. Three ornate peacocks roamed the grounds; a belle in white gown was being courted by two gentlemen of leisure; and the master was relaxing after an afternoon ride. It was hardly the average working plantation common to North Georgia in 1861. In fact, searching through Clayton County, which the author had used for her setting, Miss Mitchell found only one columned house from the prewar era. The most the advisers, Myrick and Kurtz, could do in the face of the company's obstinance was to insist on the more common squared rather than rounded columns. It was a small victory, particularly in light of the even more pretentious set for the Twelve Oaks Plantation for the Wilkes family. Selznick knew the nation as a whole desired the image, and the South in particular would embrace it wholeheartedly, even to the extent of claiming that Twelve Oaks was "just like the mansion my grandpappy had that Sherman burned."[9]

Though she would not interfere directly, Miss Mitchell upon occasion did express her fears to Susan Myrick. Realizing the course that Selznick was taking and how the South itself would

[9]Behlmer, *Memo*, 202; Harwell, *Letters*, 36, 137, 249-50, 358, 406-07; see also Lambert, *GWTW*, 69-70; and Flamini, *Scarlett*, 146, 148, 210.

warmly receive the nostalgic romanticism he was so carefully creating, she regretted the excesses. She especially feared the opening scenes would include field hands suddenly erupting in joyous song, as they had in so many films. Both she and her husband were weary "at seeing the combined Tuskegee and Fisk Jubilee Choirs bounce out at the most inopportune times and in the most inopportune places . . . ," as such groups had done from *Hearts in Dixie* (1929) to *Jezebel* (1938). Worse than the singing would be "the inevitable wavings in the air of several hundred pairs of hands . . . ," a tradition born as early as the Edison Company's 1903 version of *Uncle Tom's Cabin*.[10]

She was not far wrong, for though the movie contained no mass chorales, every other stock ingredient was included. And although the picture examined the antebellum lifestyle only briefly, it was similar to *Birth of a Nation* in that the entire picture utilized the plantation setting as a common reference point for comparison with the postwar period. Though the shortest segment of both films, the prewar portion was the most essential.

It is interesting to note that both *Birth of a Nation* and *Gone With the Wind* are regarded as the most memorable of the Old South pictures. Why? Certainly not simply because of their detailed, but so brief, examinations of the plantation world. If that were the case, movies now as easily forgotten as *Way Down South* would have been considered equally successful. The sheer splendor, the technical innovations, the glamorous casts also helped attract theatre goers. But *Dixiana* had new innovations and well known personalities also; the same could be said of countless others. No, as alluring as the techniques and personalities were, the unique comparisons both Griffith and Selznick included of the old as opposed to the new were crucial.

The South was portrayed as an uncomplicated society, in marked contrast to each story's postwar alterations. The two pictures presented far better than any other production an impossible dream with which many viewers were fascinated; they placed a conservative ideal against the encroaching urban, commercial, and racial despair which followed the South's demise and which was so distressingly familiar to the audiences. That the

[10]Harwell, *Letters*, 271-72; see also 406-07.

message could be nestled in a retrospective film which laid claim to being an epic presentation of American history made the lesson all the more palatable. The reviews and popularity of the productions were loud testimony to the releases' conservative influence.

The studio's advertising stressed that the production was from Margaret Mitchell's "story of the Old South," rather than of a period encompassing Reconstruction as well. For the initial release period, 1939-1940, instead of relying on the standard poster motif, Selznick International presented advertisements in the style of a formal, printed invitation at the top of which was a small pen and ink drawing—usually of a belle, a finely dressed gentleman, and an officer standing before an antebellum house.[11] Later posters transposed a picture of Scarlett in her low-cut white gown onto a scene in which she wore a drab dress; it appeared the mythological image simply had to be included in the advance advertising campaigns.[12]

The beginning of the picture itself confirmed that the legend would be presented unchanged as a dreamlike existence lovingly recalled. The film's introduction revealed that "There was a land of Cavaliers and cotton fields called the Old South," which in all its magnificence was a "pretty world" of "gallantry" and "knights and their ladies fair." And again, the viewer was reminded that the movie was from a "story of the Old South."

In the fields, the blacks plow unsupervised by any onlooking white. In fact, the slave Big Sam claimed "Ah's de foahman" and "de one dat sez when it's quittin' time at Tara." Like its many forebears, the scene upheld the myth that the Negroes were not only well treated but had important responsibilities. Viewers discover later in the movie how grateful and attached to the system the black was when in Atlanta Big Sam proudly tells

[11]See for example, *Baltimore Sun*, Jan. 26, 1940; *St. Louis Post-Dispatch*, Jan. 24, 1940; *Detroit Free Press*, Jan. 24, 1940; *Meridian Star*, March 24, 1940; *Manchester* (N.H.) *Union*, Feb. 9, 1940; *Santa Fe New Mexican*, Feb. 20, 1940; *Newark Star-Ledger*, Jan. 25, 1940; *Portland Oregon Daily Journal*, Jan. 21, 1940; *Seattle Post-Intelligencer*, Jan. 24, 1940; *Providence* (R.I.) *Journal*, Jan. 25, 1940; *Sioux Falls Daily Argus-Leader*, Feb. 25, 1940; *Memphis Commercial Appeal*, Jan. 26, 1940; *Pittsburgh Press*, Jan. 25, 1940.

[12]*Gone With the Wind* (n.d., rerelease) Poster, LC-PPD.

Scarlett that he and his fellows were to dig trenches for the Confederates, "to help 'em win de war."

The slaves were also closely allied to their master's family and played a considerable part in its activities. The O'Hara clan conducted evening prayer with their house servants, though the blacks stood at the back of the room. Hattie McDaniel as Mammy displayed not only the black concern for the white family but her influence within it. Scarlett was as much her responsibility as Mrs. O'Hara's. After chiding the feisty girl for having "no mo' mannahs 'dan a fiel' han'," Mammy laments such behavior "aftah me an' Miss Ellen don' labored wid yo'." And later when Mrs. O'Hara is late arriving home, the servant performs as ruler of the household, expressing that her mistress was "actin' like a wet nurse to 'dem low down po' white trash instead of bein' here eatin' her supper." The O'Haras and Tara were indeed her family. As she later tells Scarlett, "Ef yo' don' care whut fo'ks says 'bout dis fambly, ah does."

Beyond the confines of the family, the South as a whole was also shown as an idyllic society, content with its status and unwilling to tolerate encroachments. As Gerald O'Hara told his daughter, it made no difference whom she wed, "so long as he's a Southerner and thinks like you." At nearby Twelve Oaks, passersby were warned not against trespassing, but that "anyone disturbing the peace on this plantation will be prosecuted."

The barbecue at Twelve Oaks, the grand estate of John Wilkes and his son Ashley, amply demonstrates the facets of the legend. The hoop-skirted ladies are consistently alluring and intent on proving their charms. Scarlett herself in a pique of jealousy over Ashley Wilkes decides to take revenge by flirting outrageously with the other ladies' beaux. She draws them around her by means of a rapid banter, calling Charles Hamilton a "handsome old thing," telling Frank Kennedy his new whiskers were "dashing." By lunch, she had a veritable circle of admirers, many culled right from under the eyes of their ladies. It was odd that these gentlemen, who were otherwise known as ready fighters, skilled horsemen, and individuals of refinement, were portrayed as so helpless in the face of a beautiful woman. The characterization was a familiar one, and heightened the reputation of the Southern belle. Everett Marshall in *Dixiana*, Bing Crosby in

Mississippi, Robert Cummings in *So Red the Rose*, and George Brent in *Jezebel* all become shadows of their true selves under the gaze of a charming Southern lady.

The gathering at Twelve Oaks also said much of the local society. Scores of finely clothed people mill about, awaiting the arrival of friends in fine carriages. The social position of the men is confirmed in a conversation which makes the South appear as if it were peopled by none other than the planter elite. While the planters over drinks and cigars argue the probability of war, one fellow declares that "gentlemen can always fight better than rabble"—a statement which reveals first a conception of the North as lacking in any social graces and also a stereotyped view of the overall Southern population.

As the first part of the picture attempted to demonstrate, the South was in Melanie's words, "a whole world that only wants to be graceful and beautiful." If the region's physical beauty was to be destroyed, the changes wrought would be so significant as to threaten the South's very ideals. And throughout the remainder of the film, the audiences saw what happens when a society's very foundations crumbled. The analogy to the viewers' own times was not easily missed. As a result, the South's example took on even more force.

The latter half of *Gone With the Wind*, including the years of Reconstruction, repeatedly accentuated the differences between the plantation world and the postwar society. One of the recurring symbols of the changes wrought by the war was the use of the staircases of Twelve Oaks, Tara, and Rhett and Scarlett's Victorian home. The grand, wide, beautifully curving stairway of the Wilkes home represented all that was gracious in the antebellum South. The passage was sparkling white, airy, and full of the ebb and flow of a cultured society. There Rhett first spied Scarlett on the staircase; Scarlett herself ensnared some of her admirers on the steps. The stairwell area was the meeting place of bowing servants and their betters. There Melanie displayed her Christian charity in defending her cousin Scarlett's designs; there too Ashley encountered the flirtatious O'Hara. One of the widely used publicity stills pictured the stairs full of belles descending to meet awaiting gentlemen. It was the plantation world at its best.

But the war would change all that. The movie refrained from

Hattie McDaniel and Vivien Leigh in *Gone With the Wind*. BELOW: Clark Gable in *Gone With the Wind*.

showing much of the actual fighting, confining the war to panoramic shots of a subdued or burning Atlanta or of Scarlett driving a wagon across a field strewn with military debris and the dead. But all the horror and destruction of war were nonetheless powerfully captured in the scene of Scarlett, cornered on the ruined staircase of Tara, repelling the Yankee looter. In that moment the horrifying extent of the culture's alteration was depicted.

The region was no longer the same; Tara's once graceful interior has been ravaged and ruined. The symbolic structure is dark, weakened, narrow, and leads to only further darkness and ruin in the once proud estate. Scarlett stands on the stairway, confused; at its bottom waits what appears to the mistress of the house as the cause of all the destruction. The resulting pistol shot echoes the South's frustration; whatever price was exacted upon the enemy, the culture's fate had already been sealed.

The Southerners' perseverance would sustain them, however, and bring eventual recovery, but at a woeful price. Even though Scarlett and Rhett maintain a fortune built upon Scarlett's new found entrepreneurial talents and Rhett's wartime blockade running, the lifestyle they enjoy never matches that which had been so recently destroyed. Their new mansion does not reflect the refinement of the South but instead the crass materialism of a commercial society. The red brick, Victorian style house seems out of place, and dominating its interior is a wide, dark-stained, red-carpeted staircase leading from a gloomy, foreboding hallway up to what often appeared total darkness. The comparative crassness of the new, overdone, and heavily ornate grandeur was in garish contrast to the splendor of say Twelve Oaks. It was the stairway over which raged many an argument, and it was the passage down which Scarlett rushed in pursuit of Rhett who has declared that even he who was once viewed as a prewar oddity for his callous disregard of the antebellum conventions was "going back to Charleston, back where I belong" to find if there was not "something left in life of charm and grace." Down the stairs he retreats to a past. As she watches him, Scarlett also realizes her salvation is with the old culture; thus the ideals of Tara in the end emerge victorious.

One scene in particular points to how the overwhelming

quality of life in the South had been accepted as the normal lifestyle. Having left what was once a handsome estate supporting dozens of fieldhands and eight house servants, Mammy (Hattie McDaniel), the butler Uncle Peter (Eddie Anderson), and Prissy (Butterfly McQueen) arrive at the new Atlanta mansion. Life on the old estate must have seemed a particularly average existence for the three who must staff the new home: while they gape incredulously, Prissy gasps, "Lawsy, we's rich *now!*"

Perhaps the best symbol of the South's desperate longing to cling to the old culture was Ashley Wilkes (Leslie Howard), the quintessential Southern gentleman whose only concerns had been with his immediate surroundings and his loved ones. Content to remain a gentleman farmer forever, Ashley is stunned by the changes. Just recently home from the war, he repeatedly mourns the passing of the pleasant, agrarian way. Ax in hand, dirty, tired, and frustrated, he admits to Scarlett that he can hardly "bear" the reality of the situation, can hardly tolerate the fate of his beloved land.

He is even more aghast while working for Scarlett as manager of the lumber business she inherited from her second husband, Frank Kennedy. Ashley protests that he has no head for accounts and business, and is disturbed that Scarlett would stoop to using convict labor. He is deeply hurt to watch the gaunt, chained men file through the work yard. To his objections, Scarlett points out that it is no different a system than slavery. But Ashley objects; neither he nor his father ever treated "our darkies" in such a manner. Ashley's comments constitute a slight against the Northern industrial wage slavery that many had been so fond of stressing was probably worse than the benign plantation mode of bondage. Ashley adds that, had it not been for the war, his father would have freed the slaves anyway.

His pleas of the system's innocence and concern for the blacks' welfare were moving but not credible. Contained within his protest were the contradictions so prevalent in all the genre's films. They presented a genteel society, accustomed to comfort and supported by happy slave labor, which had escaped the rapaciousness of commerce, and more importantly, the evils of labor so evident elsewhere. Audiences and reviewers repeatedly failed to ask how such large plantations existed without considerable commercial drive and some degree of business ability which fictional Southerners were so wont to accuse their Northern brethren of overemphasizing. Also, Ashley's statement that all would have continued unchanged after his blacks were freed points to the naive belief in the contented Negro who would maintain the status quo regardless of his new station. What was remarkable was the absence of comment by critic and viewer alike upon the dream's fallacy.

To the vast majority, the film was a testimony to the culture's charms. Throughout his days Ashley could only feign interest in the affairs of business and continually recalled the pastoral ideal. Firmer evidence of the South's superiority was of course Rhett's final realization that he was wrong to have denied his region's obvious attractions. And Scarlett, awakened to her proper course as well, goes home to Tara, to the land, still dominated by a rebuilt mansion and still tended by a band of faithful Negroes.[13]

The resounding message was that a society strong enough in its beliefs could survive almost anything. And audiences, North and South, flocked to the theatres to view the eagerly awaited epic. Particularly in the South was there a sense of pride, even vindication. At the December 15, 1939, Atlanta premiere, the populace poured forth its heartfelt emotion.

A million people streamed into Atlanta for what the Governor had declared an official state holiday. There were huge gatherings at the airport to greet each plane of film executives and stars; a motorcade through downtown Atlanta drew thousands of cheering citizens. Luncheons, formal functions, press conferences—a whirlwind of activities—whetted the public's appetite for the first showing. The Junior League Charity Ball utilized the movie's Confederate bazaar set, to which was added a group of singing "plantation darkies."

Film critics from all over the nation were in the city for the event. The Grand Theatre boasted a new facade, made to resemble Twelve Oaks. People wore period costumes. The celebrations continued for three days. Adoring crowds showered attention on

---

[13]Dialogue and Cutting Continuity, *Gone With the Wind* (1939), LC-MPS Copyright File LP-9390; Richard B. Harwell, ed., *GWTW: The Screenplay* (New York: Macmillan, 1980).

Clark Gable, Vivien Leigh, and Olivia DeHavilland—all of whom were at times bewildered by what they had wrought. Leigh, an Englishwoman, even failed to understand the significance of the film to many. Fortunately local reporters did not quote her response upon hearing a local band strike up "Dixie"—that the band was playing "that song from the picture." Tickets for the premiere, at $10.00 apiece, were treasured social assets. By opening night, scalpers were asking as much as $200.00 per admission.

GWTW, as the movie became known, was hailed in the Georgia capital as a giant step toward healing sectional wounds. In an editorial in the *Atlanta Constitution*, Robert Quillen exclaimed that the story "by the simple expedient of telling the truth, has won the admiration and affection of all America." Forgiven and finally understood, the spirit of the region and of Georgia would "march through all America, conquering hearts as it goes." A later editorial praised the tale's refraining "from caricature, either the romantic exaggeration of Southern partiality or the impossible nobility of visionary Northerners." As a result, the production would be viewed "as the exact historic recording of its place and time." The editor of the *Atlanta Journal*, the newspaper for which Miss Mitchell had once worked, agreed wholeheartedly; the film chronicled an age that "seems never to have died—or, rather, to have died and risen in new strength and beauty." Margaret Mitchell's fears of modern Southern romanticism had been well grounded.[14]

Local advertisements boasted of the plantation culture's "gracious life" which had survived for so long, "till one soft Southern night there was blood on the moon and catastrophe swept over all." Reliving that glory and disaster, audiences in Atlanta openly wept, cheered until hoarse, and rose repeatedly to the strains of "Dixie."[15]

Elsewhere in the South the response was similar. For weeks, local newspapers touted the production's arrival date and adver-

[14]*Atlanta Constitution*, Dec. 13, 14, 15, 16, 1939; *Atlanta Journal*, Dec. 14, 15, 1939.

[15]*Atlanta Constitution*, Dec. 15, 16, 1939; *Atlanta Journal*, Dec. 14, 15, 1939.

tised the release as a "great story of the Old South without deviation." So eager was the public that theatres received reservation requests from all over the state. Theatres were sold out before a print even arrived. Local showings were repeatedly extended, with some theatres beginning performances at 10:00 A.M.[16]

And as in Atlanta, audiences reacted quite viscerally: they cheered, hissed, or cried at each development in the plot. Other cities staged their own gala premieres. In Dallas, the walk in front of the theatre was covered with a red carpet, and "an old Negro footman in costume" greeted the guests. A staff of twenty-eight ushers attired as "Cavalier gentlemen" bowed for the season's debutantes, each with three escorts.[17]

Consistently, regional critics viewed the picture as a "superlative" effort which would withstand close scrutiny and the test of time.[18] A Richmond commentator was especially pleased with the treatment of the slavery issue, as it was "in accord with all the stories and legends of slavery-time Negroes." More importantly, the release was "a journey back through the years, a reliving of a gracious age of chivalry" which accurately depicted the planters and their ladies. Thus *GWTW* "should give the dream reality, and bring it back for the delectation of a whole new generation."[19]

It was evident that Southerners saw the spirit of the antebellum society evoked throughout the entire film rather than merely in its beginning. For example, a Louisville reporter believed that there was in the entire film "a just accent upon the once beautiful civilization of the Old South." The continued loyalty of the blacks after freedom was regarded as normal and expected. Hattie McDaniel as Mammy was "a joy, a thoroughly convincing Negro

[16]See, for example, *Birmingham News*, Feb. 4, 1940; *Montgomery Advertiser*, Jan. 28, 29, 1940; *Little Rock Arkansas Democrat*, Feb. 25, 1940; *Meridian Star*, March 24, 1940; *Raleigh News and Observor*, Feb. 11, 28, 1940.

[17]*Dallas Morning News*, Feb. 7, 1940.

[18]See, for example, *Miami Herald*, Jan. 18, 1940; *Charlotte Observor*, Jan. 30, 1940.

[19]*Richmond Times-Dispatch*, Feb. 3, 1940.

woman of the Old South, some of whom survive in many communities."[20]
Selznick's masterpiece was dubbed as "deeply moving and tremendously effective" in communicating the region's ideals. And testimonies mounted as to the story's authenticity. One critic reported that thirty-eight survivors of the Civil War emerged from the theatre convinced that the movie was "true . . . to the South of their own childhoods." A ninety-two year old Confederate veteran could only mutter, "It's the gol-darndest thing I ever saw."[21]
But the film was more than the recreation of the prewar South as many wished to remember it. The story also contained a lesson which many commentators pointed out. Although one reviewer pointed to the issue of slavery and warned that in light of the world economic and political situation, the master-slave relationship was not necessarily a dead issue, such critical insights were extremely rare.[22] There was more to heed in the antebellum era and its aftermath than what was termed its "flamboyant magnificence." For example, several reviewers perceived Scarlett's excessive business greed built upon sprawling urban growth as appalling. Henry Martin, a Memphis critic, viewed Vivien Leigh's change in character as one which served as a "study of the South's descent into Gethesemane and its return from Calvary." And Gable's final awareness of the culture's significance was the "personification of man's regeneration through belated awakening to the call of a cause greater than one's own self."[23]
Though Southerners such as Mrs. W. D. Lamar, President-General of the United Daughters of the Confederacy, believed GWTW was "wonderfully faithful to the traditions" of the section, for national import the production had to prove popular and meaningful in the North and West as well.[24] And popular it

[20]*Louisville Courier-Journal*, Jan. 27, 1940.

[21]*New Orleans Times-Picayune*, Jan. 27, 1940; *Memphis Commercial Appeal*, Jan. 27, 1940; *Nashville Banner*, Dec. 16, 1939.

[22]*Dallas Morning News*, Feb. 8, 1940.

[23]*Houston Post*, Feb. 11, 1940; *Memphis Commercial Appeal*, Jan. 27, 1940.

[24]*Nashville Banner*, Dec. 16, 1939.

certainly was. In Boston, for instance, a record crowd of 17,000 persons viewed the film its first day; the line for tickets had formed at 6:00 A.M. and by the second day of the run over 50,000 advance bookings were sold. Audiences and critics alike were unanimous in their praise, even to the extent of comparing it to *Birth of a Nation*, as the only other film worthy of all the adjectives applied to it.[25] Heady praise indeed, but did non-Southerners grasp the theme of the plantation ideal and the contemporary lesson of spiritual survival at any cost?

Most reviewers did stress the production's period flavor. In Los Angeles, the critics were particularly pleased with the background color. A San Francisco commentator also marvelled at the society and its demise, "how completely the gracious, patrician life of the Old South, the life of Tara and Twelve Oaks, has been shattered, never to be reclaimed." There seemed geniune sorrow at the death of such a culture. Though regretting what he interpreted as the film's bitterness against Northerners, a Chicago reviewer remarked that the war was "in pathetic and terrible contrast to episodes of the lazy, carefree prewar era in a South of Cavaliers and ladies and gracious living. . . ."[26]

Particularly noteworthy about the reviews were the overwhelming assumptions that the South was a section of noblesse oblige, that Tara was indicative of the upcountry, middle-class planter existence, and that the cotton planter class was representative of the region as a whole. A Midwestern critic labeled the film as accurate; the atmosphere was "faithful" and "startingly beautiful in pastoral scenes." Remarkably, practically all described the production's view as perfect in its recreation of the plantation as a "graceful culture" or a "gorgeous panorama." After decades of similar settings, the myth bordered on being an historical fact. As the film was overdone, so too was the acceptance of "the magnolia-scented days of the Old South." To non-Southerners the society was without doubt one of "wealth and

[25]*Boston Daily Globe*, Dec. 22, 1939; see also *Indianapolis News*, Jan. 27, 1940; *Butte Montana Standard*, Feb. 22, 1940; *Newark Star-Ledger*, Jan. 26, 1940.

[26]*Los Angeles Times*, Jan. 1, 1940; *San Francisco Chronicle*, Jan. 26, 1940; *Chicago Daily Tribune*, Jan. 26, 1940.

distinction," with the attendant "hospitable manners, broad acres, beautiful women and chivalrous men and the faithful old mammies who served them."[27]

If the lifestyle had become so laudatory, so fantastically alluring, it was then but a short step to grieve at its passing, regret its treatment by the victors, and finally praise its determination and example. It was quite a turnabout only seventy-five years after the nation's bloodiest conflict. The films could take a great deal of responsibility for the change. Movies aided enormously the affirmation of the South as the most distinctive region of the country, with a rural character which presented an alternative economic system to recall with nostalgia. So attractive was the section, especially as seen in *GWTW*, that non-Southerners continued to enjoy the films with little hesitation or awareness of the social repercussions.

Many reviewers, such as one in Topeka, insisted that *GWTW* presented its theme without undue favoritism toward the South, a judgment which revealed the extent of the mythology's credibility. *GWTW* and its predecessors made a strong case that the region was not solely responsible for the Civil War; both sides were defending a lifestyle, a mode of society. The oversimplified pictures made the point, as a Connecticut writer phrased it, that people "merely misunderstood the motives underlying two completely different types of people" of two "contrasting sets of ideals." Once the sincerity of the Confederate cause was understood and its way of life so lovingly recreated, even a Northerner could—as a Boston writer postulated—"rise up and whistle 'Dixie' along with the rabid Yankee-hating Georgians." The film in its presentation of "the finest qualities of the old South" constituted a moving argument that the section was misunderstood.[28]

What a Midwesterner termed the region's "dreamy appeal of

---

[27]*Cleveland Plain Dealer*, Jan. 27, 1940; *Portland* (Me.) *Press Herald*, Feb. 9, 1940; *Detroit Free Press*, Jan. 24, 1940; *Portland Oregon Daily Journal*, Jan. 26, 1940; *Salt Lake Tribune*, Jan. 29, 1940; *Seattle Post-Intelligencer*, Jan. 26, 1940.

[28]*Topeka Daily Capital*, Feb. 21, 1940; *Hartford* (Conn.) *Times*, Feb. 3, 1940; *Boston Daily Globe*, Dec. 22, 1939.

baronial magnificence" became a vision for Depression audiences. Viewers also faced what the defeated South had encountered, "the rise of a new and unhappy age," as a Cleveland writer described it. And in the defeated people's very survival lay the lesson. A Philadelphia critic believed strongly that the example merited considerable attention, that "even a dyed-in-the-wool Yankee must—and can afford to—give a rebel yell for *Gone With the Wind*." The epic had served to demonstrate that one "courageously, stubbornly, and painfully built upon the ashes of crushed hopes and ruined lands . . . ," a feat many hoped to duplicate.[29]

The romantic films of the Old South during the 1930s, of course, did not alone ameliorate the low spirits of numerous viewers, but the contribution towards such an end was evident. Moreover, and more essential, releases such as *GWTW* which praised the fortitude of the South furnished a popular example of recovery from adversity. The movies of the 30s verified legend and presented an apologia more sweeping than any the section had constructed. By the outbreak of World War II, the many myths, the racial and cultural conservatism, had reached an apex of cinematic reevaluation begun so humbly and unintentionally in 1903. The marvel was that the process, with a few exceptions, was still so misguided; the stories were simply the studios' reflection of popular tastes which craved films of romance and flair. But in their innocence what a message pictures such as *GWTW* bore; their very popularity revealed the persistence of a legend which decreed that an opulent South and its beliefs were being enjoyed at the expense of progress nationally in race relations and in a more accurate perception of the South's past and present problems.

---

[29]*St. Louis Post-Dispatch*, Jan. 28, 1940; *Cleveland Plain Dealer*, Jan. 27, 1940; *Philadelphia Inquirer*, Jan. 19, 1940; see also *Pittsburgh Press*, Jan. 27, 1940.

V

Hollywood and
the Reinterpretation of the South

REFORM AS GOOD BUSINESS, 1941-1980

A slave woman holds her newborn child over the dark, swirling waters of the Mississippi levee. Her owner stares, frozen in fear that both mother and child will fall to their deaths. Furious, and clutching her boy, the woman in a halting voice cries out, "Him man-child, him warrior, him die—but him no slave, never!" Then hesitating no longer, she turns and leaps, carrying her child to freedom in death. The film was *The Foxes of Harrow* and the year was 1947.[1]

A decade later, in 1957, Clark Gable played a rakish ex-slave trader ashamed of his African exploits in *Band of Angels*. To assuage his guilt, he takes under his care a young black, Rau-Ru, who grows to manhood and a responsible position on the plantation under his master's benign tutelage. It was another remarkable alteration from the usual story line which seldom even mentioned the slave trade, much less criticized it. Equally as astounding was the planter's liason with a woman of mixed blood whom he had purchased at a New Orleans slave market.[2]

In a 1965 production a Virginia family of farmers steadfastly opposes what they perceive as a planters' war and its paramount issue, slavery. In fact, one member of the family advises a young black to escape to freedom. Eventually the lad enlists in the Union army and fights beside white youths in a skirmish against

---

[1]Dialogue and Cutting Continuity, *The Foxes of Harrow* (1947), LC-MPS Copyright File LP-1437.

[2]*Band of Angels* (Warner Brothers, 1957), LC-MPS.

obviously stereotyped Southerners, led by an officer on a white charger. The rebels had incomprehensibly thick accents and drooping moustaches dripping with tobacco juice. The film was *Shenandoah*, and it would rank among the top pictures of the year.[3]

These three movies, spanning the twenty-five years since the presentation of *Gone With the Wind*, appeared light years away from the shuffling dances of *Hearts in Dixie*, the baronial magnificence of *Dixiana*, the romance of *Mississippi*, the outspoken propaganda of *So Red the Rose*, and the facile charm of *Jezebel*. And the productions of the postwar South were even more altered.

To be sure, there were still some productions of unabashed romanticism such as *Virginia* (1941), starring Fred MacMurray as "Stonewall" Elliot, Madeleine Carroll, Sterling Hayden, and Louise Beavers. The Paramount film charmed many critics, "and how those scribes come flocking—like pickaninnies when a new barrel of molasses is being broken out." Filmed in the Old Dominion, the picture was advertised with handbills printed to represent Confederate money, with contests for the "cutest Virginia accent," and with such poster captions as, "There's somethin' 'bout our Virginia climate just makes gentlemen romantic." The movie went so far as to include a scene of an old black returning to die on the plantation, site of his happy days as a slave.[4] *The Vanishing Virginian* (1941) included a similar scene.

Other productions such as *Lady From Louisiana* with John Wayne and Ona Munson sought to capture the spirit of postwar New Orleans and succeeded so well that many thought the splendor could only have belonged to the antebellum era.[5] In

---

[3]*Shenandoah* (Universal, 1965), LC-MPS; see also Dialogue and Cutting Continuity, LC-MPS Copyright File LP-33414. The film by the conclusion of its initial distribution grossed $7.75 million, and ranked 243rd on the list of all-time money-makers; *Variety*, Jan. 5, 1977.

[4]*Virginia* (Paramount, 1941), U/16; see also Poster, LC-PPD. Despite studio claims to the contrary, some reviewers were convinced someone had "read too much Thomas Nelson Page in their youth"; see *New York Times*, Jan. 29, 1941; *Time*, Feb. 17, 1941; *New York World Telegram*, Jan. 29, 1941; *Variety*, Jan. 15, 1941.

[5]Synopsis, *Lady From Louisiana* (1941), LC-MPS Copyright File LP-10455. For representative reviews, see *New York Times*, May 15, 1941; *New York*

addition, movies such as *The Romance of Rosy Ridge* (1947), starring Van Johnson and Janet Leigh (in her first movie role), praised the cohesive spirit of the Southern small towns.[6] The drama *Saratoga Trunk* (1945) included "lush, late '70's settings of exotic Old New Orleans."[7] *The Toast of New Orleans* (1950), with David Niven and Mario Lanza, returned to the city in a musical extravaganza.[8] *Showboat* (1951) showcased the singing talents of Howard Keel in yet another melodic journey to the Southland.[9] John Ford's comedy *The Sun Shines Bright* (1954) was a remake of the amusing *Judge Priest*, and included the seemingly irrepressible Stepin Fetchit in a predictable role.[10]

But such innocent films with their nostalgic views of the South were becoming scarcer. The majority of movies presented a postwar South populated by pitifully poor farmers, unrepentent bigots, sadistic rednecks, sex objects, and greedy, ambitious members of a corrupt upper class. Some pictures, such as *Swamp Water* (1941), were failures as effective examinations of the region, despite a serious tone highlighted by posters painted by Thomas Hart Benton.[11] Others like *Wild River* (1960) sought to balance the needs of progress with the region's rural lifestyle, but also failed commercially. But most of the releases were hardhitting dramas which shocked audiences more accustomed to films like *Virginia*. *The Southerner* (1945), for instance, set in Texas, was akin to *The Grapes of Wrath* in its depiction of regional destitution and desperation.

In earlier years probing films such as *They Won't Forget* (1937), with Claude Raines as a prejudiced and unscrupulous lawyer, were rarities among the dozens of productions devoted to a more

Herald Tribune, May 15, 1941; *New York Post*, May 15, 1941; *Variety*, May 21, 1941; see also Poster, LC-PPD.

[6]*New York Times*, Sept. 12, 1947.

[7]*Time*, Nov. 26, 1945.

[8]Studio Press Book, *The Toast of New Orleans* (1950), MOMA-FSC. See also *Time*, Oct. 23, 1950; *Variety*, Aug. 30, 1950.

[9]*Showboat* (MGM, 1951), LC-MPS; see also *New York Times*, July 20, 1951; *Time*, July 2, 1951.

[10]*New York Times*, March 17, 1954.

[11]Studio Press Book, *Swamp Water* (1941), MOMA-FSC.

pleasant view of the contemporary South. The content changed drastically after 1945.

These revisionist films on the postwar South included releases such as *Pinky* (1949), a financial gamble dealing with that "more noted area of racism, the Deep South." Others attacked the problem with biting humor, the satiric *Gone Are the Days* (1963), for example, with Ruby Dee, Ossie Davis, Godfrey Cambridge, and Alan Alda. Audiences were moved by white injustices in *The Young Ones* (1961), *The Intruder* (1962), *To Kill a Mockingbird* (1963), and *Nothing But a Man* (1964).[12]

Additional movies examined not only the white Southerners' racial shortcomings, but their sexual and psychological ones as well. In *Hot Spell* (1958), Shirley Booth, Anthony Quinn, Earl Holliman, and Shirley MacLaine suffer from stupidity, arrogance, and petty fears. The region even became a haven for the heretofore unexplored excessively ambitious politician and entrepreneur. James Cagney in *A Lion is in the Streets* (1953), Gary Cooper in *Bright Leaf* (1950), and Broderick Crawford in *All the King's Men* (1949) were far removed from the grandfatherly Lionel Barrymore of the 30s. Revenge fed by blind rage was the theme of several films such as *Cape Fear* (1962) in which a degenerate Robert Mitchum stalked his nemesis Gregory Peck.[13]

But how in just a few short years could the thematic direction of *Gone With the Wind* be so changed in *The Foxes of Harrow*, so abandoned in *Shenandoah*? How could the pleasant nostalgia found in even films of postwar settings such as *The Little Colonel* or *In Old Kentucky* be so shattered in *The Intruder*? Had the nation's view of the South and the black changed so radically that the

[12]See *New York Times*, Sept. 30, 1949; *Gone Are the Days* (Hammer Bros., 1963), LC-MPS. For representative critical reviews of such films, see *Commonweal*, Feb. 10, 1961; *New York Herald Tribune*, Jan. 19, 1961; May 15, 1962; Dec. 28, 1964; *New York Times*, Jan. 19, 1961; Sept. 21, 1964; *Variety*, Feb. 1, 1961; May 14, 1962; Dec. 12, 1963; *Villager*, Feb. 14, 1963; *Village Voice*, March 7, 1963; *Time*, Jan. 15. 1965.

[13]See Studio Press Book, *A Lion is in the Streets* (1953), MOMA-FSC; for the typical critical response to such pictures, see *Time*, June 26, 1950; *Cue*, June 17, 1950; *Variety*, May 24, 1950; Sept. 5, 1952; March 1, 1962; *New York Herald Tribune*, Jan. 18, 1953; April 19, 1962; *New York Times*, Sept. 18, 1958.

newer films were economically viable and an accurate reflection of general feelings? Indeed, much had changed by the mid-60s. First, the return of more prosperous times reduced the need for countless escapist films.[14] Depression era films had routinely dealt with the question of racial injustice by stating that the problem did not exist or that it was a false issue. And the general public found little fault with the omissions. But after 1945, changes in the relationship between the races came at a dizzying pace. The studios were confronted with a problem, whether to maintain a view traditionally acceptable or to face the reality of change. Films on the antebellum and postwar South would bear the brunt of the decision.

The single decade after World War II had seen the integration of the armed services, the instigation of fair hiring guidelines in the Federal bureaucracy, and several Supreme Court decisions barring discrimination, the most noteworthy being the 1954 *Brown* v. *The Board of Education* decision. Blacks were entering such white dominated enclaves as the professions. In the arts new Negro intellectuals and literary spokesmen were emerging. In 1950 a black won the Pulitzer Prize and the rapidly growing *Ebony* magazine reflected a keen interest in social commentary. The Congress of Racial Equality had by 1947 staged its first organized protests and during the 1950s many schools of higher education began to accept Negroes. By 1960, twenty states had enacted fair employment laws. The Congress in 1957, 1960, and 1964 passed Civil Rights acts. The Twenty-Fourth Amendment to the Constitution ended the use of the poll tax, long used to deny the black his rightful vote. And the first years of the 1960s were a period of yet more sit-ins, freedom rides, and protest marches to Washington and Southern state capitals. Productions such as *Way Down South* seemed hardly possible any longer.

However, to declare that the post-Depression films mirrored current liberal politics would be as erroneous as to say that the many legislative and individual actions taken against racial bias were universally successful. In the South, federal troops at the Little Rock public schools and the murder of civil rights workers

[14]For an overview, see Andrew Bergman, *We're in the Money: Depression America and Its Films* (New York: NYU Press, 1971).

served as grim testimony to the region's opposition to change. Nationally, the posturings and filibusterings of politicians and the general backlash of white Americans revealed just how hollow the initial victories were. Where did the movies' interpretation rest—on the side of change? Or was the industry on the side of the majority, who were either bewildered, or adamantly opposed, or only slowly and begrudgingly beginning to change? For business reasons, past films of the South had been uniformly a vehicle of conservative sentiment. There was little reason to expect that the movies of the post-Depression decades would support without question the difficult, albeit belated, changes. In fact the productions reflected the indecisions, the uncertainties, of the society. Hollywood's motives in dealing at all with the nation's racial problems were more financial than liberal. Actually, in the first years of World War II, the industry found the changes imposed from outside.

Not only was the film colony required in the 40s to produce a steady playbill of entertaining fare, plus pool its talents for government training and propaganda films; it also had to be more cautious with each production's content. Fighting a conflict for the free world democracies and against totalitarianism, the nation had to be careful of the image it presented on film. To safeguard that image, a watchdog Bureau of Motion Pictures under the Office of War Information insured that new releases did not damage the view of America as a stalwart defender of justice.[15]

Certainly, pictures of Negro slavery, whether pleasant or not, hardly fit the prescribed message. Films of the Old South quite suddenly dropped references to the institution. But Hollywood, knowing full well the economic returns gained from antebellum themes, could not entirely forsake producing these films. Instead, the slave character was reshaped or eliminated, not necessarily from any charitable designs but to insure the continuation of a lucrative plot structure within guide lines imposed from the

---

[15]For an overview of the wartime role of the government in Hollywood, see Clayton R. Koppes and Gregory D. Black, "What to Show the World: The Office of War Information and Hollywood, 1942-1945," *Journal of American History* 64 (June 1977), 87-105; see also Allan M. Winkler, *The Politics of Propaganda: The Office of War Information, 1942-1945* (New Haven: Yale Univ. Press, 1978), especially 57-60.

outside. It was a key transition nonetheless, for although the industry motives were economic, the ramifications were of enormous social significance. At last the view of the black would change and, with it, conceptions of the South as well.

At first, the studios seemed unsure of the direction to take. A good example of the vacillations and wartime difficulties to come was *The Flame of New Orleans* (1941). The production was highly touted as another vehicle for Marlene Dietrich and as the first American film directed by the masterful French specialist in light comedy, Rene Clair. The picture had its moments of interest in its glimpses of 1840 New Orleans waterfront low life as boisterous and gay compared to the staid, proper atmosphere of high society. The picture also included a new characterization: Teresa Harris as a slave girl was more adviser and friend than maid to her mistress Miss Dietrich.

Supported by a cast including Bruce Cabot, Andy Devine, and Clarence Muse, the plot held the promise of a unique and gentle poke at southern aristocracy. But any satiric value was lost in a perplexing production of bizarre details. For example, the low-lying New Orleans was surrounded in the movie by high rolling hills. And the city was dominated by architecture which could only have been leftover from Universal's many horror pictures set in Bavarian villages.[16]

The public had to have been confused by more than just the setting. Many advertisements gave the impression that the story had a modern setting. Trading upon Dietrich's sultry image, bulletins presented her in a black gown of modern design, with long blonde hair styled in a contemporary manner, and reclining on a chaise while lightly waving a long-stemmed cigarette holder.[17] It was no surprise that the movie did no better than second billing in many communities.[18]

[16]*The Flame of New Orleans* (Universal, 1941), U/16; see also Synoposis, LC-MPS Copyright File LP-10438.

[17]See, for example, *Phoenix Arizona Republic*, May 7, 1941; *San Francisco Chronicle*, May 15, 1941; *Miami Herald*, May 16, 1941; *Indianapolis News*, May 1, 1941; *Butte Montana Standard*, June 29, 1941; *Manchester* (N.H.) *Union*, May 28, 1941; *Philadelphia Inquirer*, May 16, 1941; *Sioux Falls Daily Argus Leader*, May 17, 1941; *Memphis Commercial Appeal*, May 1, 1941. .

[18]See, for example, *Indianapolis News*, May 1, 1941; *Boston Daily Globe*, May 29, 1941; *St. Louis Post-Dispatch*, May 7, 1941.

When well received by the critics, it was not the film's different viewpoint that was heralded but the spectacular, though inaccurate, settings. The studio had only claimed that the movie was one of "beautiful belles, bold philanderers, dashing lovers and gay ladies—all in a Mardi Gras of romance in the gaiety capital of the world." Reviewers emphasized the appeal of prewar "elegance and leisure," thus displaying a surviving affection for the traditional image, despite the film's gropings for something different.[19]

On the other hand, *Dixie* (1943) marked a return to a more familiar New Orleans. With Bing Crosby and Dorothy Lamour, the picture was a light musical biography of Dan Emmett, the Northern minstrel trouper and composer of "Dixie." Essentially a high-spirited collection of humor and song inspired by the film's locale, it was popular with the soldiers abroad. Stateside audiences as well thought it achieved its primary purpose of providing an entertaining look at "the carefree days and romantic nights in gay New Orleans."[20] Again, the Southern motif was serving as a pleasant release from contemporary tensions. It was a success, held over in many areas to rave reviews and receptive audiences as "a delightful piece of nostalgia and as American as the song that inspired it."[21]

Both films reveal the subtle change occurring. *The Flame of New Orleans* included a characterization of the black as more friend than servant. *Dixie*—shown extensively overseas for troops—

[19]See, for example, *Los Angeles Times*, May 24, 1941; *Atlanta Journal*, June 15, 1941; *Louisville Courier-Journal*, May 24, 1941; *Portland* (Me.) *Press Herald*, May 19, 1941; *Nashville Banner*, May 29, 1941; *Houston Post*, May 10, 1941; *New York Daily News*, April 26, 1941; *New York Post*, April 26, 1941.

[20]See Studio Press Book, *Dixie* (1943), LC-MPS Copyright File LP-12571.

[21]*Cleveland Plain Dealer*, July 15; Aug. 4, 1943. See also *Richmond Times-Dispatch*, June 30; July 14, 1943; *Los Angeles Times*, Aug. 3, 15, 1943; *Boise Idaho Daily Statesman*, Aug. 5, 11, 1943; *Indianapolis News*, July 13, 27, 1943; *Louisville Courier-Journal*, July 1, 14, 1943; *New Orleans Times-Picayune*, July 3, 16, 1943; *Boston Daily Globe*, July 8, 28, 1943; *Charlotte Observor*, July 4, 15, 1943; *Newark Star-Ledger*, July 13; Aug. 10, 1943; *Portland Oregon Daily Journal*, Sept. 3, 20, 1943; *Philadelphia Inquirer*, Aug. 19, 31, 1943.

omitted completely scenes of slave labor or subservience. But it would be a mistake to assume that Hollywood or the public because of temporary disappearances of standard plots had mended their ways. Both the industry and the audience too quickly returned to the theme of the Old South romance after 1945.

Walt Disney's *Song of the South* (1946), based on the folk tales collected by the Georgian Joel Chandler Harris, was evidence of the continued existence, believability, and profitability of the fictional plantation. Around a collection of animated cartoons of Uncle Remus's beloved characters, Brer Rabbitt, Fox, and Bear, ran a thin thread of a plot. But the lightness of the story could not mask the Disney studio's enthusiasm for recreating the antebellum scene. A magnificent mansion was built to Disney's specifications, overlooking a long row of quarters for the blacks, who were as devoted as in any previous production. The grandson of the mistress plays happily with one of the young blacks, who live a rather comfortable existence of fishing and instructing the white folks' children in the area's attractions.

In the big house, the Academy-Award-winning Hattie McDaniel again played the happy servant—in this release joyfully bouncing about the kitchen laughing and baking pies to the everlasting pleasure of the household and Uncle Remus. James Baskett, an experienced radio performer, played Uncle Remus, a clever old fellow who with charm and a bit of wily reasoning had his run of the plantation. Revered as a wise and perceptive individual, he occupied a private cabin. Retired after a life of devoted service, he had the free time to indulge in story-telling and general relaxation.

It was appealing to both children and adults—the beautiful setting, the faithful workers, the proud mistress of the house. The ingredients had become practically a litany. When the young master becomes bedridden, the blacks—as expected—amble to the big house emotionally singing for the boy's recovery.[22] It was a scene reminiscent of *Jezebel, So Red the Rose, Mississippi,* and many others.

Of course, the Disney studio could not be expected to do

[22]*Song of the South* (Walt Disney, 1946), LC-MPS.

Teresa Harris and Marlene Dietrich in *Flame of New Orleans*. BELOW:
James Baskett and Bobby Driscoll in *Song of the South*.

otherwise. The company's forte had always been technical and artistic innovations rather than interpretive ones. But the very fact that the movie was so enormously popular once again revealed that the public found little fault with the studio's perception. Disney himself had dictated that his "musical drama of the romantic Old South" capture the mood and magnificence so many had come to appreciate—the "traditional beauty, simplicity, and romance of many Southern homes."[23] It was also the theme of the advertising, which stressed the regional lifestyle complete with enormous houses, cotton picking, singing Negroes, beautiful maidens, and aristocratic finery in general.[24]

Of course, in the South the response was predictably enthusiastic, especially in Harris's native state. The Atlanta premiere attracted journalists from the leading Southern newspapers, and a first night audience of five thousand burst into applause on fifteen occasions for the "golden film of the Old South's glory." And as had been the case so often before, an ex-slave was procured to provide the proper subservient tone. The Uncle Remus Memorial Association employed a ninety-five year old Pike County black to sit on the front porch of a simple cabin and regale the little white children with folk tales.[25]

The Southern critical and popular response was expected: "definitely one of the best pictures ever made."[26] But the Northern response also showed little change from the 1930s. In fact,

[23]Souvenir Booklet, *Song of the South* (1946), LC-MPS Box C-26.

[24]Many advertisements included drawings of courting lovers, mansions, magnolias, and carriages with liveried drivers; other drawings showed blacks picking cotton. See, for example, *Miami Herald*, Jan. 30, 1947; *Atlanta Constitution*, Nov. 10, 1946; *Des Moines Register*, Dec. 24, 1946; *Louisville Courier-Journal*, Dec. 25, 1946; *Albuquerque Journal*, Feb. 28, 1947; *Cleveland Plain Dealer*, Dec. 25, 1946; *Nashville Banner*, Nov. 28, 1946; *Salt Lake Tribune*, Dec. 22, 1946; *Washington Post*, Dec. 26, 1946; see also *Motion Picture Herald*, Nov. 9, 1946.

[25]*Atlanta Journal*, Nov. 13, 1946; *Atlanta Constitution*, Nov. 13, 1946; see also *Richmond Times-Dispatch*, Nov. 17, 1946; *Memphis Commercial Appeal*, Nov. 13, 14, 1946; *Birmingham News*, Nov. 13, 17, 1946.

[26]See, for example, *Montgomery Advertiser*, Nov. 17, 1946; *Louisville Courier-Journal*, Dec. 25, 1946; *Memphis Commercial Appeal*, Nov. 14, 1946; *Nashville Banner*, Dec. 12, 1946.

the movie achieved extended runs in such diverse areas as Boise, Chicago, Des Moines, Boston, Minneapolis, Omaha, and Salt Lake City.[27] A Los Angeles critic in fact dismissed as an overreaction any criticism of the Uncle Remus characterization as "the stereotype of the lazy, shiftless (but admittedly lovable) Southern Negro." Obviously moved by the picture's nostalgia, a Cleveland reviewer wrote that one of the release's greatest attractions was "its vivid recordings of a beautiful way of living."[28]

The protests were only scattered. The NAACP expressed regret over the film's "idyllic master-slave relationship" which only "perpetuated a dangerously glorified picture of slavery." The National Negro Congress picketed New York's Palace Theatre carrying placards reminding onlookers of black contributions to the nation and chastising Disney for his product. Many blacks called for a Negro Legion of Decency to combat such caricatures as Baskett and McDaniel had been compelled to deliver.[29] Unfortunately, neither the organizations nor their sympathizers emphasized two aspects of the film generally overlooked.

First, the plot was actually set in the postwar period, which explained why Uncle Remus near the picture's end could entertain thoughts of simply packing a few belongings and strolling away. The audiences, not realizing the time frame, found slavery unconfining. Though a few critics realized the period, no one questioned the validity of a happy estate in a period of general reconstruction, relative poverty for the planters, and new found independence for the blacks.[30]

---

[27]*Boise Idaho Daily Statesman*, Dec. 25, 1946; Jan. 3, 1947; *Chicago Daily Tribune*, Dec. 23, 1946; Jan. 10, 1947; *Des Moines Register*, Dec. 25, 1946; Jan. 8, 1947; *Boston Daily Globe*, Dec. 23, 1946; Jan. 10, 1947; *Minneapolis Star and Journal*, Jan. 16, 29, 1947; *Omaha Morning World-Herald*, Dec. 26, 1946; Jan. 7, 1947; *Salt Lake Tribune*, Dec. 22, 1946; Jan. 7, 1947.

[28]*Los Angeles Times*, Jan. 31, 1947; *Cleveland Plain Dealer*, Dec. 29, 1946; see also *Newark Star-Ledger*, Dec. 19, 1946.

[29]*New York Times*, Nov. 28; Dec. 14, 1946.

[30]A few reviewers commented on the time frame, but none made any conclusions concerning its significance; most nevertheless still referred to the setting as "the Old South." See, for example, *Los Angeles Times*, Jan. 31, 1947; *Time*, Nov. 18, 1946.

Secondly, much could have been made of the fact that the picture's animated fables were indeed moralistic and symbolic tales of African and American slave origin. Though often told to the white folks, the tales also cleverly masked the danger, frustration, guile, and dreams of the black. Many a master had unwittingly laughed at the defeat of Brer Bear or Fox who in their cruel, wicked ways well matched the system's manner of race control.[31] The tales, therefore, served as a safe form of rebellion. Whatever solace the Negroes and their white supporters could have taken from the film rested on their stressing this coincidental inclusion of the Afro-American culture into cinema. The tactic might have gone far to defuse some of the bias, but the realization of the potential was rare, though one black commentator in Pittsburgh lamented the missed opportunity.[32]

But the mood of at least a minority of white Americans was obviously changing. Some critics who in the 1930s had heaped praise upon many mythological epics now abruptly terminated their blind devotion to the old ideal. Though their numbers were pitifully few, they did represent the first rumblings from the industry's critics beyond the isolated swipes of previous decades. It was a beginning.

An Indianapolis critic remarked that the story was patently obvious and was "hardly improved by the aura of magnolias, contented slaves, pillared mansions, poor white trash and other cliches of the Old South." In agreement, a Detroit writer attacked the excess of "old Southern corn and ham, dripping with syrup"; a Philadelphia commentator added that it was "soupily sentimental." Even a New Orleans observer grew tired of "the Old South in sticky pastels." Far harsher were those reviews which came down squarely upon the problem of the repeated cinematic view, its "nauseating symbol of an ultra-contented slave." However, such comments against "magnolias and nostalgia in bloom, darkies on de old plantation, and the usual assort-

[31]For an analysis of the role and scope of such folk tales, see Lawrence Levine, *Black Culture and Black Consciousness: Afro-American Folk Thought From Slavery to Freedom* (New York: Oxford Univ. Press, 1977), especially 81-83, 106-20.

[32]*Pittsburgh Courier*, Jan. n.d., 1947, MOMA-FSC Files.

ment of Hollywood cliches" were still scattered and failed to stem the tide of patrons. Just how much the national perception of the Negro and the South had to change was evident in the fact that those very few areas which provided the sharpest critiques also furnished the local theatres with some of the longest runs and most enthusiastic audiences for *Song of the South*.[33]

How is it, then, that the very next year *The Foxes of Harrow* included a scene of black rebellion and desperation so strong that death was preferable to life in a society previously presented as so kind? At first glance, the movie loomed as an abrupt change of perspective, particularly so since the film was adapted from a novel of the same title by the talented black author Frank Yerby.

The picture was different in many ways beyond its instance of slave resistance. Whereas previous films had revolved around the planter of gentlemanly bearing, *The Foxes of Harrow* related the rise from obscurity of one Stephen Fox, an illegitimate Irishman who had grown to manhood in the South. Played by Rex Harrison, the rake had won his fortune and title to the plantation Harrow on a riverboat gaming table, and had been compelled to shoot the loser. Eager to gain acceptance into society, he had wed an aristocratic Creole beauty, played haughtily by Maureen O'Hara. Disturbed at his low-life friends and their carousing on her wedding night, she argues with Fox. Enraged, he ravishes her and then storms from the room. From that violent encounter, she gives birth to a son as crippled as was their love. For years, Fox finds affection elsewhere and his wife Odalie dotes on the boy. In the end, spurred on by financial reverses, efforts to save his land, and later the tragic death of their son, the two are reconciled.

It was a bizarre story. However, its adaptation to the screen was prompted more by business considerations than any desire to provide a ground-breaking study of the South in the 1830s. Hollywood was undergoing profound changes which would affect far more than just movies on the prewar South.

A few years before the release of *The Foxes of Harrow*, Hol-

---

[33]*Indianapolis News*, Feb. 27, 1947; *Detroit Free Press*, Jan. 10, 1947; *Philadelphia Inquirer*, Dec. 26, 1946; *New Orleans Times-Picayune*, Dec. 26, 1946; see also *New York Times*, Nov. 28, 1946; *New Masses*, Dec. 17, 1946; *Musical Digest*, Jan. 1947.

Rex Harrison in *The Foxes of Harrow*. BELOW: Kim Hunter, Vivien Leigh, and Marlon Brando in *A Streetcar Named Desire*.

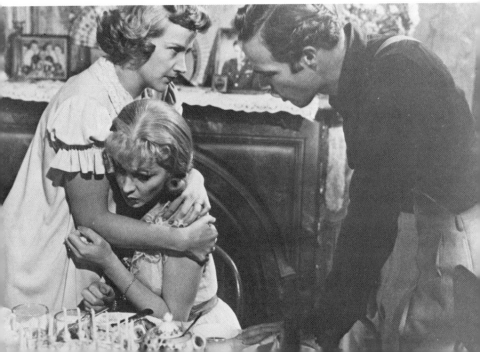

lywood had decided to learn more about its viewers, and the resulting study revealed that the character of the audience had changed significantly between 1935 and 1945, a period during which attendance had greatly increased. During the late Depression and the war a growing number of movies were created to appeal to the affluent, educated viewer—sophisticated comedies, historical romances, etc. These films were intended to broaden the foundation for customers, who up until then had come primarily from the working classes.

The new surveys provided evidence that by the end of World War II those films of more substance had in fact attracted the more perceptive, demanding audience. But the growth was at the expense of the original ticket buying groups. Thus it was logical that the next step to increase attendance was to reinterest the less economically secure, less educated public. The danger, though, was to go too far to the other extreme and alienate the new higher class of viewers.

Tragically, Hollywood misjudged the opportunity and too often produced films catering primarily to its first supporters. To compound the problems, the industry frequently failed to adjust to differences in American culture after 1945. Investigations in 1941, 1943, and 1947 by the House Un-American Activities Committee had taken their toll.

There were still strong suspicions of Communist influence in the movie business, and movie makers were careful not to offend any potentially vocal conservative audience. Unfortunately the industry believed that survival depended on stories that would appeal to that broad, traditional foundation of customer support—the less prosperous and schooled but loyal ticket holder.[34]

In addition, Hollywood was faced with a new competitor, television. In 1946, only 8,000 American families could boast of owning a television. However, by 1949, there were 940,000 televisions, and over the same period the weekly motion picture attendance dropped by twenty million. At first, the film studios were complacent: television was a fad and could not sustain its

[34]For an overview of the post-1945 demise of film, see Sklar, *Movie-Made America*, 269-304; and Jowett, *Film*, 333-51, 364-73.

initial growth. But by 1949 it became obvious that the film industry was facing its greatest challenge. Various attempts were made to draw the viewer from the small to the big screen. Studios tried epics such as *Samson and Delilah* (1949) and *Ben Hur* (1959). For a brief time "3-D" films such as *The Charge at Feather River* were the rage. The curved, wide-screen pictures such as *This Is Cinerama* and *Cinerama Holiday* did well. The Cinemascope process doubled the screen's width and was first used in 1953 for *The Robe*. Yet another method to loosen television's tightening grip on the public was to provide characters and situations which were as yet unimagined or not permissible for television.[35] The Southern themes fell easily into this category.

And while the nation became more educated, more suburbanized, and progressively more oriented towards television by the early 1950s, films slowly began to lose the very patrons that the industry most needed to maintain a quality product. Instead, productions catered more and more to a group largely unsympathetic to didactic causes in their entertainment. It was an audience attracted by plots which had to be all the more sensational to overcome the lure of television. The industry was desperate. The year 1946 had been one of peak theatre attendance, but quite soon thereafter ticket sales dropped precipitously and by 1953 receipts were half what they had been in 1946.[36]

Films on the South, old and new, exhibit Hollywood's financial problems and indecisions about how to approach the customers. The industry went to great lengths to produce numerous works on the region by renowned writers who had contributed bestselling books and well-received plays. It was hoped that such productions would retain as customers the very people the studios had so recently earned. It was assumed to be good business to offer the educated, professional individual stories by William Faulkner, Tennessee Williams, Erskine Caldwell, Robert Penn Warren, and Lillian Hellman.

Several of Faulkner's writings were produced: *The Story of*

[35]Jowett, *Film*, 347-60; see also Erik Barnouw, *Tube of Plenty: The Evolution of American Television* (New York: Oxford Univ. Press, 1975).
[36]Sklar, *Movie-Made America*, 269-74; Jowett, *Film*, 347-73.

Temple Drake (1933), *Intruder in the Dust* (1949), *The Long, Hot Summer* (1958), *The Sound and the Fury* (1959), *Desire in the Dust* (1960), *Sanctuary* (1961), and *The Reivers* (1969). Two of Warren's novels, *All the King's Men* and *Band of Angels*, were filmed in 1949 and 1957 respectively. Miss Hellman's plays reached the screen as *The Little Foxes* (1941), *Another Part of the Forest* (1948), and *Toys in the Attic* (1963). The well known Erskine Caldwell provided the stories for *Tobacco Road* (1941), *God's Little Acre* (1958), and *Claudelle Inglish* (1961). The prolific Tennessee Williams added *A Streetcar Named Desire* (1951), *Baby Doll* (1956), *Cat on a Hot Tin Roof* (1958), *Suddenly Last Summer* (1959), *The Fugitive Kind* (1960), *Summer and Smoke* (1961), and *Sweet Bird of Youth* (1962).[37]

It was a laudable effort, but Hollywood failed to take into account how different the themes were compared to earlier films.

[37]The films on the South became so numerous, reviewers were often confused as to their meaning—whether the movies were an indictment of the section itself, or a study of humanity in general, or merely shocking amusement. A consensus seldom emerged; see, for example, *Tobacco Road*: *Variety*, Feb. 26, 1941; *New York Times*, Feb. 20, 1941; *New York Post*, Feb. 21, 1941; *The Little Foxes: New York Sun*, Aug. 22, 1941; *New York Herald Tribune*, Aug. 22, 1941; *New York Times*, Aug. 24, 1941; *Variety*, Aug. 13, 1941; *New York News*, Aug. 22, 1941; *Another Part of the Forest*: *Newsweek*, May 31, 1948; *Time*, May 31, 1948; *Variety*, April 21, 1948; *Intruder in the Dust*: *Hollywood Reporter*, Oct. 11, 1949; *Variety*, Oct. 12, 1949; *All the King's Men*: Variety, Nov. 9, 1949; *A Streetcar Named Desire: Variety*, June 20, 1951; *Time*, Sept. 17, 1951; *New York Herald Tribune*, Nov. 20, 1951; *Baby Doll: New York Herald Tribune*, Dec. 19, 1956; *The Long Hot Summer*: *New York Herald Tribune*, April 4, 1958; *Cat on a Hot Tin Roof: Variety*, Aug. 13, 1958; *The Sound and the Fury: Variety*, March 4, 1959; *New York Herald Tribune*, March 28, 1959; *Saturday Review*, March 7, 1959; *Suddenly Last Summer: New York Times*, Dec. 23, 1959; *The Fugitive Kind: New York Herald Tribune*, April 15, 1960; *Variety*, April 13, 1960; *New York World Telegram*, April 15, 1960; *Sanctuary: Variety*, Feb. 22, 1961; *New York Herald Tribune*, Feb. 22, 1961; *Claudelle Inglish: Variety*, Aug. 30, 1961; *Summer and Smoke*: *Variety*, Sept. 6, 1961; *Sweet Bird of Youth: New York Times*, April 8, 1962; *Variety*, Feb. 20, 1962; *Toys in the Attic: New York Times*, Aug. 1, 1963; *New York Herald Tribune*, Aug. 1, 1963; *Time*, Aug. 9, 1963.

Many in the audience were unfamiliar with contemporary literature. Even the hugely successful *Gone With the Wind* had not been read by a majority of the critics who reviewed the film. To insure the industry's profitability, the studios had to make the new movies palatable to a broad clientele. Therefore, the film companies reconstructed most of the stories, often using their shocking scenes or plots as nothing more than a new thrill rather than as the tactic the writers had used to point out humanity's shortcomings.

Even so, the films' symbolic Southerners—destitute, depraved, and often ensnared in a once proud but now bankrupt tradition—provided a needed new perspective; at first they were welcomed. As one critic remarked in a review of *The Little Foxes*, such movies served as a "most powerful indictment of a certain kind of human being, Southern, parvenu, money-mad and vicious" and were "an antidote to all the flood of romanticism concerning the Old South. . . ."[38]

But too often these movies concentrated on the sensational effect, threatening any message the already emasculated adaptations retained. For example, several critics saw films such as *Tobacco Road* not as criticism but only as a money-making production, a diluted "saga of poh white trash in the Ole South" or "too much slapstick substituted for drama." Films such as *Baby Doll* generated storms of protest. Other pictures were labeled as only "grim and humorless" or only "folk comedy." By the late 1950s, the commentators and many viewers saw these plots as no more than a "simmering story of life in the Deep South, steamy with sex and laced with violence and bawdy humor," "a form of Peyton Place." In order to survive commercially, the "engineered soap operas" had hidden their important lessons in lurid trappings.[39]

Other films on the South could not even claim origins in

[38]*New York Post*, Aug. 22, 1941.
[39]See, for example, *Variety*, Feb. 26, 1941; May 14; March 5, 1958; Sept. 14, 1960; June 26, 1963; *New York Post*, Feb. 21, 1941; April 15, 1960; *Commonweal*, Jan. 11; Feb. 1, 1957; *New York Herald Tribune*, Aug. 14, 1958; Sept. 21, 1961; *Life*, April 20, 1959; *New York Times*, March 29, 1962.

important literature. Though there were still a few excellent films, such as *Inherit the Wind* (1960) concerning the Scopes trial in Tennessee, many movies were illustrious only in their potential for drawing customers. *The Defiant Ones* (1958) was an effort to expose prejudice as rooted in ignorance and misunderstanding, but was marred by exaggerated advertising and an obvious story. The much publicized *Black Like Me* (1964), concerning the exploits of a Texan who underwent skin treatments to pass for black, was regarded more as a piece of clever journalism than as a blow for human dignity.

Some, such as *Swamp Woman* (1941) or *Swamp Women* (1956), did not even pretend to bear a message; the former starred a burlesque performer. Many were simply embarrassing. *Angel Baby* (1961) exploited faith healing, while *Common Law Wife* (1963) flaunted sexual promiscuity as did *White Trash on Moonshine Mountain* (1964).[40] Such films, though drastically altering the public perception of the South, could do little in developing a better understanding of the region and its problems. The pictures made money, and that seemed justification enough.

Thus, *The Foxes of Harrow* too represented far more the changes Hollywood was undergoing than any attempt to reexamine the South. Any flavorings of an expose were more to entice than to enlighten. The advertising of the late 1940s and 1950s made it particularly apparent that titillation and not reevaluation was the prime influence. *The Foxes of Harrow* and its later counterparts such as *The Mississippi Gambler, The Gambler From Natchez, Duel on the Mississippi,* and *Band of Angels* were no exceptions.

Frequently, the advertisements for *The Foxes of Harrow* pictured Harrison as Stephen Fox, crashing through a heavy door to his lady's boudoir. In other bulletins he held her in a vice-like grip while glancing at his prize with a seductive air. The captions told of the lust, of "the veneer of a gentleman stripped off—and once again he was the renegade of the river boat, a man of savage

[40]*Village Voice*, Dec. 10, 1958; *Variety*, Dec. 31, 1941; Oct. 31, 1956; Aug. 6, 1958; May 10, 1961; May 20, 1964; *New York Herald Tribune*, Sept. 25, 1958; May 21, 1964; *Time*, May 8, 1964; *New York Times*, Dec. 27, 1941; *New York Post*, Dec. 27, 1941; *New York Daily News*, Dec. 27, 1941.

Sidney Poitier and Tony Curtis in *The Defiant Ones*.

passions." A Midwestern theatre promised "emotions as violent as the era that spawned them." A Southern advertisement revealed that "to Odalie, he was still a savage whose violence repulsed her, as it pulled her breathlessly to him." Other bulletins had even less subtlety, holding out the promise of "thrills—when Stephen Fox breaks down his bride's door."[41]

Amazingly enough, to many Southerners the South's charms emerged unscathed. Many Southern critics praised the "fabulous spectacle of magnificent wealth." A Miami writer said the movie had "some of the greatness of *Gone With the Wind*." As "an expansive mural of one of the South's most turbulent, exciting eras," the production was hardly regarded by the region as any slight.[42]

Other areas expressed similar approval. Very few observers even commented upon the changes represented by the inclusion of the black mother's suicide or a slave voodoo ritual. In Washington a reviewer lamented that *The Foxes of Harrow* had "every magnolia cliche," but the film nonetheless was held over. A similar opinion in Los Angeles failed to diminish the story's popularity or profits, as the release played at four theatres simultaneously and also merited an extended run. In the East, it was "smashing all records." Most critics simply enjoyed the fun.[43] As a Midwestern commentator admitted, the standard ingredients

[41]*Motion Picture Herald*, Sept. 13, 1947; *Topeka Daily Capital*, Oct. 18, 1947; *New Orleans Times-Picayune*, Sept. 20, 1947; *Newark Star-Ledger*, Oct. 27, 1947; see also *Washington Post*, Oct. 8, 1947; *Birmingham News*, Oct. 14, 1947; *Boise Idaho Daily Statesman*, Oct. 8, 1947; *Indianapolis News*, Nov. 11, 1947; *Louisville Courier-Journal*, Nov. 28, 1947; *Baltimore Sun*, Sept. 27, 1947; *Meridian Star*, Oct. 2, 1947; *Albuquerque Journal*, Nov. 7, 1947; *Charlotte Observor*, Nov. 2, 1947; *Salt Lake Tribune*, Oct. 9, 1947; and *The Foxes of Harrow* (1947) Poster, LC-PPD.

[42]*Richmond Times-Dispatch*, Oct. 2, 1947; *Miami Herald*, Oct. 2, 1947; *Atlanta Constitution*, Oct. 30, 1947; *Atlanta Journal*, Oct. 24, 1947; *Louisville Courier-Journal*, Nov. 27, 1947; *New Orleans Times-Picayune*, Sept. 30, 1947; see also *Memphis Commercial Appeal*, Oct. 10, 1947; *Houston Post*, Oct. 10, 1947.

[43]*Washington Post*, Oct. 10, 1947; *Los Angeles Times*, Oct. 11, 1947; *Hartford* (Conn.) *Times*, Oct. 9, 14, 1947; *Philadelphia Inquirer*, Oct. 4, 1947; *Pittsburgh Press*, Oct. 6, 1947; see also *Newark Star-Ledger*, Oct. 27,

were still enormously entertaining, because "if you like the proud Southern beauties in hoopskirts and ringlets, devil-may-care gamblin' men, white pillared mansions plentifully staffed with slaves—all the old moonlight and magnolia formula . . . —this lavish and glossy production" was ideal. In fact, many reviewers were convinced that the melodrama would "find a lot of favor with discriminating audiences."[44]

The protesting voices were few, and ironically a Southern review alone pointed out how different and valuable the film was. Despite its intent as exciting rather than revisionist entertainment, *The Foxes of Harrow* was important because the "revealed operations of slavery . . . should convince even the United Daughters of the Confederacy that it was wrong."[45] The Old South as a topic, however, was still difficult. Its conservatism simply was not to be attacked too seriously even if the subject of slavery had to be down played or avoided. In *The Mississippi Gambler* (1953) and *The Gambler From Natchez* (1954), plots revolved around urban life and used blacks merely as decorative details. *Duel on the Mississippi* (1955), set on a plantation, also managed to ignore the slave system.

Productions such as *The Mississippi Gambler* continued to stress the romantic. Tyrone Power as a Northern gentleman comes South to find the honor lacking in his homeland. Posters again were intended to be alluring, whether they matched the actual story or not. Power was always pictured in a well-cut white suit, attending grand balls where his touch was "a wildfire temptation

1947; *Providence* (R.I.) *Journal*, Oct. 11, 1947; *New York Herald Tribune*, Sept. 25, 1947; *New York Times*, Sept. 25, 1947.

[44]*Chicago Daily Tribune*, Oct. 20, 1947; see also *Indianapolis News*, Nov. 13, 1947; *Des Moines Register*, Oct. 19, 1947; *Portland* (Me.) *Press Herald*, Oct. 2, 5, 1947; *Boston Daily Globe* , Oct. 31, 1947; *Omaha Morning World-Herald*, Oct. 10, 1947; *Manchester New Hampshire Morning Union*, Oct. 25, 1947; *Cleveland Plain Dealer*, Oct. 6, 1947; *Seattle Post-Intelligencer*, Oct. 18, 1947; *New York Daily Mirror*, Sept. 25, 1947.

[45]*Dallas Morning News*, Oct. 10, 1947; see also *New York Post*, Sept. 25, 1947; *Portland Oregon Daily Journal*, Nov. 12, 1947; *San Francisco Chronicle*, Oct. 10, 1947; *Louisville Courier-Journal*, Nov. 28, 1947; *St. Louis Post-Dispatch*, Oct. 12, 1947.

to every woman, his luck a challenge to every lusty river man."[46] The critical reactions represented a denial of any demand for a change from the "horribly cliched legend." It was a step backward only a few reviewers were willing to block. Many Southern movie houses persisted in announcing that "there will be a second premiere for Negroes." One Western writer openly praised the return of the romantic plot. A New England paper heralded the release as "one of the year's greatest hits." A Cleveland reporter welcomed it, as the story "reflects the leisure pace and the intermittently eventful life of the South's era of knighthood." A vast majority agreed.[47]

Hollywood's direction and the general audience approval signalled a considerable lack of fortitude in placing blame for current racial dilemmas. Several reviewers labeled the following year's *Gambler From Natchez* as only "innocent fun." The film did, after all, scrupulously avoid the slavery issue and relied on a rapid-paced plot of honor and duelling with Dale Robertson,

[46]*The Mississippi Gambler* (Universal, 1953), LC-MPS. For representative advertising motifs, see *Washington Post*, Feb. 8, 1953; *Birmingham News*, Feb. 8, 1953; *Wilmington* (Del.) *Journal-Every Evening*, Feb. 12, 1953; *Atlanta Constitution*, Jan. 28, 1953; *Boise Idaho Daily Statesman*, Feb. 25, 1953; *Baltimore Sun*, Feb. 25, 1953; *Minneapolis Star*, Feb. 19, 1953; *Meridian Star*, Jan. 15, 1953; *Butte Montana Standard*, March 8, 1953; *Omaha Sunday World-Herald*, Feb. 8, 1953; *Charlotte Observer*, Feb. 8, 1953; *Sioux Falls Daily Argus-Leader*, March 10, 1953; *Nashville Banner*, Feb. 4, 1953.

[47]*Memphis Commercial Appeal*, Jan. 11, 1953; for favorable reviews, see *San Francisco Chronicle*, Feb. 7, 1953; *Los Angeles Times*, Feb. 7, 1953; *Manchester* (N.H.) *Union-Leader*, Feb. 26, 1953; *Cleveland Plain Dealer*, March 7, 1953; see also *Variety*, Feb. 12, 1953; *Miami Herald,* Feb. 1, 1953; *Atlanta Journal*, Jan. 30, 1953; *Louisville Courier-Journal*, April 3, 1953; *New Orleans Times-Picayune*, Jan. 16, 1953; *Houston Post*, Jan. 30, 1953; *Indianapolis News*, Feb. 5, 1953; *Des Moines Register*, Feb. 22, 1953; *Portland* (Me.) *Press Herald*, Feb. 11, 1953; *Boston Daily Globe*, March 12, 1953; *Newark Star-Ledger*, Feb. 11, 1953; *Portland Oregon Daily Journal*, March 5, 1953; *Philadelphia Inquirer*, Feb. 6, 1953; *Providence* (R.I.) *Journal*, Jan. 29, 1953. Only a few critics protested the production; see *Washington Post*, Feb. 14, 1953; *Chicago Daily Tribune*, Jan. 28, 1953; *St. Louis Post-Dispatch*, Jan. 18, 1953; *New York Times*, Jan. 30, 1953; but criticism did little to discourage audiences, as in all the above areas the film achieved extended runs.

Tyrone Power in *The Mississippi Gambler*. BELOW: Dale Robertson in
The Gambler from Natchez.

Debra Paget, and Woody Strode. In fact, the picture was so devoid of references to bondage that several writers assumed it was set in the postwar South. It was a culture that the advertisements promised had women striving for the gamblers, "lusty and gusty as their fiery women." It was no wonder the public remained attracted to such "swashbuckle and crinoline adventure."[48]

When Warner Brothers acquired the rights to the novel *Band of Angels* by the distinguished Southern writer Robert Penn Warren, there was cause for hope that an important project was in the making. The novel dealt with questions of individual identity and freedom by following the experiences of a young woman who discovers that her mother was of Negro ancestry. Sold into slavery, wed for a time to a Union officer in whose whiteness she sought herself, and finally the companion of an ex-slave, the daughter struggles to find herself. It was a powerful work, but the studio's response, though significant, verified the industry's reluctance to alter the traditional conception. Too much too soon endangered business and fomented anger; it was still dangerous to lead.

Band of Angels was a turning point of sorts in that it was the first movie to portray white and black as neither all good nor all evil under the system of slavery. The relationship between Hamish Bond (Clark Gable) and his ward, overseer, and slave

---

[48]Dialogue Continuity, *The Gambler From Natchez* (1954), LC-MPS Copyright File LP-4007. The confusion as to time period was somewhat evident; see *Atlanta Constitution*, Aug. 13, 1954; *Newark Star-Ledger*, Sept. 23, 1954; *Sioux Falls Daily Argus-Leader*, Oct. 10, 1954. For instances of the advertising hyperbole, see, for example *Albuquerque Journal*, Oct. 15, 1954; *Butte Montana Standard*, Oct. 6, 1954; *Baltimore Sun*, Sept. 29, 1954; *Birmingham News*, Aug. 26, 1954. The complimentary reviews were many; see *New York Times*, Aug. 14, 1954; *New York Herald Tribune*, Aug. 14, 1954; *Newark Star-Ledger*, Sept. 23, 1954; *Portland Oregon Daily Journal*, Sept. 17, 1954; *Philadelphia Inquirer,* Sept. 2, 1954; *Providence* (R.I.) *Journal*, Sept. 25, 1954; *Sioux Falls Daily Argus-Leader*, Oct. 10, 1954; *Variety*, Aug. 11, 1954; *Richmond Times-Dispatch*, Sept. 16, 1954; *Miami Herald*, Oct. 2, 1954; *Atlanta Constitution*, Aug. 12, 1954; *Atlanta Journal*, Aug. 13, 1954; *Louisville Courier-Journal*, Sept. 17, 1954; *New Orleans Times-Picayune*, Sept. 25, 1954.

Rau-Ru (Sidney Poitier) was fraught with tension. And the hate the once proud aristocrat (Yvonne DeCarlo) bore towards her new master also said much about the evils of slavery and white bigotry. But there the uniqueness of the film ended. It was a considerable first step, but much of the impact was lost in the adaptation.

In comparison to the novel, the issues of race, slavery and miscegenation were but delicately touched upon. And though the film had its moments, much of the power was lost in the greatly revised denouement. Warren's plot was rewritten so that the mulatto beauty weds her tormentor and master, and Rau-Ru comes to feel ashamed of his unappreciative attitude, and even frees his master from a rapidly encircling column of Union forces. As the master flees, the black sergeant (in the novel he was a lieutenant) realizes that his Federal commander was actually more prejudiced than his former Southern owner.[49]

The film's revisionist aspects were damaged in advertising as well. The advertisements read as if blackness was still a condition to despise; the sexual undertones were also repeatedly emphasized. In many newspapers, Poitier was shown taunting DeCarlo that "you're the same color I am!" Other publications printed captions which left little doubt concerning the racial hierarchy; DeCarlo displayed "the beautiful Southern blueblood and the shock of her sudden dishonor." Many theatre managers harped on the theme that "a drop of blood made her a slave instead of a debutante." Other bulletins made yet a stronger point that "you're no blueblood anymore honey—the master bought you—now he's waitin'!"[50]

[49]Walter Sullivan, *Death by Melancholy: Essays on Modern Southern Fiction* (Baton Rouge: LSU Press, 1972), 36-51.

[50]See, for example, *Denver Post*, Aug. 29, 1957; *Washington Post*, Aug. 9, 1957; *Phoenix Arizona Republic*, Aug. 9, 1957; *Wilmington* (Del.) *Journal-Every Evening*, Aug. 27, 1957; *Topeka Daily Capital*, Aug. 14, 1957; *Baltimore Sun*, July 25, 1957; *Minneapolis Star*, Aug. 27, 29, 1954; *Butte Montana Standard*, Sept. 1, 1957; *Albuquerque Journal*, Sept. 5, 1957; *Providence* (R.I.) *Journal*, Aug. 13, 1957; *Richmond Times-Dispatch*, Aug. 28, 1957; *Miami Herald*, Aug. 1, 1957; *Nashville Banner*, Aug. 30, 1957; *Houston Post*, Aug. 7, 1957; *Montgomery Advertiser*, Jan. 11, 1958; *In-*

As the potpourri of thrills, the Warner Brothers film garnered large audiences throughout the nation. Towns as diverse as Charlotte and Indianapolis hailed *Band of Angels* as another *Gone With the Wind*, a statement that showed just how little of the book was retained in the script.[51] It was held over several times in cities such as Philadelphia. In Los Angeles it played at fourteen area theatres despite a growing number of disenchanted critics.[52] Here at last was a picture which broached the taboo subjects of the master's cruelty and lust. But within the context of so many pictures which attracted rather than repelled ticket sales with similar explicit characteristics, the reinterpretation was not as ground-breaking as it should have been.

The legend's staying power and its influence proved to be still considerable. In the same year as *Band of Angels*, Metro-Goldwyn-Mayer's *Raintree County* presented another opulent tribute to the South. Adapted from a novel by Ross Lockridge, Jr., the picture included several scenes of a Northerner's introduction to the grand Southern tradition. Newly married to a Southern lass, played by Elizabeth Taylor, the newcomer Montgomery Clift marvels at the region's ways. Courting abolitionist sentiments, he astounds his bride who does not understand his emotions, "'cause all you have to do is go South once and you love it." And besides, there were conditions worse than being an abolitionist, "like havin' Negra blood in ya'—just one little

---

dianapolis News, Aug. 30, 1957; *Portland* (Me.) *Press Herald*, July 30, 1957; *St. Louis Post-Dispatch*, Aug. 1, 1957; *Sioux Falls Daily Argus-Leader*, Sept. 1, 1957; *Boise Idaho Daily Statesman*, Aug. 6, 1957.

[51]*Indianapolis News*, Aug. 30, 1957; *Charlotte Observer*, Aug. 23, 1957.

[52]Extended runs were common, see *Los Angeles Times*, Aug. 7, 15, 1957; *Philadelphia Inquirer*, Aug. 7, 21, 28, 1957; see also *Denver Post*, Aug. 30; Sept. 12, 1957; *San Francisco Chronicle*, Aug. 16, 28, 1957; *Hartford* (Conn.) *Times*, Aug. 1, 9, 14, 1957; *Chicago Daily Tribune*, Aug. 2, 15, 1957; *Indianapolis News*, Aug. 30; Sept. 11, 1957; *Detroit Free Press*, Aug. 6, 26, 1957; *St. Louis Post-Dispatch*, Aug. 1, 15, 1957; *Cleveland Plain Dealer*, Aug. 23, 30, 1957; *Newark Star-Ledger*, July 30; Aug. 6, 13, 1957; *Salt Lake Tribune*, Aug. 7, 14, 20, 1957; *Little Rock Arkansas Democrat*, Aug. 25, 31; Nov. 5, 1957; *Atlanta Constitution*, Aug. 16, 29, 1957; *New Orleans Times-Picayune*, Aug. 7, 14, 22, 27, 1957; *Charlotte Observer*, Aug. 21, 31,

Elizabeth Taylor in *Raintree County*.

teeny drop and a person's all Negra."[53] The film hardly represented a blow for civil rights, and in fact the fear of Negro heritage led to the wife's paranoia and eventual death.

A 1960 version of *The Adventures of Huckleberry Finn* did little better in dispelling the old myths. Although billed as only a "boyhood adventure story" aimed at predominantly the younger viewer, the film attracted a large audience. The film showed towns still abounding in cotton, grand steamers brimming with happy passengers, folk of obvious social standing, and homes which if not mansions still expressed the overall prosperity of each small Southern hamlet. Worse, much of Jim's flight is attributed to highly unusual circumstances rather than to slavery itself. At the end, Jim (Archie Moore) and Huck (Eddie Hodges) actually fret over whether the local slaves had given them the correct directions to freedom or had directed them to an ambush by a pursuing John Carradine, Tony Randall, and Buster Keaton.[54]

Finally, in 1965 a distinctly new conception of the antebellum society appeared. However, *Shenandoah* was produced more to take advantage of the nation's Civil War Centennial than to offer

---

1957; *Houston Post*, Aug. 10, 17, 21, 1957. There was a significant majority of critics who praised the production as "a great picture of the Old South" or condemned it for its few didactic moments; see *Richmond Times-Dispatch*, Aug. 29, 1957; *Miami Herald*, July 25, 1957; *Atlanta Constitution*, Aug. 23, 1957; *Chicago Daily Tribune*, Aug. 5, 1957; *Louisville Courier-Journal*, Aug. 9, 1957; *Charlotte Observor*, Aug. 23, 1957; *Portland Oregon Daily Journal*, Aug. 3, 1957. For critical reviews of the film, see *Denver Post*, Sept. 2, 1957; *Los Angeles Times*, Aug. 8, 1957; *San Francisco Chronicle*, Aug. 17, 1957; *Detroit Free Press*, Aug. 7, 1957; *St. Louis Post-Dispatch*, Aug. 4, 1957; *Seattle Post-Intelligencer*, Aug. 5, 1957; *Philadelphia Inquirer*, Aug. 9, 1957; *Pittsburgh Press*, Aug. 14, 1957; *New York Times*, July 11, 1957; *New York Herald Tribune*, July 11, 1957; *Hartford* (Conn.) *Times*, Aug. 2, 1957; *Cleveland Plain Dealer*, Aug. 24, 1957; *Memphis Commercial Appeal*, Aug. 8, 1957; *Salt Lake Tribune*, Aug. 7, 1957. But as was so often the case, though the perceptions of the critics changed, the response did not diminish the popular reception for the exciting and romanticized film.

[53]*Raintree County* (MGM, 1957), LC-MPS.

[54]*The Adventures of Huckleberry Finn*, (MGM, 1960), LC-MPS; see also Studio Press Book, LC-MPS Box C-38.

any attack on prewar days. Well developed by the noted script writer James Lee Barrett, the picture in the spirit of the national festival took no sides. The screenplay explored both Federal and Confederate with compassion, but hidden within the story were considerable comments concerning the image of the Old South. Although some critics saw the movie as "full of cliches and overdone sentimentality behind which at any moment the reviewer expected to hear 'Dixie,'" the picture was a milestone.[55] James Stewart played a Virginia farmer who with his sons worked his five hundred acres "without the sweat of one slave." The family lived in a comfortable but simple home and only wished to be left alone. Stewart's role was a marked departure from all the planters, gamblers, duellists, and gentlemen before him. In the characterization of a prosperous valley farmer, something approaching one of the lifestyles of the region had at last been presented.[56]

Regrettably, critic and viewer alike failed to recognize the popular film's uniqueness and potential. More cinematic explorations were needed in the same vein, studies which would finally downplay the previous six decades of unrestrained mythology. The movies of the period 1941 to 1965 had marked the slow birth of a necessary reassessment, from the tentative beginnings in *The Foxes of Harrow* to the largely unappreciated *Shenandoah*.

Unfortunately, however, the changes were too frequently incidental rather than essential to a story's meaning, and thus represented little concerted effort to undo the racial bias which had since 1903 characterized the plantation theme in film. The region that pictures such as *The Intruder* or *Band of Angels* presented was without doubt different from anything seen before on film, and being so different the productions have taken on an importance which is not completely deserved. The films of the Old South actually clung to old precepts, and the sordid films of the New South were often more exciting entertainment than revealing examinations.

The seemingly unique departures from the usual were often

[55]*New York Herald Tribune*, July 20, 1965.

[56]*Shenandoah* (Universal, 1965), LC-MPS; see also Dialogue and Cutting Continuity, LC-MPS Copyright File LP-33414.

devices to enhance a film's financial success. The studios in neither their advertising nor their press releases made any pretensions regarding a production's revisionist merits. With such motives, it was almost an accidental achievement that the public learned more of the section. And what did the audiences learn? That the South was populated by Jeeter Lesters, Big Daddys, and Hamish Bonds may have dispersed much romanticism, but the image did no more than exchange one mythology for another in again lumping all Southerners into a few categories.

In addition, in explaining relationships between rich and poor, black and white, male and female as motivated by the basest or most flippant drives, the stories were hardly an indictment unique to the South. If the section were really so apart, then studies were needed which captured the origins of those evils and the essence of that civilization alone.

The need was not to be fulfilled. The years after the release of *Shenandoah* would reveal even more the necessary economic base of the film industry. The films of the 1930s earned money largely by providing highly entertaining stories. The film business after 1945 survived in part by providing excitement not to be seen on television. After 1965, the business made profits by reflecting audience desires to an even greater extent. The most recent films would have been unimagined just a few years earlier. But the response was considerable.

For example, the concluding segment of the television film *Roots* (1977) captured the medium's largest single-program audience. *Mandingo* ranked eighteenth among the hundred most profitable films of 1975, and its sequel, *Drum* (1976), returned a handsome profit as well, as did *Slaves*.[57] All were marked departures from the movies of just the previous decade. The black was the central character, portrayed as a raging, righteous foe of a system which had never before been shown in such stark outlines. Uncle Tom had become Nat Turner.

But pictures with a Southern setting were not the only radically different films. Spurred on by a period of protest against many American institutions, new characterizations were found in many traditional film genres.

[57]*Washington Post*, Feb. 2, 1977; *Variety*, Jan. 7, 1976; Jan. 5, 1977.

Clark Gable, Yvonne DeCarlo, and Sidney Poitier in *Band of Angels*.
BELOW: Stephen Boyd and Dionne Warwick in *Slaves*.

Even the long sacred western had by the 1960s evolved as a political statement. *The Wild Bunch*, for instance, in its depiction of Gringo depredations in Mexico was a thinly veiled attack on the nation's war in Southeast Asia. *Pat Garrett and Billy the Kid* was a moving censure of the law-and-order hypocrisy. *Little Big Man, Cheyenne Autumn,* and *Soldier Blue* criticized the outright theft of Indian lands and the accompanying subjugation of a minority culture. Others such as *Will Penny* and *Monte Walsh* questioned the ideal of progress and the rush to commercial modernization at the expense of our original freedom and ideals.[58]

America was examining itself, and the films of the Old South were particularly apropos, as the issue of race was never more alive. The Detroit race riots in 1967 revealed a rage born of black unemployment, persisting political impotence, slum housing, and a perceived lack of governmental concern. The assassination of Dr. Martin Luther King, Jr., a year later only heightened a sense of rebellion and confirmed a growing belief that white Americans simply did not care. Civil turmoil in Watts, Harlem, and other areas was grim testimony to a problem growing only worse.

As black audiences cheered while the slaves burned the plantation in *Slaves* and cried "Go Mandingo!" as the rebellious workers butchered the whites in *Drum*, there could be little doubt that the newest productions at the very least helped in the venting of frustrations. And the slave seasoning stations in *Drum*, the horrors of the Middle Passage aboard ship in *Roots*, the miscegenation in *The Quadroon*, the brutal beatings in *Passion Plantation*, and the breeding practices in *Mandingo* were a surprising revelation for many accustomed to films of the old mythology produced as recently as the early 60s. Television too added to the revisionism with productions such as the aforementioned *Roots* and *The Autobiography of Miss Jane Pittman*.

Hollywood, however, was catering to two distinct audiences.

[58]For an overview of the western's modern evolution, see Philip French, *Westerns: Aspects of a Movie Genre* (New York: Oxford Univ. Press, 1977); and George N. Femin and William K. Everson, *The Western: From Silents to the Seventies* (New York: Penguin, 1977).

The films from 1945 to 1965 had furnished passion and violence to maintain the customers. After 1965, the industry's audience was fragmented by more than television. There was increasingly a white suburban audience and a black inner city audience. Ever resourceful, the industry developed a product for both. Films like *Passion Plantation* (1978) exploited the urban market and quickly became known as "blaxploitation" pictures. The suburban ticket holder viewed an entirely different product.

For instance, *Reader's Digest* presented two pictures intended for family viewing, *Tom Sawyer* (1973) and *Huckleberry Finn* (1974). Both were among their respective year's most profitable releases. The reissue of *Song of the South* placed sixteenth in earnings for 1972, and *Gone With the Wind* in 1971 did well too. Such audience satisfaction with different themes did not bode well for a single, revised popular interpretation of the antebellum era. Even that highly touted television audience for *Roots* was closely followed by the audience for *Gone With the Wind*, the second largest number of viewers ever for a televised program.[59]

---

[59]In 1974, *Huckleberry Finn* grossed $1.2 million and ranked 85th of the 94 films earning at least $1 million that year, while *Tom Sawyer* in 1973 drew $6 million and ranked 25th of 111. The 1972 rerelease of *Song of the South* made $5.9 million for the Disney Studio and placed 16th of 92, and the re-release of *Gone With the Wind* in 1971 earned distribution rentals of almost $1.3 million, reaching 78th on a list of 93. This compares favorably with the competing films, as within the same period the pictures adhering to the old legends earned a total of $14.4 million as opposed to $13.2 million for the revisionist releases. *Mandingo* in 1975 grossed $8.6 million, placing 18th of 104; *Drum* in 1976 reached almost $2.2 million and a position of 71st of 116; and *The Skin Game* in 1971 brought $2.2 million and a rank of 54th of 92. The plantation films of earlier years were still profitable, but a better measure of their popularity in past, original distribution and in rerelease is more apparent when total earnings from the date of issue are examined, taking into consideration the older pictures' much lower ticket prices and the newer pictures' smaller audiences, lured elsewhere by greatly expanded entertainment options. Of the 833 movies which have achieved rental earnings of at least $1 million, *Gone With the Wind* (1939) ranks 5th at $76.7 million; *Song of the South* (1946) is 116th at $12.8 million; *Mandingo* (1975) is 209th with $8.6 million; *Shenandoah* (1965) reached 243rd and $7.75 million; *Raintree County* (1957) is 388th with $5.97 million; *Showboat*

The critics also welcomed an occasional return to a less complicated, more romantic South. Although the region's racial conservatism was an anathema to many, few could deny that the comfortable settings had entertainment value. Produced as a musical comedy, the 1973 version of *Tom Sawyer* with Johnny Whitaker, Celeste Holm, and Warren Oates was regarded as a unique work of "local history and folklore." The "breath of fresh nostalgia" was still appreciated.[60] The more serious *Huckleberry Finn* the following year, with Paul Winfield as Jim, downplayed the issue of slavery. That hardly diminished its popular reception. In fact, only Roberta Flack's rendition of the musical introduction, "Freedom," lent any social significance to the production.[61]

The persistent popularity of discredited interpretations was attributable to several factors. For some die-hards rereleases such as *Gone With the Wind* were more than cinema classics; they were an instance of "old times there are not forgotten." Others sought in *Song of the South*, for example, more innocent entertainment for children than was available at most theatres. But the newer pictures such as *Slaves*, though profitable, satisfied the desires primarily of blacks. For whites, the newer stories were exciting diversions, but the plots did not hold the significance as history that they did for the blacks.

On the other hand, because films such as *Mandingo* were obviously more popular with black audiences did not mean that a white majority watching *Gone With the Wind* in 1971 and 1976

(1951) is 509th at $5.53 million; and *Tom Sawyer* (1973) is 603rd with $4.9 million. *Uncle Tom's Cabin* (1965), *Slaves* (1969), *The Quadroon* (1971), *The Skin Game* (1971), and *Drum* (1976) are not listed among the top 833. The returns for *Birth of a Nation* (1915) are difficult to estimate; the most recent calculation is $5 million, placing it 561st. See *Variety*, Jan. 5, 1972; Jan. 3, 1973; Jan. 9, 1974; Jan. 8, 1975; Jan. 7, 1976; Jan. 5, 1977.

[60]For appreciative comments, see *New York Times*, March 16, 25, 1973; *Variety*, March 14, 1973; *Newsweek*, April 9, 1973; there were some dissenting voices; see *Time*, April 2, 1973; *New Yorker*, April 7, 1973; *Women's Wear Daily*, March 16, 1973.

[61]The critics were generally appalled; see *New York Times*, May 25, 1974; *Variety*, April 3, 1974; *Newsweek*, June 3, 1974; *Time*, June 17, 1974.

saw its fictional lifestyle as the answer to the way slavery and the South had worked. The point, however, was that as lamentable and unsatisfying as the traditional view was, it was essentially the only other one the popular culture offered in comparison to the newer *Slaves*, *The Quadroon*, or *Passion Plantation*. The new presentations depicted cruelty and lust as rampant as benevolence had been in the earlier films.

Ironically, perhaps the only film to strike a middle ground was a comedy, *The Skin Game* (1971). A picaresque tale of a white confidence trickster (James Garner) and his black partner (Lou Gossett), it was advertised as a tale of "the old West." Actually, it was a fascinating story of Missouri in the 1850s, pitting the protagonists against both slave traders and abolitionists. But it was an exception amidst the "blaxploitation" films.[62]

The result of confronting one view with another—the romanticized versus the revisionist—was that it was too easy to lose sight of the crucial lesson. Whether the master was a Walter Connolly dispensing favors in *So Red the Rose* or a Stephen Boyd in *Slaves* administering the lash, the audience was not exposed to an essential point. The fact was that slavery, benign or savage, was

---

[62]The film was widely praised as a "beacon of sane humor in the dark that has gathered around the racial question." See, for example, *Philadelphia Inquirer*, Oct. 8, 1971; *Washington Post*, Oct. 9, 1971; *Denver Post*, Oct. 15, 1971; *Richmond Times-Dispatch*, Oct. 15, 1971; *Little Rock Arkansas Democrat*, Oct. 22, 1971; *San Francisco Chronicle*, Oct. 21, 1971; *Atlanta Constitution*, Nov. 8, 1971; *Chicago Tribune*, Oct. 19, 31, 1971; *Christian Science Monitor*, Oct. 18, 1971; *Boston Globe*, Oct. 14, 1971; *Detroit Free Press*, Oct. 13, 1971; *Omaha World Herald*, Oct. 17, 1971; *Charlotte Observor*, Oct. 12, 1971; *Providence* (R.I.) *Journal*, Oct. 13, 1971; *Houston Post*, Oct. 29, 1971; *New Yorker*, Oct. 9, 1971. Criticism was widely scattered; see *Louisville Courier-Journal*, Oct. 7, 1971; *St. Louis Post-Dispatch*, Oct. 17, 1971; *Cleveland Plain Dealer*, Oct. 14, 1971; *Memphis Commercial Appeal*, Oct. 16, 1971. There were numerous theatres that used the "Old West" theme advertisements; see, for example, *Montgomery Advertiser*, Nov. 5, 1971; *Wilmington* (Del.) *Evening Journal*, Oct. 22, 1971; *Miami Herald*, Oct. 23, 1971; *Atlanta Constitution*, Nov. 8, 1971; *Boise Idaho Daily Statesman*, Oct. 17, 1971; *Chicago Tribune*, Oct. 19, 1971; *Des Moines Register*, Oct. 17, 1971. The film, however, repeatedly refers to a Southern setting, see *The Skin Game* (Warner Brothers, 1971), LC-MPS.

Jeff East, Warren Oates, and Johnny Whitaker in *Tom Sawyer*.
BELOW: James Garner and Lou Gossett in *The Skin Game*.

by definition dehumanizing, unjust, a crime against man's natural rights. It was a system in which both black and white were trapped. But film provided no middle ground, no place to study the guilt, doubts, remorse, complex racial relationships, deep emotions, and even satisfactions of the participants. Film stated either that slavery was a justifiable, paternalistic institution which ennobled the master and depersonalized the slave, or that it was a vicious system in which the black found spiritual uplift in murder and mayhem and the white in depravity and miscegenation. Both were oversimplifications.

The productions of the 1930s were incorrect to make every planter a man of wealth whose benevolence earned the undying devotion of his simple slaves. It was just as wrong in the most recent pictures to make every black a budding Nat Turner in the face of a degenerate owner who sleeps with his workers' women, drinks to excess, and orders harsh punishments without hesitation. Small wonder there could be no majority sentiment expressed on the origins of the nation's racial crisis. The movies added to the dilemma.

Caught between the two extremes, the critics uniformly found both wanting. The contemporary domestic scene had convinced the last of the romanticists that it was sheer folly to hold onto the tenets of the supposedly glorious past. But current events also convinced the critics that presentday views were being imposed on long past historical situations. As films once asked for unquestioning admiration for the Old South's social order, the newest movies required, at times demanded, unwavering hatred of all things white and Southern. Knowing the former was unpalatable did not make the latter any easier to swallow.

As if making up for lost time, the tone of many films became so severely critical that the postwar South became more bizarre than it had been in the releases of the 50s and early 60s. It was as if it were not enough to attack the South of slavery. The post-Civil War South had been as racist and was as open to attack. There were few films which examined the South without a trace of bitterness or superiority. Film repeatedly provided audiences with the view that the South, not the nation, was responsible for the racial turmoil.

There were, however, a few more tasteful productions, such as

Sounder (1972), which heralded the plucky nature of Southern blacks in the Depression, or *Conrack* (1974), which followed the efforts of a sometimes overenthusiastic Dixie liberal as a teacher of black children. Some such as *The Flim-Flam Man* (1967) with George C. Scott or *W. W. and the Dixie Dance Kings* with Burt Reynolds were rollicking affairs which soft-pedalled incisive examinations into regional poverty, ignorance, bigotry, and fundamentalism.[63] Other Reynolds films such as *Gator* (1976) and *Smokey and the Bandit* (1978) used the Southern settings for exciting action or engaging humor. The local color "hick flicks" made their points in a far more subtle manner. But most still followed a far blunter course.

Racial animosity was violently presented in films like Otto Preminger's *Hurry Sundown* (1967), with Michael Caine as a Southerner so consumed by greed that he is willing to ruin both white and black alike. *The Klansman* (1974), which featured Lee Marvin and Richard Burton, was a tale of racial rape and murder. The reviewers finally saw such productions as no less overdone than those from the 30s. *Hurry Sundown* merited little critical praise, being regarded as "de Stereotyped South dat you and me done love since ol' Massa Caldwell and Faulkner done see all dat decay down yonder. . . ." The releases were perceived as less and

---

[63]*Sounder* was an enormously popular picture which some saw as a welcome relief from the "blaxploitation" productions. See *New York*, Oct. 2, 1971; *New York Times*, Oct. 15, 1972; *Variety*, Aug. 16, 1972; *New Yorker*, Sept. 30, 1972; *Newsweek*, Oct. 2, 1972; *Time*, Oct. 9, 1972. There was a minority which viewed it as "crude" and "sanctimonious"; see *New Republic*, Oct. 14, 1972; *Rolling Stone*, Jan. 18, 1973; *Village Voice*, Oct. 12, 1972; *Real Paper*, Dec. 27, 1972; *New York Times*, Nov. 12, 1972. *Conrack* as well merited wide support, but also earned its share of criticism for what some perceived to be a strong condescending tone; see *Variety*, Feb. 20, 1974; *Real Paper*, April 24, 1974; *New York Times*, March 28; April 21, 1974; *Rolling Stone*, April 11, 1974; *Village Voice*, April 18, 1974; *New Yorker*, March 11, 1974. *The Flim-Flam Man* was general enough to be reviewed as a bit of "Americana" rather than locked to a Southern setting; see *Time*, Sept. 1, 1967; *New York Daily News*, Aug. 23, 1967; *Variety*, July 12, 1967; *New York Post*, Aug. 23, 1967; *Village Voice*, Oct. 19, 1967. *W. W. and the Dixie Dance Kings* was inoffensive and "ebullient" to most; see *New York Times*, July 24, 1975.

less sincere, as only stories "facing up to one of the Deep South's many exploitable problems."[64] Many more pictures postulated that the region was characteristically violent. The violent films reached a peak with *Walking Tall* (1973), from which "anyone looking to set up a neighborhood vigilante group can get a good jolt of moral inspiration." Easily as nefarious was *Macon County Line* (1974), a story of a sheriff billed as one who "doesn't like punk kids, strangers, or smart alecks from up North." Though both films were "pitched at a mentality that finds roadside reading an intellectual labor," the two earned enormous profits.[65] The South was sinking deeper into a mire of stereotypes.

And there was to be more of the same. *The Chase* (1966), from a screenplay by Lillian Hellman, contained an excess of bigotry, adultery, and religious fanaticism. *Shanty Tramp* (1967) included the expected nubile sharecropper's daughter. *The Devil's Eight* (1969) unleashed a pardoned Southern chain gang in pursuit of bootleggers. *Buster and Billie* (1974) set out to assure the viewer that little had changed in the Georgia backwoods.[66] Others such as *The Last American Hero* (1973) stressed cars and booze as the

[64]For the poor response to *Hurry Sundown*, see *World Journal Tribune*, March 24, 1967; *Look*, April 14, 1967; *New York Post*, March 24, 1967; *Time*, March 31, 1967; *Newsweek*, March 31, 1967. Few reviewers praised the film; see *Variety*, Feb. 15, 1967; *New York Times*, Aug. 21, 1967. *The Klansman* fared little better; see *Variety*, Nov. 6, 1974; *New York Times*, Nov. 21 1974; *Time*, Nov. 25, 1974.

[65]For derogatory reviews of *Walking Tall*, see *Time*, May 21, 1973; *New York*, Feb. 18, 1974; *Village Voice*, Feb. 21, 1974; *New York Times*, Feb. 9, 1974. For complimentary reviews, see *Rolling Stone*, April 26, 1973; *Variety*, Feb. 28; Aug. 1, 1973. See also Studio Press Book, *Macon County Line* (1974), MOMA-FSC; *Variety*, April 24, 1974; *Time*, Oct. 14, 1974; *New York Times*, Jan. 16, 1975; *New York*, Dec. 9, 1974.

[66]For representative reviews of *The Chase*, see *Village Voice*, April 7, 1966; *New York Herald Tribune*, Feb. 19, 1966; *Variety*, Feb. 2, 1966; *Time*, Feb. 25, 1966. *The Devil's Eight* rarely even attracted critical attention; see *Variety*, March 14, 1969; *New York Post*, June 19, 1969. The same could be said for *Buster and Billie*; see *Time*, Sept. 16, 1974; *Variety*, June 12, 1974; *New York News*, Aug. 4, 1974.

main ingredients of the Southern rural scene like its predecessor, and now classic *Thunder Road* (1958).

More probing higher quality movies of the section such as the acclaimed *In the Heat of the Night* (1967), or *Deliverance* (1972), or releases of regional locale but national insights such as Robert Altman's *Nashville* (1975) or *Norma Rae* (1979) were too few to offset the damage that the highly exaggerated and less well-paced productions inflicted.

Physical force and stubbornness became characteristic of the region. It was thus an easy adaptation to create an Old South of like characteristics. With often the best of intentions, producers depicted the slave owners as sadistic, merciless bigots, made in the image of their modern white counterparts in film. As a result, not only were the whites as narrowly defined as they had always been in films of the antebellum years, but the blacks were as well—an often overlooked facet of the revisions in the haste and satisfaction of overturning the Hollywood legacy. Negroes were never to be condemned in the new films.[67] Their blemishes of character, if any, were accepted simply as the result of white injustice. Therefore, their virtues were not a product of free choice but of a personality awarded them by liberal cinematic propaganda. The conservatives such as Griffith, Pollard, Selznick, Vidor, and others had once shaped the same perfect character for the planter.

It was not that the producers were insincere; rather they were extremely eager to take a stand. Conditions made the filmmakers' views far easier to present without a studio censoring the product. Theatres faced declining attendance—brought about by factors ranging from competing pastimes such as television to the relocation of the population away from the cavernous urban movie houses—and by the 1950s Hollywood's studios were no longer the huge enterprises they had been. For example, in 1949 only 370 actors were under regular contract versus 750 in 1946.[68] Increasingly, the once proud companies found themselves distributing the creations of smaller independent producers. With

[67]For a broader discussion of the problem, see *Village Voice*, Aug. 17, 1967.
[68]Jowett, *Film*, 353.

the new found autonomy from corporate dictates, freedom of expression grew. The most outspoken statement of purpose was delivered by Kroger Babb, distributor of the European-made *Uncle Tom's Cabin* (1965/U.S. distribution, 1968). Perhaps full of righteous indignation that no American company had wanted to film the Stowe classic, Babb exclaimed that his version told "the story of slavery in the Deep South with amazing accuracy and tremendous spectacle," and that it also explained "what no teacher can." He added that such an important effort was "equally as entertaining and informative" for children as for adults, black and white.[69]

The producer of *Slaves* was no less enthusiastic about his film's lofty purpose. Phillip Langer proudly testified that "many liberal exhibitors in Northern cities" congratulated him on the picture, though he was shocked that some refused to show the film for fear of racial reactions. The actor Ossie Davis stressed the film's function, as it "not only has historical validity but is indirectly related to the problems of today." To add to the resoluteness of purpose, the earnest and committed Herbert J. Biberman, working on his first picture since his Hollywood blacklisting in 1954, served as the release's co-writer and director.[70]

Dino DeLaurentis was also convinced of his picture's strength of purpose. The executive producer's *Mandingo* and its sequel *Drum* were meant to reach "beyond the sentimentalized South of other films with uncompromising honesty and realism to show the true brutalizing nature of slavery. . . ." In reflecting on the planter, the actor Perry King remarked that his character could neither rise above nor even question the society which had so warped him. James Mason concurred, adding that *Mandingo* was "to enlighten the audience insofar as it exposes in dramatic terms the truth about slave labor and its adjunct, slave breeding."[71]

[69]Studio Press Book, *Uncle Tom's Cabin* (1965), LC-MPS Box C-32.

[70]*Pictures*, June 11, 1969; *New York Times*, Jan. 19; July 3, 1969; *Washington Post*, May 21, 1969; *Hartford* (Conn.) *Times*, July 10, 1969; *Baltimore Sun*, May 4, 1969. See also Studio Press Book, *Slaves* (1969), LC-MPS Box C-16.

[71]Studio Press Book, *Mandingo* (1975), LC-MPS Box C-90. See also *Atlanta Constitution*, May 5, 1975; *Chicago Tribune*, May 25, 1975.

Perry King and Ken Norton in *Mandingo*.

Unfortunately the film companies diminished whatever significance their films might have had by resorting to the most sensational advertising techniques. The advertisements were obviously intended to attract not an audience receptive to new ideas but one eager for exciting visual entertainment. It was no accident that the movies were rated "R" or "X." The poster for *Uncle Tom's Cabin*, for example, was dominated by a very scantily clad slave girl in the eager clutches of Simon Legree. Worse, whatever sorrow one experienced at the hanging of the slave Andy or the maiming of Napoleon by an alligator was demeaned in calls to "Come along . . . swing with Andy . . . swim with Napoleon!" And a movie which in the same advertising could exhort the prospective ticket buyer to "have fun, dance with the Natchez folks, sing with Uncle Tom," while also calling one to "see the bull-whipping of black females" hardly deserved thoughtful consideration.[72]

The bulletins for *Slaves* were as disappointing in maintaining the tone of purpose the actors and producers insisted was there. The most commonly used poster depicted the master Stephen Boyd with an open shirt and an unmistakable look, with his nude black mistress, Dionne Warwick, standing before him. Some newspapers were compelled to cover her figure. Captions ranged from "desire knew no color in the savage world of the Old South" to "See! Feel! Taste! The Bloody Whip of Truth" in a picture which "rips through the moonlight and magnolias to give the blistering passion."[73]

Mandingo was most blunt in its contrast to earlier films by utilizing the poster motif of the rereleases of *Gone With the Wind*. The studio hired the same artist who had painted the *GWTW* advertisement, showing Rhett carrying a reclining Scarlett, and disseminated the poster widely. In the same style, the new work

[72]*Uncle Tom's Cabin* (1965) Poster, LC-PPD; see also Studio Press Book, LC-MPS Box C-32.

[73]Local captions varied widely, but the tenor remained the same; see, for example, *Birmingham News*, July 30, 1969; *Richmond Times-Dispatch*, July 30, 1969; *Baltimore Sun*, June 1, 1969; *Albuquerque Journal*, July 29, 1969; *Newark Star-Ledger*, July 16, 1969; *Philadelphia Inquirer*, July 11, 1969; *Nashville Banner*, July 18, 1969; *Milwaukee Journal*, Aug. 6, 1969.

portrayed the master carrying his black concubine while his favorite slave bore his master's wife. The bulletin's wording was no less explicit. The viewer was warned to "expect the savage, the sensual, the shocking," to be prepared for "all that the motion picture screen has never dared to show before—expect the truth."[74] The hyperbole for *Drum* rivalled that of its predecessor, for after all—as the advertisements stated—it "out-Mandingoes *Mandingo*." Promises that "it scalds, it shocks, it whips, it bleeds, it lusts" maintained a steady business.[75] *The Quadroon* (1971) held out the excitement of "one quarter black, three quarters white, all woman."[76] *Passion Plantation* (1978), where "your real roots were," promised that "anything could happen."

The emphasis on multi-racial sex was one ploy to draw customers, but once seated within the theatre the audience discovered the heavy-handed story line was hardly conducive to reasoned reflection. For example, in *Slaves* the master in a pique of anger endangers the life of one of his slave women in childbirth.[77] Certainly, some owners may have been so ignorant and unfeeling. But, for economic if not humanitarian reasons, the action was a poor example of the usual type of cruelty inflicted. To embellish the horrors of bondage not only called into question the accuracy of the individual act but jeopardized the veracity of the overall interpretation.

In *Mandingo*, James Mason resided at Falconhurst—a seedy plantation which in appearance belittled the myth of planter munificence. The point was well made in light of the repeated finery in earlier films. But the significance was lost, as every other homesite overflowed with wealth, from the huge country mansions to the fine New Orleans houses.[78] The sequel, *Drum*, in fact, was set amongst the finest structure yet seen in a movie of the prewar setting.

[74]*Mandingo* (1975) Poster, LC-PPD.

[75]See *New Orleans Times-Picayune*, Aug. 10, 1976; *Boston Globe*, Aug. 20, 1976; *Minneapolis Star*, Aug. 9, 1976; *Omaha World Herald*, Aug. 20, 1976; *Charlotte Observor*, Aug. 13, 1976.

[76]See, for example, *Atlanta Constitution*, Oct. 22, 1971.

[77]Synopsis, *Slaves* (1969), LC-MPS Box C-16.

[78]*Mandingo* (Paramount, 1975), LC-MPS.

James Mason in *Mandingo*.

Granted, the importance of the films rested not in their complete accuracy, but the repeated omissions or unreasonable assumptions once combined did detract from the message. At other times, the message was hammered home relentlessly. In *Mandingo*, for instance, the slave market of degraded capitalism and brutal whippings was appropriately dubbed "Price and Birch."

As attempts to rectify the industry's past romanticism, the productions were in earnest. The producers, directors, script writers, and actors delved into racial themes with obvious liberal political leanings and moral commitments. That made their failure all the more regrettable. Critics who banded together at long last to decry the conservative nature of such films as *Gone With the Wind*, reissued in 1967, 1971, 1974, and 1976, were greatly disappointed that the liberal revisionists had fallen into the same errors of distortion practiced so assiduously by their predecessors. Griffith's concept of white nobility and black bestiality had simply been reversed.

As a "mawkish, cliched piece of drivel," *Slaves* disappointed many who realized that its hopes and ambitions had been as great as the need. Instead, the picture was generally received as either "a horrendous boxoffice exploitation of a horrendous historical exploitation," or as a "cinematic carpetbagging project in which some contemporary moviemakers have . . . attempted to impose . . . their own attitudes that will explain 1969 black militancy." What frightened many about *Slaves* was the lesson in what was obviously a rewritten form of Harriet Beecher Stowe's *Uncle Tom's Cabin*. The gentle, obedient servant in the end brought about rebellion. The inference that violence was a traditional and successful means of altering one's status within a society was a dangerous doctrine, especially after the previous two decades of ghetto riots.[79]

[79]For a sampling of the wideranging attacks, see *Denver Post*, June 16, 1969; *Wilmington* (Del.) *Evening Journal*, July 5, 1969; *Atlanta Constitution*, June 24, 1969; *Chicago Tribune*, July 1, 1969; *Christian Science Monitor*, July 28, 1969; *Hartford* (Conn.) *Times*, July 10, 1969; *Louisville Courier-Journal*, Aug. 9, 1969; *Boston Globe*, July 17, 1969; *Detroit Free Press*, July 4, 1969; *Charlotte Observer*, Aug. 22, 1969; *New York Times*, July 3, 1969; *Film Daily*,

Mandingo fared no better critically. It was taken as a racist "conspiracy of depraved minds" who produced nothing more than "the most salacious miscegenation-inspired sex fantasies."[80] The interracial sex, nudity, and murders were equally as offensive in *Drum*, a film "less interested in information than titillation, which, in turn, reflects contemporary obsessions rather more than historical truths."[81]

It was time the slave persona was given his due measure of nobility and human emotion, but the productions went too far in creating another character just as unbelievable as the initial ones. Just as all antebellum blacks did not fall within the characterizations given by Clarence Muse, Bill Robinson, Eddie Anderson,

---

June 27, 1969. Reviews in praise of the film were quite rare; see *Cleveland Plain Dealer*, May 14, 1969; *Variety*, May 7, 1969.

[80]The production was viciously criticized; see, for example, *Variety*, May 7, 1975; *Washington Post*, May 21, 1975; *Richmond Times-Dispatch*, May 22, 1975; *Montgomery Advertiser*, July 20, 1975; *Los Angeles Times*, May 22, 1975; *San Francisco Chronicle*, May 22, 1975; *Hartford* (Conn.) *Times*, May 31, 1975; *Miami Herald*, May 27, 1975; *Atlanta Journal*, May 28, 1975; *Chicago Tribune*, June 2, 1975; *Christian Science Monitor*, May 8, 1975; *Louisville Courier-Journal*, May 29, 1975; *Boston Globe*, May 22, 1975; *Detroit Free Press*, May 26, 1975; *St. Louis Post-Dispatch*, June 1, 1975; *Omaha World Herald*, May 28, 1975; *Charlotte Observor*, May 29, 1975; *Cleveland Plain Dealer*, June 5, 1975; *Newark Star-Ledger*, June 1, 1975; *Portland Oregon Journal*, May 23, 1975; *Seattle Post-Intelligencer*, May 25, 1975; *Philadelphia Inquirer*, May 23, 1975; *Providence* (R.I.) *Journal*, June 1, 1975; *Memphis Commercial Appeal*, May 22, 1975; *Milwaukee Journal*, May 25, 1975; *Charleston* (S.C.) *News and Courier*, May 25, 1975; *Pittsburgh Press*, May 29, 1975; *New York Post*, May 8, 1975; *Real Paper*, June 4, 1975; *New York Times*, May 8, 1975; *Village Voice*, May 26, 1975.

[81]The reviews were uniformly bad; see *Variety*, Aug. 4, 1976; *New York Times*, July 31, 1976; *Washington Post*, Aug. 11, 1976; *New Orleans Times-Picayune*, Aug. 10, 1976; *Chicago Tribune*, Aug. 20, 1976; *Los Angeles Times*, Aug. 4, 1976; *Boston Globe*, Aug. 21, 1976; *Cleveland Plain Dealer*, Aug. 14, 1976; *Newark Star-Ledger*, Aug. 2, 1976; *Portland Oregon Journal*, Aug. 27, 1976; *Seattle Post-Intelligencer*, Aug. 17, 1976; *Philadelphia Inquirer*, Aug. 16, 1976; *Providence* (R.I.) *Journal*, Aug. 28, 1976; *Memphis Commercial Appeal*, Aug. 22, 1976; *Houston Post*, Aug. 9, 1976; *Dallas Morning News*, Aug. 15, 1976; *Charleston* (S.C.) *News and Courier*, Nov. 6, 1976.

or Stepin Fetchit, neither did they conveniently conform to the rebellious stud portrayals given by Ken Norton or Yaphet Kotto.

And neither did Clark Gable, Randolph Scott, Henry Walthall, George Brent, or Bing Crosby as gallant gentlemen in ruffled shirts capture any better the essence of Southern manhood than did Stephen Boyd, James Mason, Warren Oates, or John Colicos as sadists, degenerates, and fops.

Both views suffered from the common deficiency of oversimplification made so apparent from the adaptations of *Uncle Tom's Cabin* in 1903 or 1927 to those of 1965 and 1969. And as *Gone With the Wind* was a story of white people among black, so the newer films were not a story of black-white relations, but of blacks among whites. No film thus far has adequately utilized both races as equally central to the theme of slavery.

In the rush to romanticize or to destroy, the collective body of cinema all but totally ignored the complexities of the South and the institution of slavery. To state that slavery was indeed a viable institution is a necessary admission which does not defend bondage, but rather surrenders to the realization that it cannot be examined from either a white or a black perspective alone. The history of the South has too easily discredited the assumption that either race can live apart from the other.

Of course, motion pictures did not create the racial problems so much a part of the contemporary scene, but cinema shared a large responsibility for confirming and reinforcing the beliefs for so many. For sixty years the popular culture bolstered society's concept of the Negro and salved any guilt by showing white kindness and concern for the simple workers who were expected to remain grateful and loyal for the attentions bestowed upon them. It was a relationship confirmed again and again. Sometimes it was no doubt intentional, as in *His Trust Fulfilled, Birth of a Nation,* or *Topsy and Eva.* At other times it was accomplished more innocently, as in *Hearts in Dixie, Mississippi,* or *Jezebel.* And when the opportunity finally arose for productions which could destroy the old mythology, it was no surprise that they too reflected the emotional themes of their period, and as bitterly—though justifiably expected—as did D. W. Griffith in *Birth of a Nation.*

And through all the praise and denunciations, the images of

the white Southerner had been carried along also, sometimes quite willingly as in *So Red the Rose*, and at other times with trepidation as in *Drum*. The white Southerner had been represented by every sort of character, from the perennial colonel, Lionel Barrymore, to the superstitious slave breeder, James Mason.

But ironically whatever the image, benign or evil, the cinema insured that the South was a distinct section which drew unrelenting curiosity. The Old South survived if not in reality, then at least in the popular imagination. Despite the growth of urban centers and heavy industry in the region, despite the disappearance of an overwhelming reliance on the land, despite the change in population patterns diluting the section's traditional peoples, and despite the national rather than sectional slant of everything from television to advertising, the South has remained and will remain a section apart, established and sustained for better or worse by a popular culture of film. The survival of the South in the popular imagination owes more to the cinema than any other force.

Those films have exposed much of what the nation as a whole has believed about contemporary problems addressed in the movies—the racial hierarchy, economic hard times, the role of the family, and the agrarian lifestyle versus an industrial society. The same films exposed much that was wrong in contemporary America too. As social documents without parallel for their popularity, films over the next decades will reveal the long awaited changes in American society that the earliest films sought to prevent.

Afterword

The romantic themes of films set in the Old South proved popular for decades. More than just popular though, movies like *Hearts in Dixie* or *Jezebel* were escapes, entertainment seemingly without taint. Actually, the films did much to reinforce a conservative strain within the general public.

The productions of the 1920s, the 1930s, even the 1940s, simply did not attempt to change the audiences' perceptions concerning the South's distinct problems. Those dilemmas had in some cases become of national importance. In particular, the racist assumptions of Hollywood's plantation stories were accepted as fact by the viewers and forestalled any attitudinal change. It took protests and violence to do that.

Film in its heyday was not the medium for change, however. The motion picture industry in its quest for profit was understandably not obsessed with social transformation on a regular basis. Movies such as Shirley Temple's *The Little Colonel* and *The Littlest Rebel*, or *Gone With the Wind*, even *The Foxes of Harrow* and *Raintree County* involved audiences with their favorite stars, attractive settings, and romantic plots.

It was not until the post-1945 period that Hollywood more frequently and assiduously attempted to arouse a new social consciousness. Seeking renewed attendance in the face of competing entertainment options like television and beset with altered demographics, the industry turned with significantly increased interest to new views of old subjects. The plantation South was, in fact, only one of many themes reinterpreted.

John Ford's *The Searchers* (1956), for example, starkly explored the mythology of the white man's settlement of the

West, whereas John Huston's direction of *The Misfits* (1961) exposed much of the contemporary region. War, often glorified, was by the late 40s under reexamination. *The Best Years of Our Lives* (1946) discussed the serviceman's difficult readjustment to civilian life. Stanley Kubrick's *Paths of Glory* (1957) was as much anti-militarist as anti-war.

Other films presented a life far from the carefree musicals, comedies and other light fare which filled the Depression-era theatres. *Marty* (1955) was set around ordinary, almost mundane, human situations. Director Elia Kazan's *Pinky* (1949), *On the Waterfront* (1954), and *East of Eden* (1955) pitted the individual against his physical and psychological environment.

Thus the later films of the antebellum South such as *Band of Angels* were part of an overall reevaluation within cinema rather than a concerted effort to rectify that genre's interpretation alone.

But despite the overwhelming need for a reappraisal, relatively little attention has been paid to the prewar South when compared with the attention given other subjects. Since the late 60s, the major film productions include only *Uncle Tom's Cabin, Slaves, The Quadroon, Skin Game, Mandingo, Drum,* and *Passion Plantation.* The television networks, frequently presenting made-for-TV motion pictures, have released only a few also, for example *The Autobiography of Miss Jane Pittman* (1974), *Roots* (1977), *Roots: The Next Generations* (1979), and *Freedom Road* (1979), none of which included an extended view of the mid-1800's plantation setting.[1]

The debate over the multi-part television adaptation of the

---

[1] *The Autobiography of Miss Jane Pittman* was generally well received; see *New York Times*, Jan. 31; Feb. 10; March 3, 1974. The critical and popular response to *Roots* was considerable; see *New York Times*, Jan. 21, 23, 26, 28; Feb. 2, 3, 5, 8, 9, 10, 20, 25, 27; March 6, 19, 20; June 7; July 19, 1977. For the reaction to the continuation, *Roots: The Next Generations*, see *New York Times*, Feb. 15, 16, 18, 20, 21, 25, 28; March 8, 18, 1979; *New Yorker*, March 26, 1979; *Time*, Feb. 19, 1979; *Newsweek*, Feb. 19, 1979; *Encore*, Feb. 5, 1979. For a sampling of the public reaction to *Freedom Road*, see *New York Times*, Oct. 28, 29, 30, 1979; *Encore*, Oct. 15, 1979.

novel *Beulah Land* well demonstrates the problems involved in further examinations of the antebellum South. The production has been attacked by such organizations as the National Urban League as at best a reactionary interpretation.[2] The stereotypes, the bad associations brought to mind, are volatile subjects still. Whereas *Freedom Road* addresses the black strivings for economic and individual freedom, a production like *Beulah Land* persists in interpreting slavery as a benign institution. Both make large segments of the population uncomfortable.

The Old South as a topic for film is thus disappearing and is being supplanted by the "hick flicks." These less offensive films draw their origins from television series such as *Andy Griffith, Mayberry R.F.D., Petticoat Junction,* and *The Beverly Hillbillies* and movies such as the *Ma and Pa Kettle* series at one extreme and *Thunder Road* at the other.

The productions include the attractions of the Old South romances without quite the prejudice of the antebellum plots. The problem of race is subordinated, but the region's supposedly strong claim to independence and individualism is sustained in films of truckers, moonshiners, and forthright country folk. And if the images of wealth are to be sacrificed too, then perhaps contemporary audiences can better relate to the "down-home" characters than the rich planters once so attractive in early film or the 1930s but now somewhat embarrassing and jaded in a period of diminishing expectations and increased awareness of the legacy of slavery and racism.

Thus the mythology is being adapted to the times. The productions in theme are still rural, free-wheeling, rollicking, sometimes touchingly romantic; the land is still unspoiled and unique. *The Waltons, Carter Country, Sheriff Lobo, Palmerstown USA,* the *Dukes of Hazzard* pit the average man, white or black, against those who would infringe upon his inherent Southern values. The stance is no different from the gentlemen's dinner conversations in *Jezebel, Gone With the Wind, Raintree County,*

[2]For an analysis of the protest against the interpretation of *Beulah Land*, see *Panorama*, May, 1980. See also *Time*, March 10, 1980; *Variety*, July 2, 1980; *TV Guide*, April 22, 1980.

and countless other films. Now the debate is carried on in a more common atmosphere; witness the Burt Reynolds characterizations in *Smokey and the Bandit, Gator, White Lightnin'*, and *W. W. and the Dixie Dance Kings*.[3] The mythology survives, only the trappings have changed.

[3]For a broad examination of the contemporary, rural Southern setting in film, see Richard Thompson, "What's Your 10-20?" *Film Comment* 16 (July-Aug. 1980), 34-42.

Bibliography

Films

The following is a list of films which were of particular use to the study. The list does not include every motion picture screened or script read. Many films used to study the general theatre offerings of a specific period have been omitted, and thus the filmography includes only those pictures referred to directly in the text.

Not all the films listed are readily available. Though most are included in the collections of the Library of Congress, the Museum of Modern Art, and the International Museum of Photography/George Eastman House, other pictures may be procured only by rental. A few films were viewed in public theatres or on television. Some productions, especially silent films, are simply too difficult to locate. Some productions no longer even exist. In such cases, scripts, outlines, reviews, and stills are necessary means of research.

For each title, research whenever possible included a studio's publicity publications, souvenir booklets, stills, advertising posters and lobby cards, dialogue and cutting continuities, and trade announcements.

Adventures of Huckleberry Finn, The (1960)
Adventures of Tom Sawyer, The (1938)
All the King's Men (1949)
Angel Baby (1961)
Another Part of the Forest (1948)
Autobiography of Miss Jane Pittman, The (1974)
Baby Doll, (1956)
Band of Angels (1957)
Banjo on My Knee (1936)
Battle, The (1911)
Birth of a Nation, The (1915)

Black Like Me (1964)
Bride of Hate, The (1916)
Bright Leaf (1950)
Broken Chains (1916)
Buster and Billie (1974)
Cabin in the Cotton (1932)
Can This Be Dixie? (1936)
Cape Fear (1962)
Carolina (1934)
Cat on a Hot Tin Roof (1958)
Chase, The (1966)
Claudelle Inglish (1961)
Colonel Carter of Cartersville
  (1915)
Common Law Wife (1963)
Confederate Spy, The (1910)
Conrack (1974)
Cool Hand Luke (1967)
Cotton Pickin' Days (1930)
Coward, The (1915)
Debt, The (1912)
Defiant Ones, The (1958)
Deliverance (1972)
Desire in the Dust (1960)
Devil's Eight, The (1969)
Dixiana (1930)
Dixie (1924)
Dixie (1929)
Dixie (1943)
Dixie Days (1928)
Drum (1976)
Duel on the Mississippi (1955)
Fighting Coward, The (1924)
Flag of Two Wars, A (n.d., si-
  lent)
Flame of New Orleans, The
  (1941)
Flim-Flam Man, The (1967)
For Massa's Sake (1911)
Foxes of Harrow, The (1947)
Free and Equal (1915)
Freedom Road (1979)

Fugitive Kind, The (1960)
Gambler From Natchez, The
  (1954)
God's Little Acre (1958)
Gone Are the Days (1963)
Gone With the Wind (1939)
Guerrilla, The (1908)
Hallelujah (1929)
Harmony Lane (1935)
Hearts and Flags (1911)
Hearts in Dixie (1929)
His Trust (1911)
His Trust Fulfilled (1911)
Honor of His Family, The (1909)
Hot Spell (1958)
House With the Closed Shutters,
  The (1910)
Huck and Tom (1918)
Huckleberry Finn (1920, 1931,
  1939)
Hurry Sundown (1967)
I Am a Fugitive From a Chain
  Gang (1932)
In Humanity's Cause (1911)
In Old Kentucky (1909)
In Old Kentucky (1935)
In Slavery Days (1913)
In the Heat of the Night (1967)
Informer, The (1912)
Inherit the Wind (1960)
Intruder, The (1962)
Intruder in the Dust (1949)
Jezebel (1938)
Judge Priest (1934)
Kentucky (1938)
Klansman, The (1974)
Lady From Louisiana (1941)
Lady's From Kentucky, The
  (1939)
Last American Hero, The (1973)
Lion is in the Streets, A (1953)
Little Colonel, The (1935)

Little Eva Ascends (1922)
Little Foxes, The (1941)
Littlest Rebel, The (1935)
Long Hot Summer, The (1958)
Love Mart, The (1927)
Macon County Line (1974)
Mammy's Ghost (c. 1911)
Mandingo (1975)
Maryland (1940)
Mississippi (1935)
Mississippi Gambler, The (1929)
Mississippi Gambler, The (1953)
My Old Kentucky Home (1938)
Nashville (1975)
Night in Dixie (c. 1930)
Norma Rae (1979)
Nothing But a Man (1964)
Old Mammy's Charge (1913)
Old Oak's Secret, The (1914)
Old South, The (1932)
Passion Plantation (1978)
Pinky (1949)
Planter's Wife, The (1909)
Quadroon, The (1971)
Rainbow on the River (1936)
Raintree County (1957)
Reconstructed Rebel, A (c. 1913)
Reivers, The (1969)
River of Romance (1929)
Romance of Rosy Ridge, The (1947)
Roots (1977)
Roots II (1979)
Sanctuary (1961)
Saratoga Trunk (1945)
Shanty Tramp (1967)
Shenandoah (1965)
Showboat (1936, 1951)
Skin Game (1971)
Slaves (1969)
Slave Days (c. 1929)
Slave's Devotion, A (n.d., silent)

Smokey and the Bandit (1978)
So Red the Rose (1935)
Song of the South (1946)
Sound and the Fury, The (1959)
Sounder (1972)
Southerner, The (1945)
Special Messenger, A (1911)
Steamboat 'Round the Bend (1935)
Story of Temple Drake, The (1933)
Streetcar Named Desire, A (1951)
Suddenly Last Summer (1959)
Summer and Smoke (1961)
Sun Shines Bright, The (1954)
Swamp Water (1941)
Swamp Woman (1941)
Swamp Women (1956)
Swanee River (1939)
Sweet Bird of Youth (1962)
They Won't Forget (1937)
Thunder Road (1958)
To Kill a Mockingbird (1963)
Toast of New Orleans, The (1950)
Tobacco Road (1941)
Tom Sawyer (1917, 1930, 1973)
Topsy and Eva (1927)
Toys in the Attic (1963)
True to Their Colors (n.d., silent)
Uncle Peter's Ruse (n.d., silent)
Uncle Tom's Cabin (1903, 1909, 1913, 1914, 1918, 1927, 1958, 1965)
Uncle Tom's Gal (1925)
Uncle Tom's Uncle (1926)
Vanishing Virginian, The (1941)
Virginia (1941)
W. W. and the Dixie Dance Kings (1975)

Walking Tall (1973)
Way Down South (1939)
When Do We Eat? (1918)
White Rose, The (1923)

White Trash on Moonshine
    Mountain (1964)
Wild River (1960)
Young One, The (1961)

Newspapers and Other Periodicals

A wide sampling of newspapers was an integral part of the overview. Whereas each studio's trade and public advertising revealed a production company's perception of the product, the newspapers often furnished another view. The publications revealed inter- and intra-sectional responses in addition to the changes or continuity over time in the impressions of individual critics and audiences.

Secondary Sources

Arvidson, Linda. "How Griffith Came to Make *The Birth of a Nation*." In *Focus on D. W. Griffith*, 80-83. Ed. by Harry Geduld. Englewood Cliffs, N.J.: Prentice-Hall, 1971.

Barnouw, Erik. *Tube of Plenty: The Evolution of American Television*. New York: Oxford Univ. Press, 1975.

Behlmer, Rudy, ed. *Memo From David O. Selznick*. New York: Viking, 1972.

Benchley, Robert. "*Hearts in Dixie*, The First Real Talking Picture." In *The Black Man on Film: Racial Stereotyping*, 46-48. Ed. by Richard A. Maynard. Rochelle Park: Hayden, 1974.

Bergman, Andrew. *We're in the Money: Depression America and Its Films*. New York: New York Univ. Press, 1971.

Bloomfield, Maxwell. "Dixon's *The Leopard Spots*: A Study in Popular Racism." *American Quarterly* 16 (Fall 1964): 387-401.

Bogle, Donald. *Toms, Coons, Mulattoes, Mammies and Bucks: An Interpretive History of Blacks in American Films*. New York: Viking, 1973.

Braudy, Leo. *The World in a Frame: What We See in Films*. Garden City, N.Y.: Anchor, 1977.

Buck, Paul. *The Road to Reunion, 1865-1900.* Boston: Little, Brown, 1937.

Carter, Everett. "Cultural History Written With Lightning: The Significance of *The Birth of a Nation.*" In *Focus on The Birth of a Nation*, 133-43. Ed. by Fred Silva. Englewood Cliffs, N.J.: Prentice-Hall, 1971.

Cash, Wilbur J. *The Mind of the South.* New York: Knopf, 1941.

Cook, Raymond A. *Fire From the Flint: The Amazing Careers of Thomas Dixon.* Winston-Salem: Blair, 1968.

————. "The Man Behind *The Birth of a Nation.*" *North Carolina Historical Review* 29 (Oct. 1962): 519-23.

Cotterill, R. S. *The Old South.* Glendale: Clark, 1936.

Cowan, Louise. *The Fugitive Group: A Literary History.* Baton Rouge: LSU Press, 1959.

Craven, Avery O. *The Growth of Southern Nationalism, 1848-1861.* Baton Rouge: LSU Press, 1953.

Cripps, Thomas J. "The Myth of the Southern Box Office: A Factor in Racial Stereotyping in American Movies, 1920-1940." In *The Black Experience in America, Selected Essays,* 116-44. Ed. by James C. Curtis and Louis L. Gould. Austin: Univ. of Texas Press, 1970.

————. "The Reaction of the Negro to the Motion Picture *Birth of a Nation.*" *Historian* 25 (May 1963): 244-62.

————. *Slow Fade to Black: The Negro in American Film, 1900-1942.* New York: Oxford Univ. Press, 1977.

Davenport, F. Gavin, Jr. "Thomas Dixon's Mythology of Southern History." *Journal of Southern History* 26 (Aug. 1970): 350-67.

Dodd, William E. *The Cotton Kingdom: A Chronicle of the Old South.* New Haven: Yale Univ. Press, 1919.

Eaton, Clement. *The Growth of Southern Civilization, 1790-1860.* New York: Harper, 1961.

Farr, Fenis. *Margaret Mitchell of Atlanta.* New York: Morrow, 1965.

Femin, George N. and Everson, William K. *The Western: From Silents to the Seventies.* New York: Penguin, 1977.

Ferro, Marc. "The Fiction Film and Historical Analysis." In *The Historian and Film*, 80-94. Ed. by Paul Smith. New York: Cambridge Univ. Press, 1976.

Field, Mary. "Making the Past Live: Inaccuracy in Historical Films." *Sight and Sound* 4 (Fall 1935): 132-34.

Flamini, Roland. *Scarlett, Rhett and a Cast of Thousands: The Filming of Gone With the Wind*. New York: Macmillan, 1975.

French, Philip. *Westerns: Aspects of a Movie Genre*. New York: Oxford Univ. Press, 1977.

Gaines, Francis P. *The Southern Plantation: A Study in the Development and Accuracy of a Tradition*. Gloucester: Smith, 1962.

Gaston, Paul. *New South Creed: A Study in Southern Mythmaking*. New York: Knopf, 1970.

Gray, Lewis C. *History of Agriculture in the Southern United States to 1860*. New York: Smith, 1941.

Gray, Richard. *The Literature of Memory: Modern Writers of the American South*. Baltimore: Johns Hopkins Univ. Press, 1977.

Hackett, Alice P., comp. *Seventy Years of Best Sellers, 1895-1965*. New York: Octagon, 1967.

Harwell, Richard B., ed. *GWTW: The Screenplay*. New York: Macmillan, 1980.

————, ed. *Margaret Mitchell's Gone With the Wind Letters, 1936-1949*. New York: Macmillan, 1976.

————, ed. "Technical Adviser: The Making of *Gone With the Wind*, The Hollywood Journals of Wilbur G. Kurtz." *Atlanta Historical Journal* 22 (Summer 1978): 7-131.

Henderson, Robert M. *D. W. Griffith: His Life and Work*. New York: Oxford Univ. Press, 1972.

————. *D. W. Griffith: The Years at Biograph*. New York: Farrar, Straus & Giroux, 1970.

Higham, Charles. *The Art of American Film*. New York: Anchor, 1974.

Hobson, Fred C., Jr. *Serpent in Eden: H. L. Mencken and the South*. Chapel Hill: Univ. of North Carolina Press, 1974.

Hubbell, Jay B. *The South in American Literature, 1607-1900*. Durham: Duke Univ. Press, 1954.

————. *Southern Life in Fiction*. Athens: Univ. of Georgia Press, 1960.

Jowett, Garth. *Film: The Democratic Art*. Boston: Little, Brown, 1976.

Karanikas, Alexander. *Tillers of a Myth: Southern Agrarians as Social and Literary Critics.* Madison: Univ. of Wisconsin Press, 1966.

Kirby, Jack T. *Media-Made Dixie: The South in the American Imagination.* Baton Rouge: LSU Press, 1978.

Koppes, Clayton and Black, Gregory D. "What to Show the World: The Office of War Information and Hollywood, 1942-1945." *Journal of American History* 64 (June 1977): 87-105.

Lambert, Gavin. *GWTW: The Making of Gone With the Wind.* Boston: Little, Brown, 1973.

Leab, Daniel J. "The Gamut From A to B: The Image of the Black in Pre-1915 Movies." *Political Science Quarterly* 88 (March 1973): 53-70.

Levine, Lawrence. *Black Culture and Black Consciousness: Afro-American Folk Thought From Slavery to Freedom.* New York: Oxford Univ. Press, 1977.

Link, Arthur. *Wilson: The New Freedom.* Princeton: Princeton Univ. Press, 1956.

McConnell, Frank D. *The Spoken Seen: Film and the Romantic Imagination.* Baltimore: Johns Hopkins Univ. Press, 1975.

Merritt, Russell. "Dixon, Griffith, and the Southern Legend." *Cinema Journal* 12 (Fall 1972): 26-45.

Munden, Kenneth, ed. *The American Film Institute Catalogue of Motion Pictures Produced in the United States: Feature Films, 1921-1930.* New York: AFI, 1971.

Noble, Peter. *The Negro in Films.* New York: Arno, 1970.

Owens, Leslie H. *This Species of Property: Slave Life and Culture in the Old South.* New York: Oxford Univ. Press, 1976.

Phillips, Ulrich B. *Life and Labor in the Old South.* Boston: Little, Brown, 1929.

————. *The Slave Economy of the Old South: Selected Essays in Economic and Social History.* Ed. by Eugene D. Genovese. Baton Rouge: LSU Press, 1968.

Pines, Jim. *Blacks in Films: A Survey of Racial Themes and Images in the American Film.* London: Studio Vista, 1975.

Powdermaker, Hortense. *Hollywood, the Dream Factory: An Anthropologist Looks at the Movie Makers.* Boston: Little, Brown, 1950.

Pressly, Thomas J. *Americans Interpret Their Civil War.* New York: Free Press, 1965.

Reid, Rachel. "What Historians Want." *Sight and Sound* 11 (Summer 1942): 23-24.

Rubin, Louis D., Jr. "The Historical Image of Modern Southern Writing." *Journal of Southern History* 12 (May 1956): 147-66.

————. *The Faraway Country: Writers of the Modern South.* Seattle: Univ. of Washington Press, 1963.

————, ed. *I'll Take My Stand: The South and the Agrarian Tradition.* New York: Harper, 1962.

————. "Southern Literature: A Piedmont Art." *Mississippi Quarterly* 23 (Winter 1969-70): 1-18.

———— and Jacobs, Robert D., ed. *Southern Renascence: The Literature of the Modern South.* Baltimore: Johns Hopkins Univ. Press, 1953.

————. *The Wary Fugitives: Four Poets and the South.* Baton Rouge: LSU Press, 1978.

Sheed, Wilfred. "Milking the Elk." *New York Review of Books* 23 (April 15, 1976): 33-35.

Simkins, Francis B. *A History of the Old South.* New York: Knopf, 1953.

Sklar, Robert. *Movie-Made America: A Social History of the American Movies.* New York: Random House, 1975.

Soderbergh, Peter A. "Hollywood and the South, 1930-1960." *Mississippi Quarterly* 19 (Winter 1965-66): 1-19.

Spehr, Paul, comp. *The Civil War in Motion Pictures: A Bibliography of Films Produced in the United States Since 1897.* Washington: Govt. Printing Office, 1961.

Stampp, Kenneth M. *The Peculiar Institution: Slavery in the Ante-Bellum South.* New York: Knopf, 1956.

Stern, Seymour. "Griffith: *The Birth of a Nation.*" *Film Culture* 36 (Spring-Summer 1965): Special Issue.

Steward, John L. *The Burden of Time: The Fugitives and Agrarians.* Princeton: Princeton Univ. Press, 1965.

Sullivan, Walter, ed. *Death by Melancholy: Essays on Modern Southern Fiction.* Baton Rouge: LSU Press, 1972.

Thomas, Bob. *Selznick.* New York: Doubleday, 1970.

Thompson, Richard. "What's Your 10-20?" *Film Comment* 16 (July-Aug. 1980): 34-42.

Thomson, David. *America in the Dark: Hollywood and the Gift of Unreality.* New York: Morrow, 1977.

Tindall, George B. *The Emergence of the New South, 1913-1945.* Baton Rouge: LSU Press, 1967.

Toll, Robert C. *Blacking Up: The Minstrel Show in Nineteenth-Century America.* New York: Oxford Univ. Press, 1974.

Van Auken, Sheldon. "The Southern Historical Novel in the Early Twentieth Century." *Journal of Southern History* 14 (May 1948): 157-91.

Van Den Ecker, Louis. "A Veteran's View of Hollywood Authenticity." *Hollywood Quarterly* 4 (Summer 1950): 323-31.

Winkler, Allan M. *The Politics of Propaganda: The Office of War Information, 1942-1945.* New Haven: Yale Univ. Press, 1978.

Wood, Michael. *America in the Movies, or Santa Maria It Had Slipped My Mind.* New York: Basic, 1975.

Index

Index

Index

Index

Index

212

The Celluloid South

was composed on the Variable Input Phototypesetter in eleven-point Garamond with one-point line spacing. Bookman Italic was selected for display. The book was designed by Jim Billingsley, set into type by Computer Composition, Inc., Nashville, Tennessee, printed offset by Thomson-Shore, Inc., Dexter, Michigan, and bound by John H. Dekker & Sons Book Bindery, Grand Rapids, Michigan. The paper on which the book is printed bears the watermark of S.D. Warren and is designed for an effective life of at least three hundred years.

THE UNIVERSITY OF TENNESSEE PRESS : KNOXVILLE